The Mostly Unfabulous Social Life of Ethan Green

by Eric Orner

ST. MARTIN'S PRESS
NEW YORK

Library of Congress Cataloging-in-Publication Data

Orner, Eric.
     The mostly unfabulous social life of Ethan Green / Eric Orner.
        p.   cm.
     ISBN 0-312-07635-5
     I. Title.
   PN6727.075M67   1992
   741.5'973—dc20   91-40159
                                                                                                      CIP

10 9 8 7 6 5 4 3 2

For my brother Peter,
whose friendship and support I am lucky to have.
And also for my mom, and for Stephen Parks.

Special thanks to Ardys Kozbial for editing and proofreading, to Stephie Sommer, to Jeff Epperly and Jim Hoover of *Bay Windows* for printing Ethan first, and to Keith Kahla of St. Martin's Press for giving me the opportunity to do this book.

Also thanks to Liz Borock and to the especially fabulous Hat Sisters.

Please return to
Kaleidoscope Youth Center
P.O. Box 8104
Columbus, OH 43201

FIRST-TIME

-AT-A-GAY-BAR-

FLASHBACK.

YOU DROVE BY THE PLACE FOR WEEKS WITHOUT ACTUALLY GOING IN...
JoJo's
CURSE CURSE
Sob SNIFFLE
SOMETHING ABOUT THE LOOKS GIVEN YOU BY THE BOUNCER'S CLIQUE MADE YOU FEEL GEEKY AND INADEQUATE...
KIR WITH LIME PLEASE

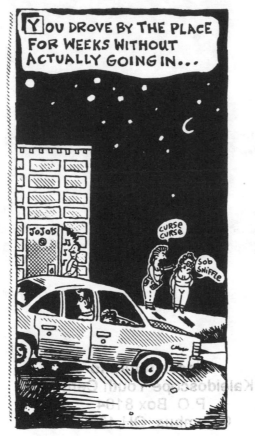

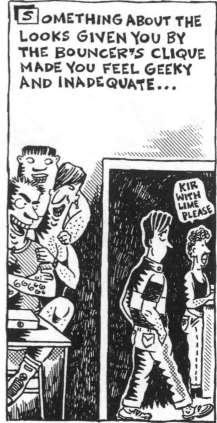

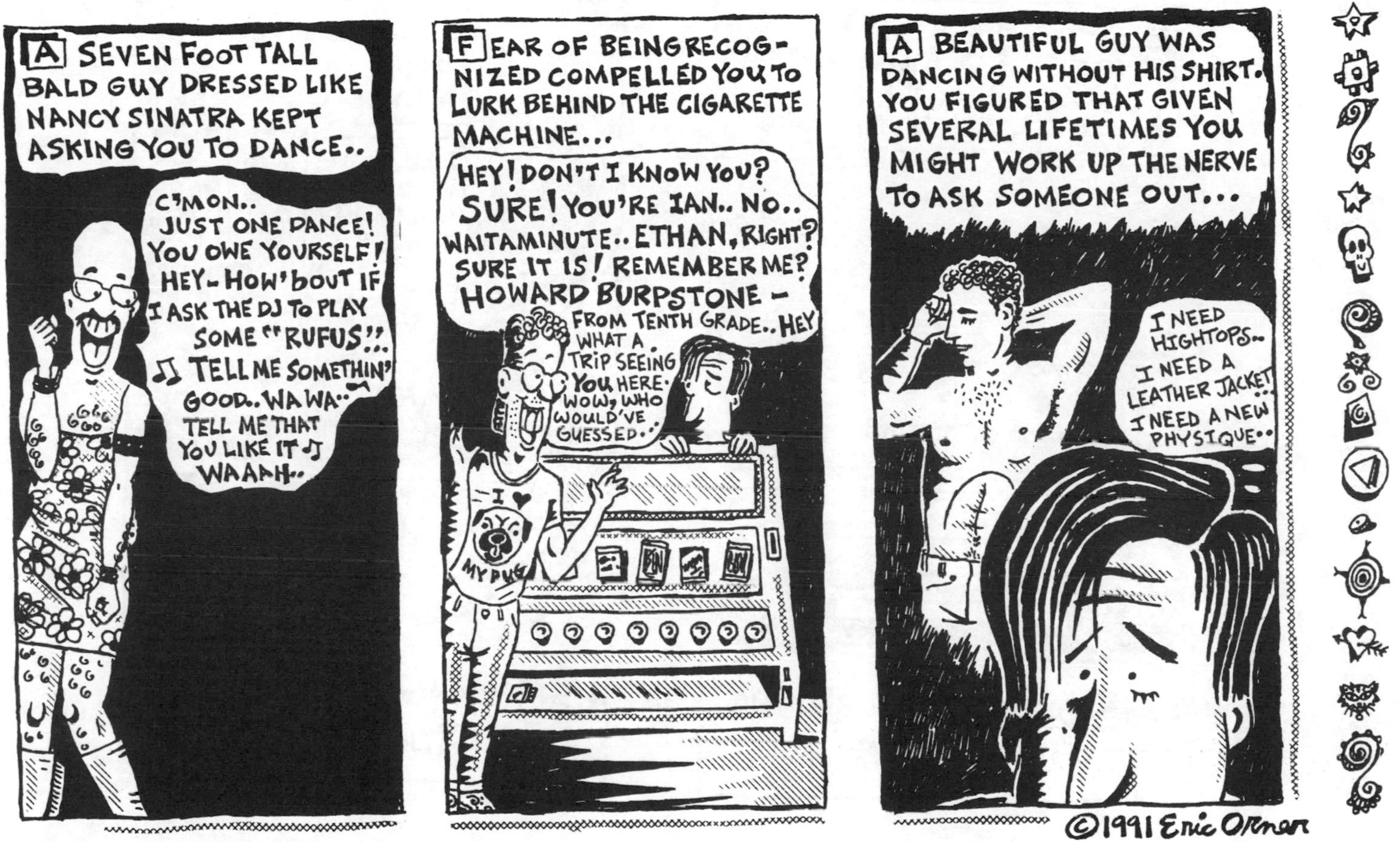
A SEVEN FOOT TALL BALD GUY DRESSED LIKE NANCY SINATRA KEPT ASKING YOU TO DANCE..
C'MON.. JUST ONE DANCE! YOU OWE YOURSELF! HEY- HOW'BOUT IF I ASK THE DJ TO PLAY SOME "RUFUS"!..
♫ TELL ME SOMETHIN' GOOD.. WA WA.. TELL ME THAT YOU LIKE IT ♫ WAAAH..
FEAR OF BEING RECOGNIZED COMPELLED YOU TO LURK BEHIND THE CIGARETTE MACHINE...
HEY! DON'T I KNOW YOU? SURE! YOU'RE IAN.. NO.. WAITAMINUTE.. ETHAN, RIGHT? SURE IT IS! REMEMBER ME? HOWARD BURPSTONE - FROM TENTH GRADE.. HEY WHAT A TRIP SEEING YOU HERE. WOW, WHO WOULD'VE GUESSED..
I ♥ MY PUG
A BEAUTIFUL GUY WAS DANCING WITHOUT HIS SHIRT. YOU FIGURED THAT GIVEN SEVERAL LIFETIMES YOU MIGHT WORK UP THE NERVE TO ASK SOMEONE OUT...
I NEED HIGHTOPS.. I NEED A LEATHER JACKET.. I NEED A NEW PHYSIQUE..

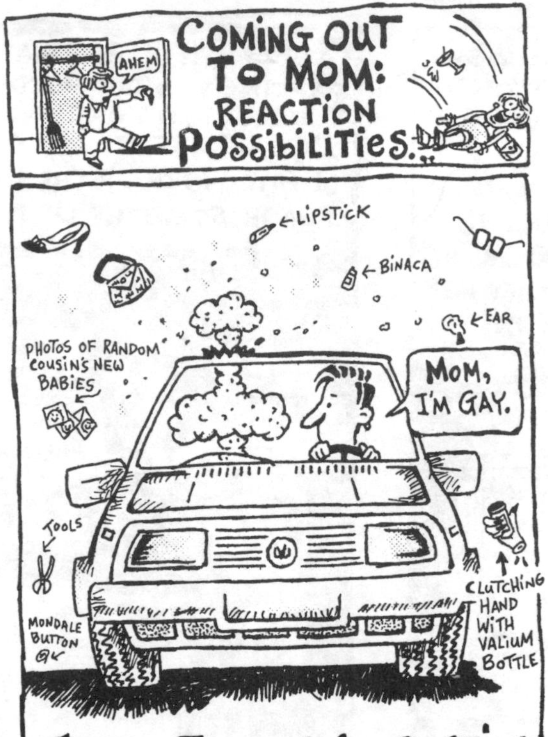
COMING OUT TO MOM: REACTION POSSIBILITIES.
AHEM
← LIPSTICK
← BINACA
← EAR
PHOTOS OF RANDOM COUSIN'S NEW BABIES
MOM, I'M GAY.
TOOLS
MONDALE BUTTON
CLUTCHING HAND WITH VALIUM BOTTLE

THE SPONTANEOUS COMBUSTION REACTION

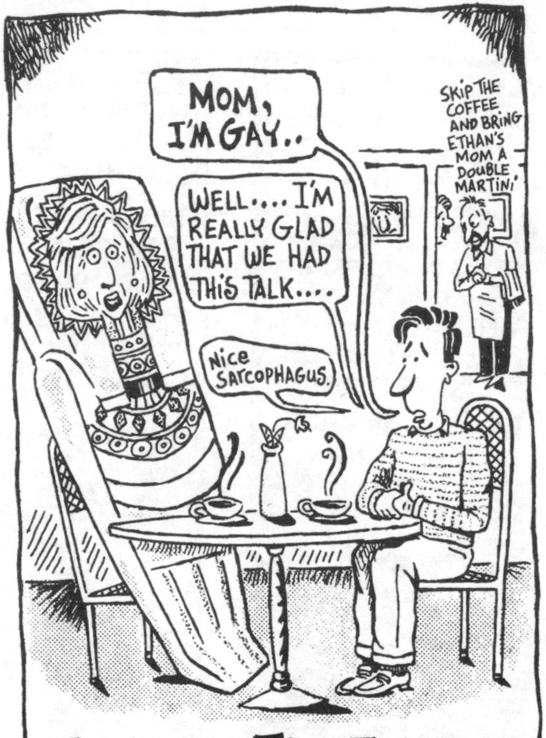
MOM, I'M GAY..
WELL.... I'M REALLY GLAD THAT WE HAD THIS TALK....
NICE SARCOPHAGUS.
SKIP THE COFFEE AND BRING ETHAN'S MOM A DOUBLE MARTINI'

THE NEEDING TIME TO ADJUST REACTION

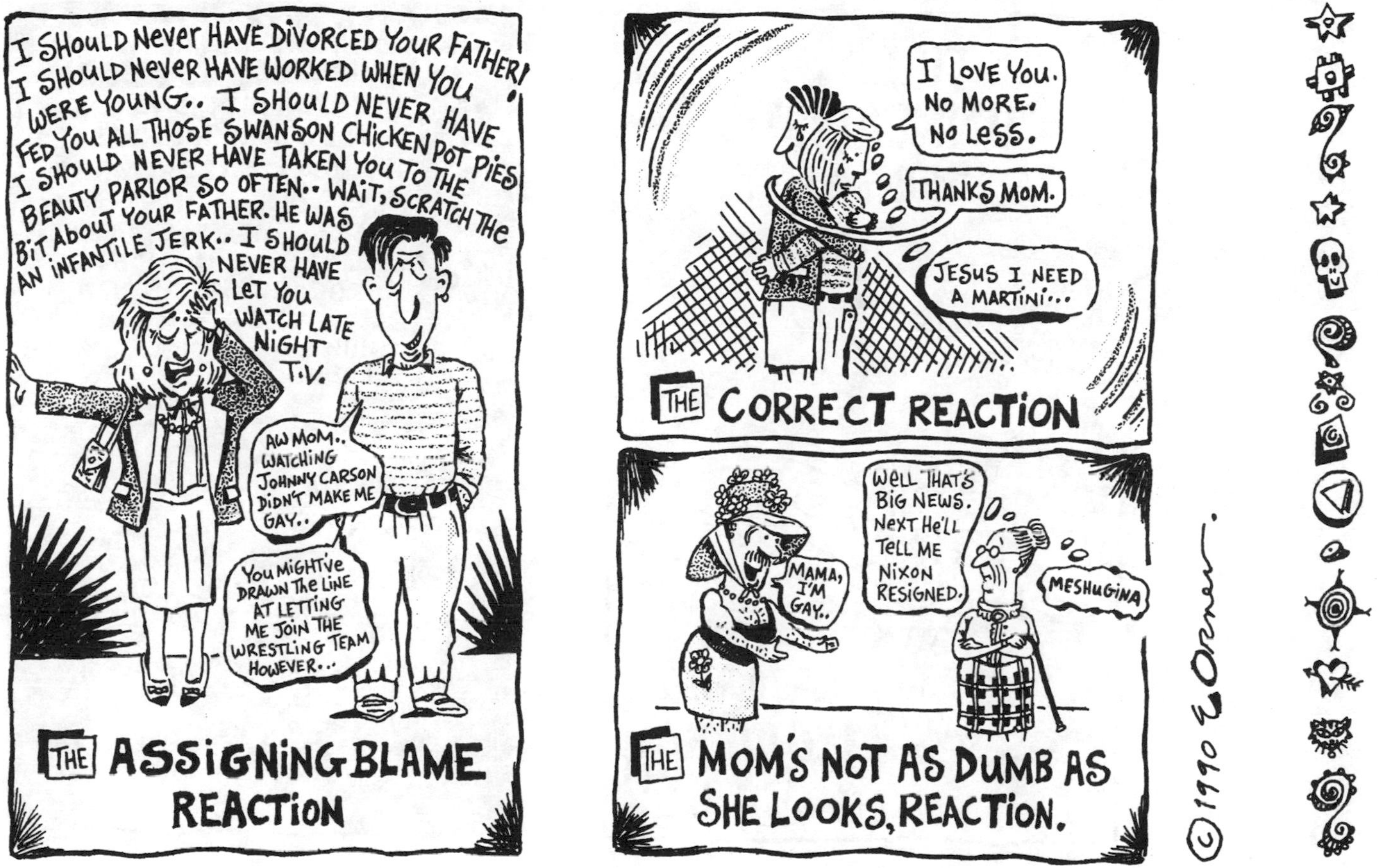
I SHOULD NEVER HAVE DIVORCED YOUR FATHER! I SHOULD NEVER HAVE WORKED WHEN YOU WERE YOUNG.. I SHOULD NEVER HAVE FED YOU ALL THOSE SWANSON CHICKEN POT PIES I SHOULD NEVER HAVE TAKEN YOU TO THE BEAUTY PARLOR SO OFTEN.. WAIT, SCRATCH THE BIT ABOUT YOUR FATHER. HE WAS AN INFANTILE JERK.. I SHOULD NEVER HAVE LET YOU WATCH LATE NIGHT T.V.
AW MOM.. WATCHING JOHNNY CARSON DIDN'T MAKE ME GAY..
YOU MIGHT'VE DRAWN THE LINE AT LETTING ME JOIN THE WRESTLING TEAM HOWEVER...
THE ASSIGNING BLAME REACTION
I LOVE YOU. NO MORE. NO LESS.
THANKS MOM.
JESUS I NEED A MARTINI...
THE CORRECT REACTION
MAMA, I'M GAY..
WELL THAT'S BIG NEWS. NEXT HE'LL TELL ME NIXON RESIGNED.
MESHUGINA
THE MOM'S NOT AS DUMB AS SHE LOOKS, REACTION.
© 1990 E. Orner

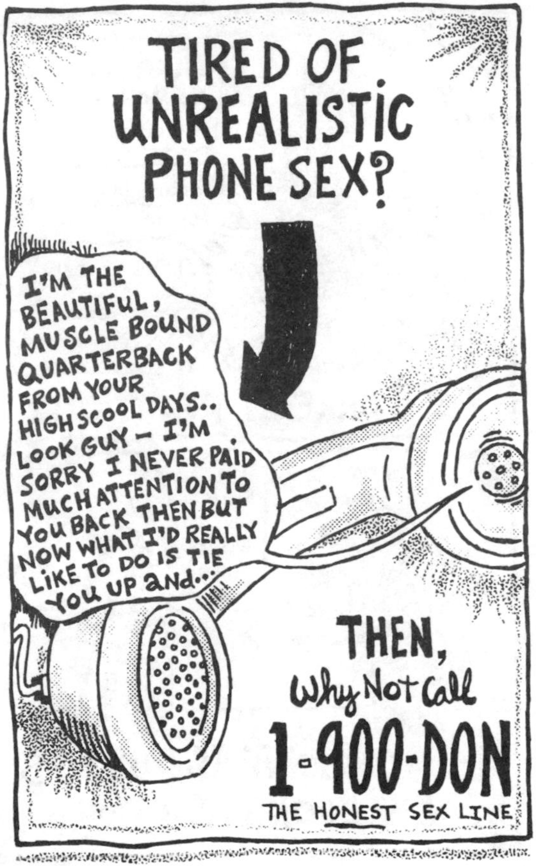
TIRED OF UNREALISTIC PHONE SEX?
I'M THE BEAUTIFUL, MUSCLE BOUND QUARTERBACK FROM YOUR HIGH SCOOL DAYS.. LOOK GUY – I'M SORRY I NEVER PAID MUCH ATTENTION TO YOU BACK THEN BUT NOW WHAT I'D REALLY LIKE TO DO IS TIE YOU UP and...
THEN, Why Not Call
1-900-DON
THE HONEST SEX LINE

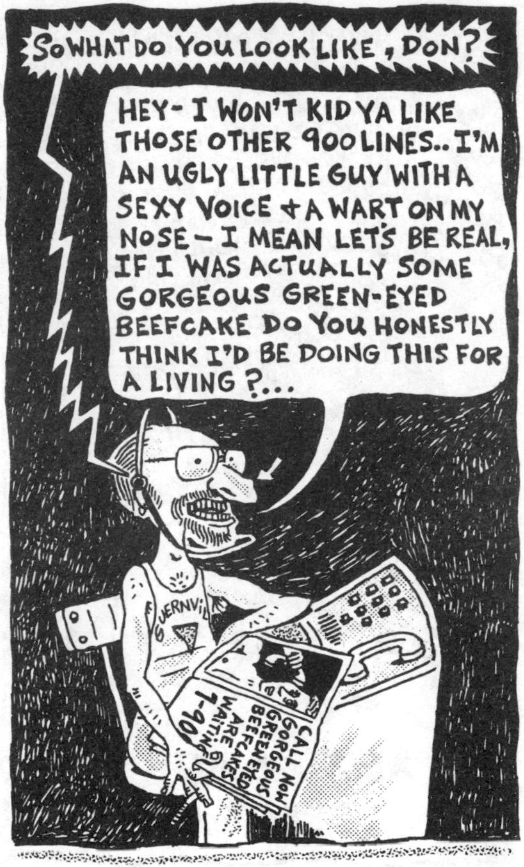
SO WHAT DO YOU LOOK LIKE, DON?
HEY- I WON'T KID YA LIKE THOSE OTHER 900 LINES.. I'M AN UGLY LITTLE GUY WITH A SEXY VOICE + A WART ON MY NOSE – I MEAN LET'S BE REAL, IF I WAS ACTUALLY SOME GORGEOUS GREEN-EYED BEEFCAKE DO YOU HONESTLY THINK I'D BE DOING THIS FOR A LIVING?...
CALL NOW GORGEOUS GREENEYED BEEFCAKES ARE WAITING

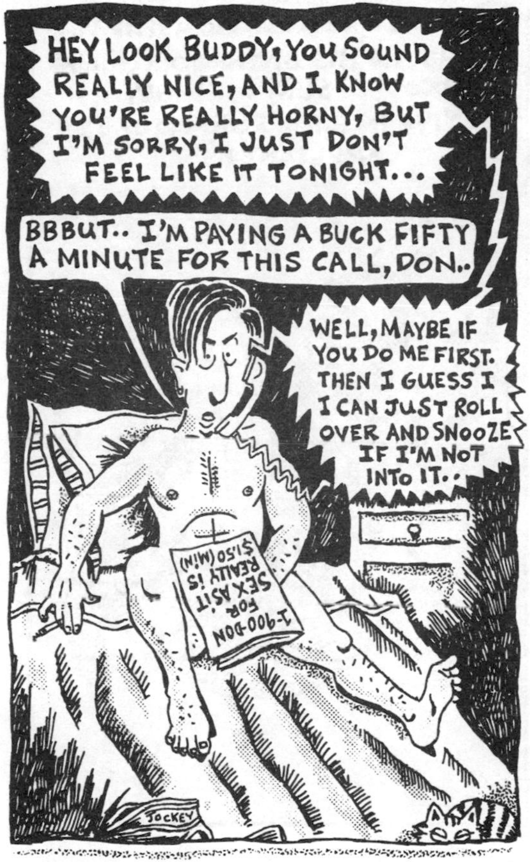
HEY LOOK BUDDY, YOU SOUND REALLY NICE, AND I KNOW YOU'RE REALLY HORNY, BUT I'M SORRY, I JUST DON'T FEEL LIKE IT TONIGHT...
BBBUT.. I'M PAYING A BUCK FIFTY A MINUTE FOR THIS CALL, DON..
WELL, MAYBE IF YOU DO ME FIRST. THEN I GUESS I I CAN JUST ROLL OVER AND SNOOZE IF I'M NOT INTO IT..
1-900-DON FOR SEX AS IT REALLY IS $1.50 (MIN)
JOCKEY

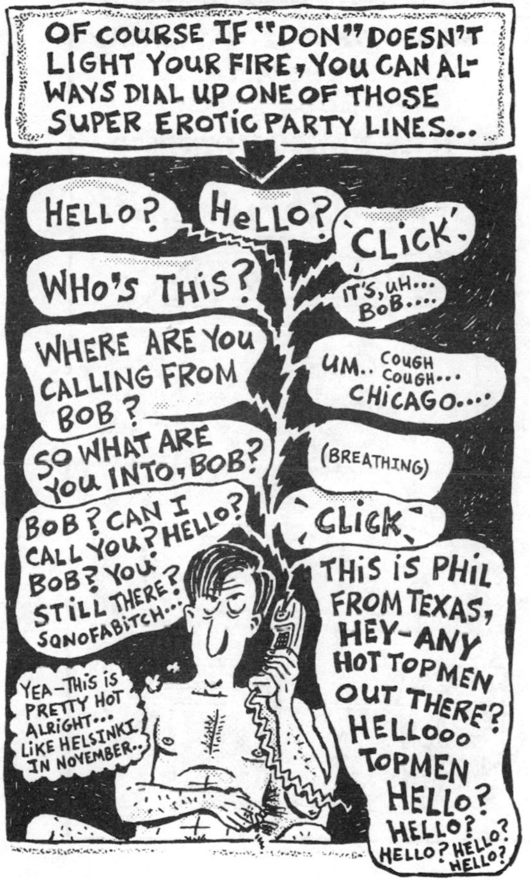
OF COURSE IF "DON" DOESN'T LIGHT YOUR FIRE, YOU CAN ALWAYS DIAL UP ONE OF THOSE SUPER EROTIC PARTY LINES...
HELLO?
HELLO?
CLICK
WHO'S THIS?
IT'S, UH... BOB....
WHERE ARE YOU CALLING FROM BOB?
UM.. COUGH COUGH... CHICAGO....
SO WHAT ARE YOU INTO, BOB?
(BREATHING)
CLICK
BOB? CAN I CALL YOU? HELLO? BOB? YOU STILL THERE? SONOFABITCH...
THIS IS PHIL FROM TEXAS, HEY-ANY HOT TOPMEN OUT THERE? HELLOoo TOPMEN HELLO? HELLO? HELLO? HELLO? HELLO?
YEA-THIS IS PRETTY HOT ALRIGHT... LIKE HELSINKI IN NOVEMBER..

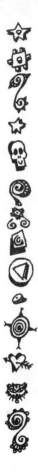

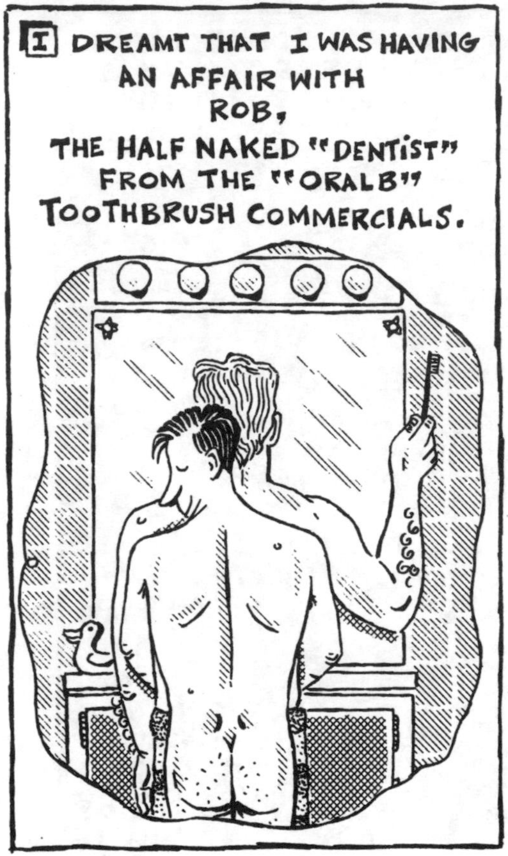
I DREAMT THAT I WAS HAVING AN AFFAIR WITH ROB, THE HALF NAKED "DENTIST" FROM THE "ORALB" TOOTHBRUSH COMMERCIALS.

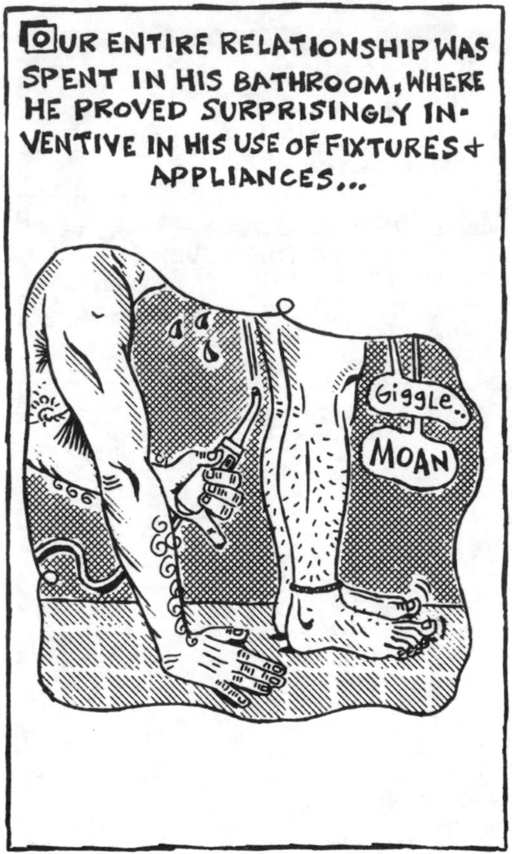
OUR ENTIRE RELATIONSHIP WAS SPENT IN HIS BATHROOM, WHERE HE PROVED SURPRISINGLY INVENTIVE IN HIS USE OF FIXTURES + APPLIANCES...
Giggle..
MOAN

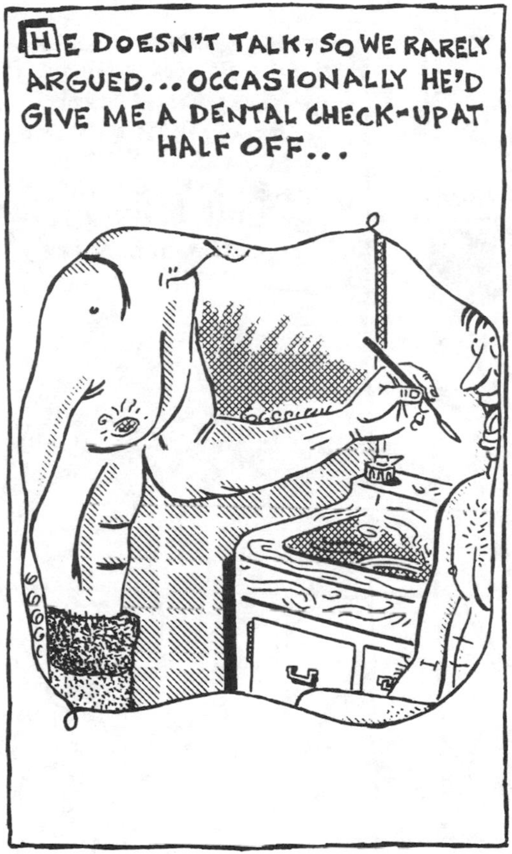
HE DOESN'T TALK, SO WE RARELY ARGUED... OCCASIONALLY HE'D GIVE ME A DENTAL CHECK-UP AT HALF OFF...

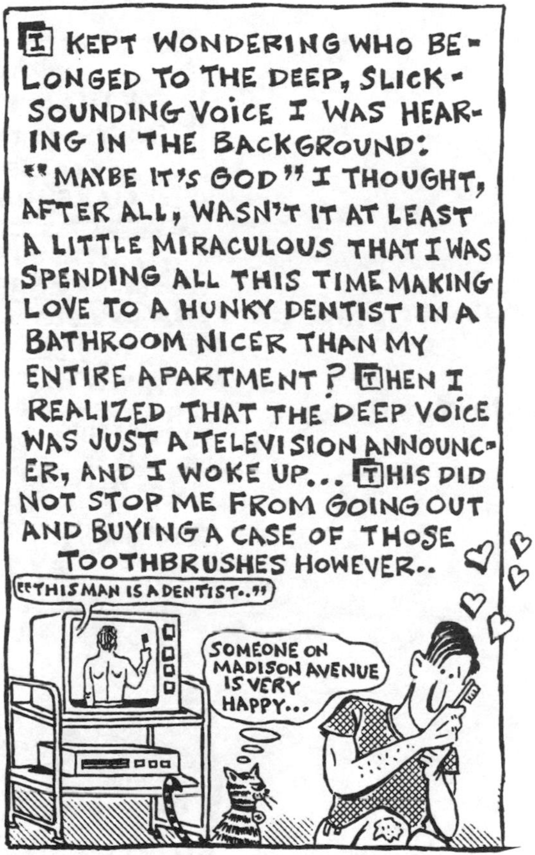
I KEPT WONDERING WHO BE-LONGED TO THE DEEP, SLICK-SOUNDING VOICE I WAS HEAR-ING IN THE BACKGROUND: "MAYBE IT'S GOD" I THOUGHT, AFTER ALL, WASN'T IT AT LEAST A LITTLE MIRACULOUS THAT I WAS SPENDING ALL THIS TIME MAKING LOVE TO A HUNKY DENTIST IN A BATHROOM NICER THAN MY ENTIRE APARTMENT? THEN I REALIZED THAT THE DEEP VOICE WAS JUST A TELEVISION ANNOUNC-ER, AND I WOKE UP... THIS DID NOT STOP ME FROM GOING OUT AND BUYING A CASE OF THOSE TOOTHBRUSHES HOWEVER..
"THIS MAN IS A DENTIST.."
SOMEONE ON MADISON AVENUE IS VERY HAPPY...

REALLY BIG

HAIR TROUBLE.

SADLY, ETHAN IS UNABLE TO THWART HIS HAIR'S CONSPIRACY TO MAKE HIM LOOK STUPID.
HE'S GETTING PRETTY DOLLED UP AINT HE?
HE'S GOT A DATE WITH SOMEONE HE MET AT THE GYM..
IS THAT SO?.. HEY.. LET'S UNDERMINE HIS CONFIDENCE BY GETTING REALLY BRITTLE + FULL OF STATIC ELECTRICITY...
AW JEEZ, WE ALWAYS DO THAT.. HOW ABOUT FAT "N" PUFFY, LIKE WHEN IT GETS REALLY HUMID..
HEY LOOK - HE'S USING THAT FANCY NEW CONDITIONER NOW REMEMBER OUR PLAN: AS SOON AS HE FINISHES DRYING US - WE COLLAPSE! 100% LIMP + LIFELESS! IT'LL BE A SCREAM!
POLYMOLECULAR SUPER HAIR STRUCTURALIZER

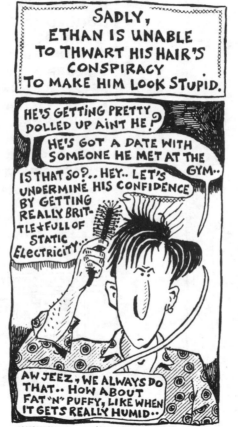

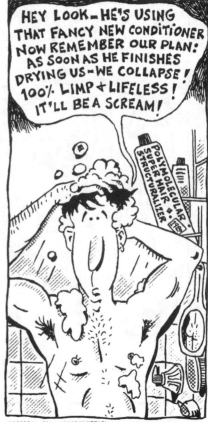

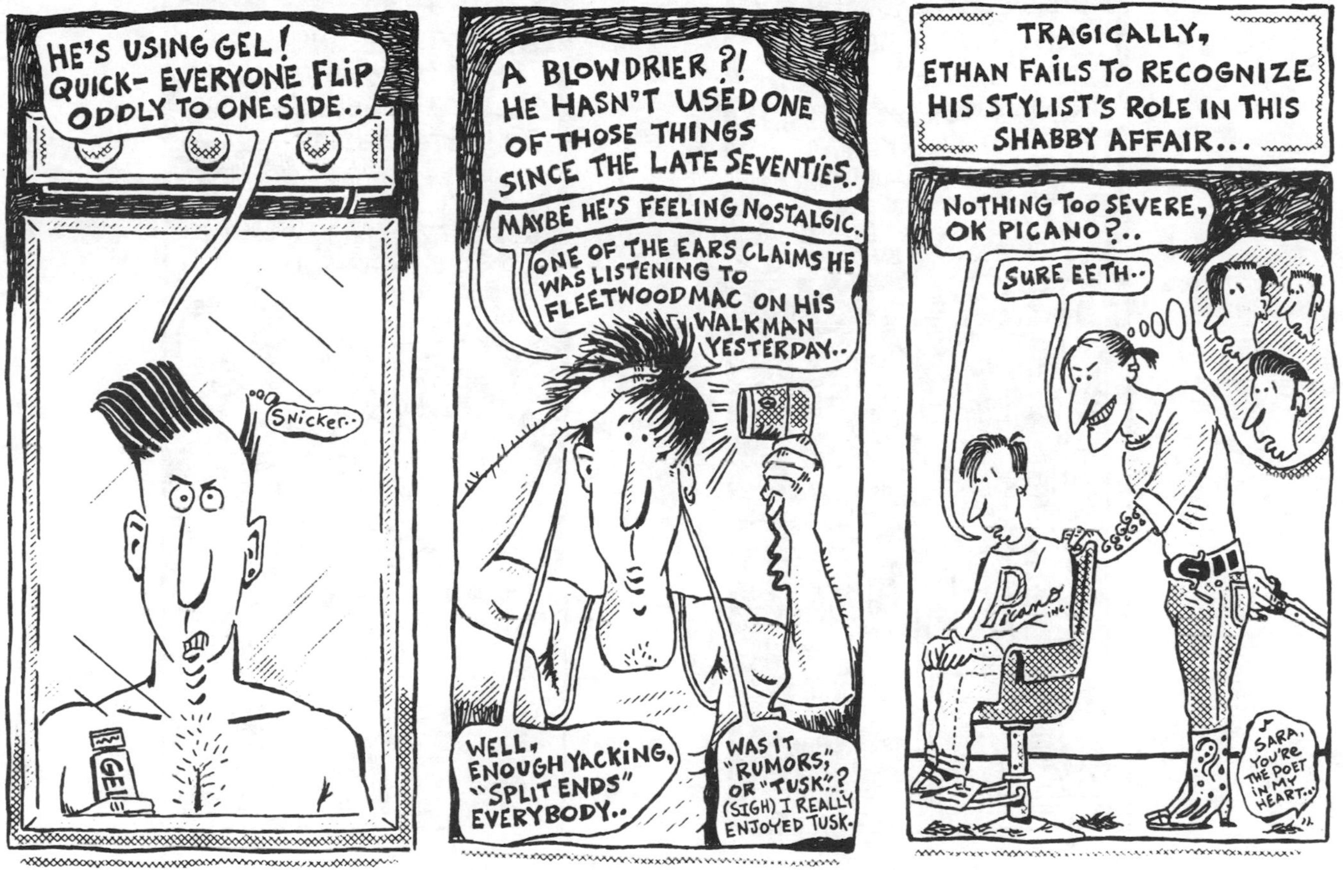
HE'S USING GEL! QUICK- EVERYONE FLIP ODDLY TO ONE SIDE..
Snicker..
GEL
A BLOWDRIER ?! HE HASN'T USED ONE OF THOSE THINGS SINCE THE LATE SEVENTIES..
MAYBE HE'S FEELING NOSTALGIC..
ONE OF THE EARS CLAIMS HE WAS LISTENING TO FLEETWOOD MAC ON HIS WALKMAN YESTERDAY..
WELL, ENOUGH YACKING, "SPLIT ENDS" EVERYBODY..
WAS IT "RUMORS," OR "TUSK"..? (SIGH) I REALLY ENJOYED TUSK.
TRAGICALLY, ETHAN FAILS TO RECOGNIZE HIS STYLIST'S ROLE IN THIS SHABBY AFFAIR...
NOTHING TOO SEVERE, OK PICANO?..
SURE EETH..
Picano INC.
SARA, YOU'RE THE POET IN MY HEART...

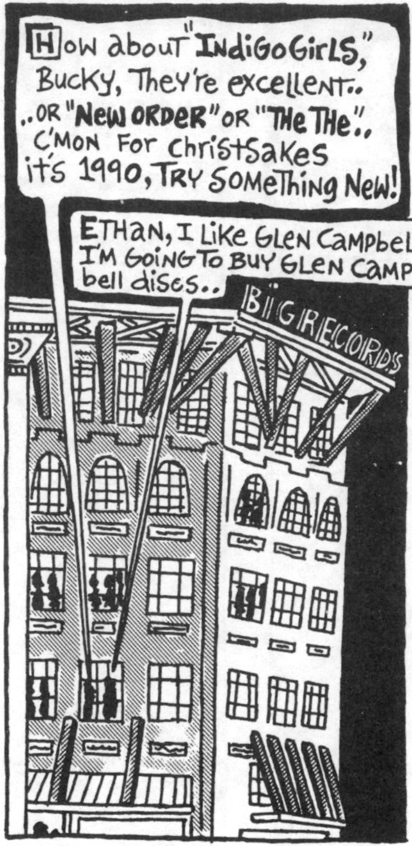
How about "IndiGo Girls," Bucky, They're excellent..
..or "New Order" or "The The"..
C'mon for Christsakes it's 1990, Try Something New!
Ethan, I like Glen Campbell. I'm going to buy Glen Campbell discs..
BIG RECORDS

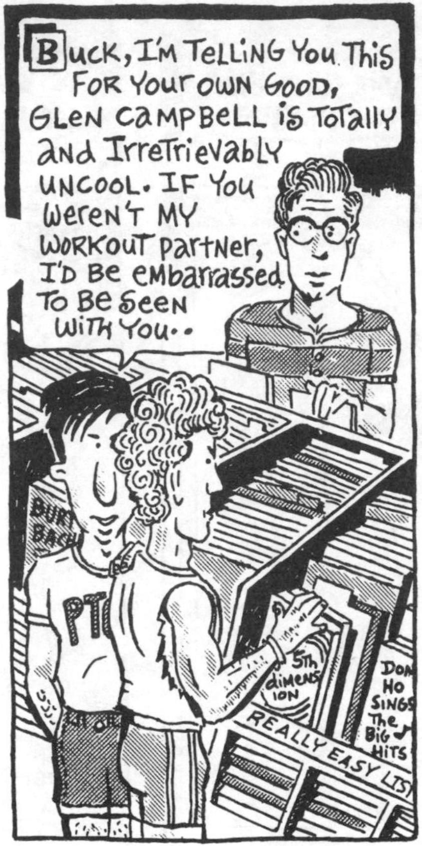
Buck, I'm telling you. This for your own good, Glen Campbell is totally and irretrievably uncool. If you weren't my workout partner, I'd be embarrassed to be seen with you..
5th dimension
Don Ho Sings The Big Hits
Really Easy

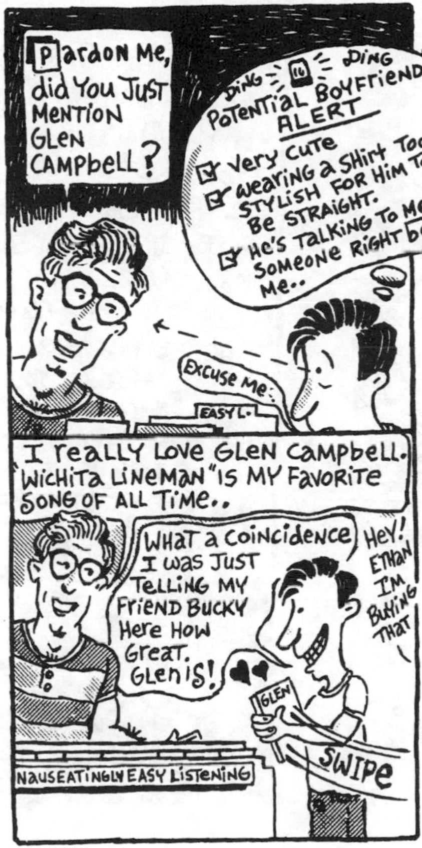
Pardon me, did you just mention Glen Campbell?
DING DING
POTENTIAL BOYFRIEND ALERT
☑ Very cute
☑ Wearing a shirt too stylish for him to be straight.
☑ He's talking to me. Not someone right behind me..
Excuse me.
EASY L.
I really love Glen Campbell. "Wichita Lineman" is my favorite song of all time..
What a coincidence I was just telling my friend Bucky here how great Glen is!
Hey! Ethan I'm buying that
GLEN
SWIPE
NAUSEATINGLY EASY LISTENING

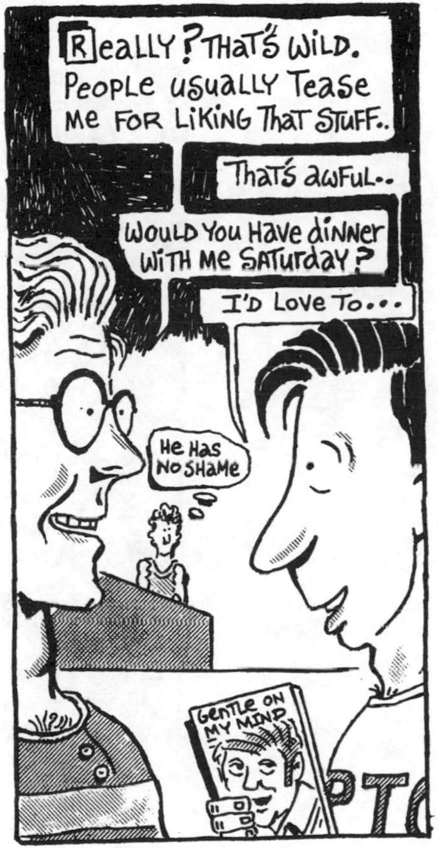
Really? That's wild. People usually tease me for liking that stuff..
That's awful..
Would you have dinner with me Saturday?
I'd love to...
He has no shame
GENTLE ON MY MIND

Enter The Netherworld

of Gay pet ownership in

DOGWALK TO HELL..

©1990 E. Orner

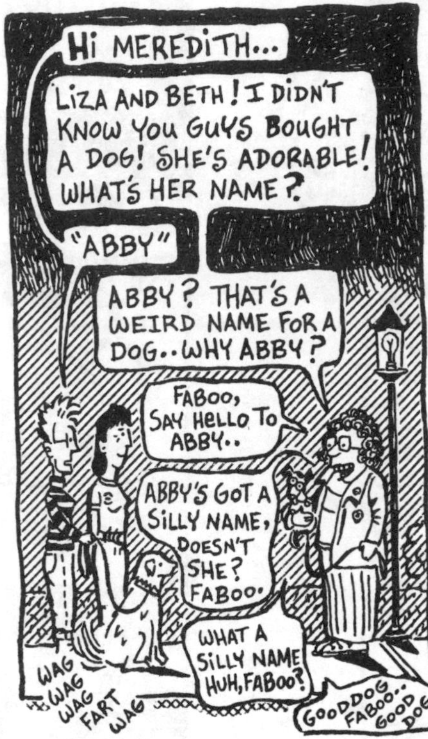

Hi MEREDITH...
LIZA AND BETH! I DIDN'T KNOW YOU GUYS BOUGHT A DOG! SHE'S ADORABLE! WHAT'S HER NAME?
"ABBY"
ABBY? THAT'S A WEIRD NAME FOR A DOG.. WHY ABBY?
FABoo, SAY HELLO TO ABBY..
ABBY'S GOT A SILLY NAME, DOESN'T SHE? FABoo.
WHAT A SILLY NAME HUH, FABoo?
GOOD DOG FABoo.. GOOD DOG.
WAG WAG WAG FART WAG

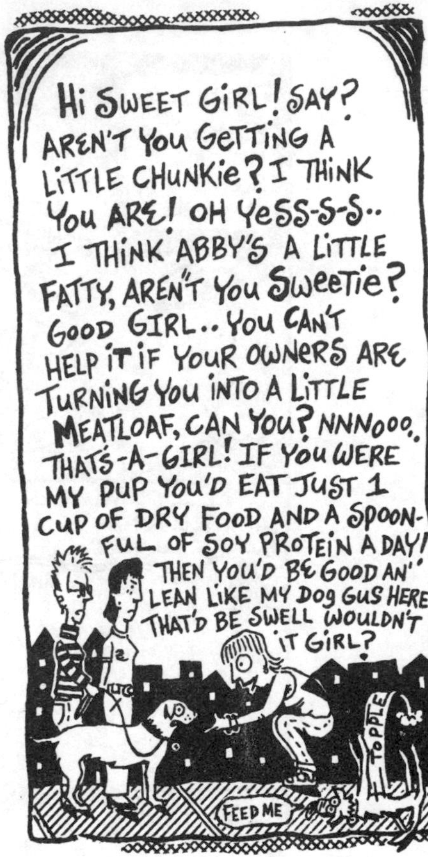

Hi SWEET GIRL! SAY? AREN'T YOU GETTING A LITTLE CHUNKIE? I THINK YOU ARE! OH YeSS-S-S.. I THINK ABBY'S A LITTLE FATTY, AREN'T YOU SWEETIE? GOOD GIRL.. YOU CAN'T HELP IT IF YOUR OWNERS ARE TURNING YOU INTO A LITTLE MEATLOAF, CAN YOU? NNNOoo.. THAT'S-A-GIRL! IF YOU WERE MY PUP YOU'D EAT JUST 1 CUP OF DRY FOOD AND A SPOON-FUL OF SOY PROTEIN A DAY! THEN YOU'D BE GOOD AN' LEAN LIKE MY DOG GUS HERE THAT'D BE SWELL WOULDN'T IT GIRL?
TOPPLE
FEED ME

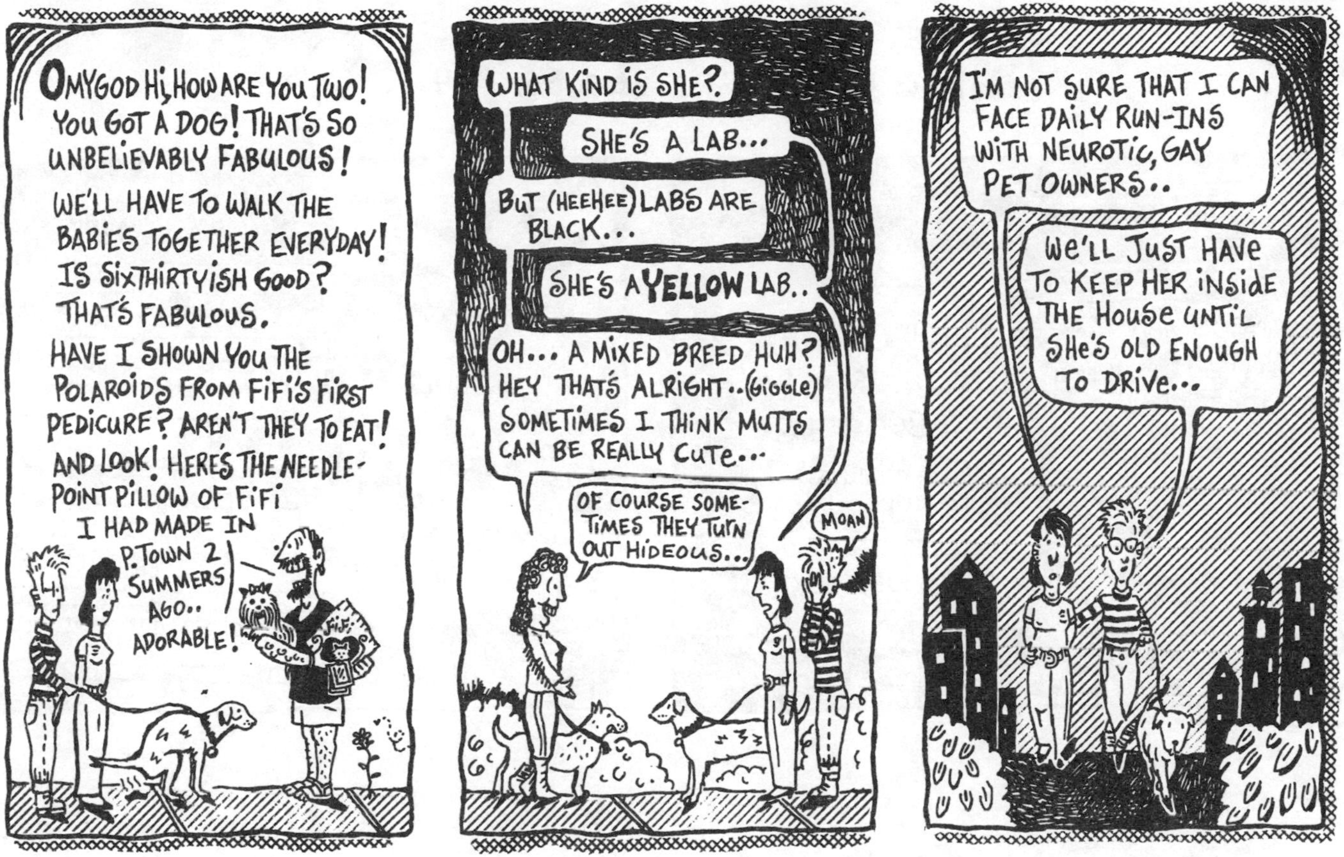
OMYGOD Hi, HOW ARE YOU TWO! YOU GOT A DOG! THAT'S SO UNBELIEVABLY FABULOUS!
WE'LL HAVE TO WALK THE BABIES TOGETHER EVERYDAY! IS SIXTHIRTYISH GOOD? THAT'S FABULOUS.
HAVE I SHOWN YOU THE POLAROIDS FROM FIFI'S FIRST PEDICURE? AREN'T THEY TO EAT!
AND LOOK! HERE'S THE NEEDLE-POINT PILLOW OF FIFI I HAD MADE IN P. TOWN 2 SUMMERS AGO.. ADORABLE!
FIFI
WHAT KIND IS SHE?
SHE'S A LAB...
BUT (HEEHEE) LABS ARE BLACK...
SHE'S A YELLOW LAB..
OH... A MIXED BREED HUH? HEY THAT'S ALRIGHT..(GIGGLE) SOMETIMES I THINK MUTTS CAN BE REALLY CUTE...
OF COURSE SOMETIMES THEY TURN OUT HIDEOUS...
MOAN
I'M NOT SURE THAT I CAN FACE DAILY RUN-INS WITH NEUROTIC, GAY PET OWNERS..
WE'LL JUST HAVE TO KEEP HER INSIDE THE HOUSE UNTIL SHE'S OLD ENOUGH TO DRIVE...

DATING NIGHTMARE # 1,500,624...

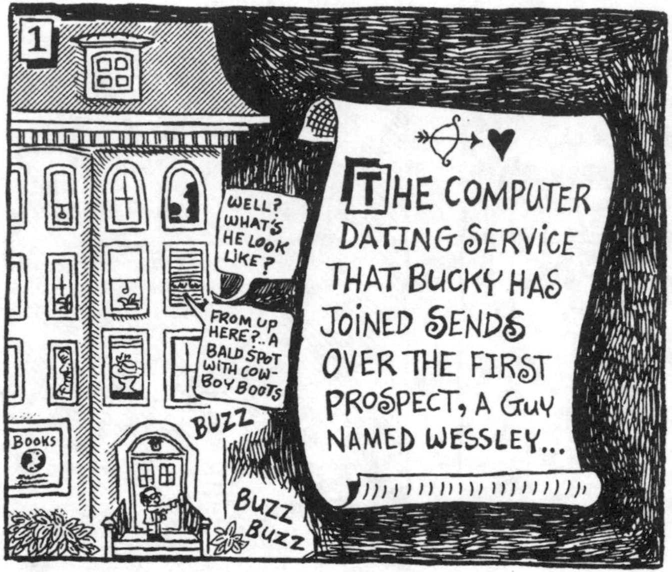
1
THE COMPUTER DATING SERVICE THAT BUCKY HAS JOINED SENDS OVER THE FIRST PROSPECT, A GUY NAMED WESSLEY...
WELL? WHAT'S HE LOOK LIKE?
FROM UP HERE?.. A BALD SPOT WITH COW-BOY BOOTS
BOOKS
BUZZ
BUZZ BUZZ
BUZZ

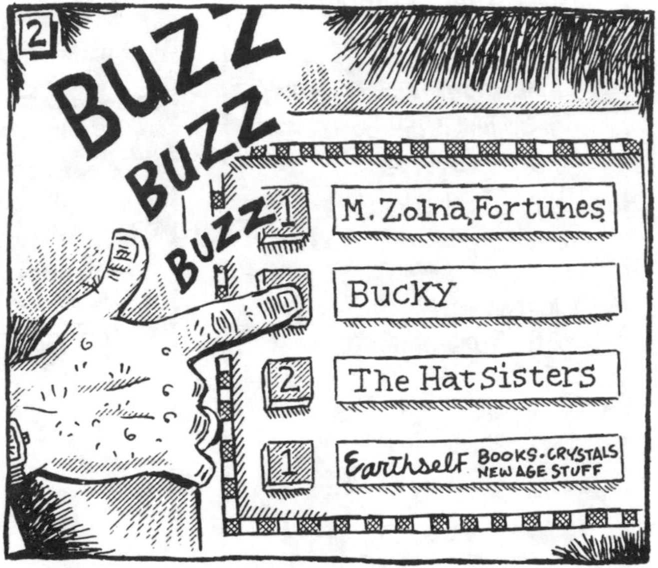
2
BUZZ
BUZZ
BUZZ
1 M. Zolna, Fortunes
Bucky
2 The Hat Sisters
1 Earthself BOOKS • CRYSTALS NEW AGE STUFF

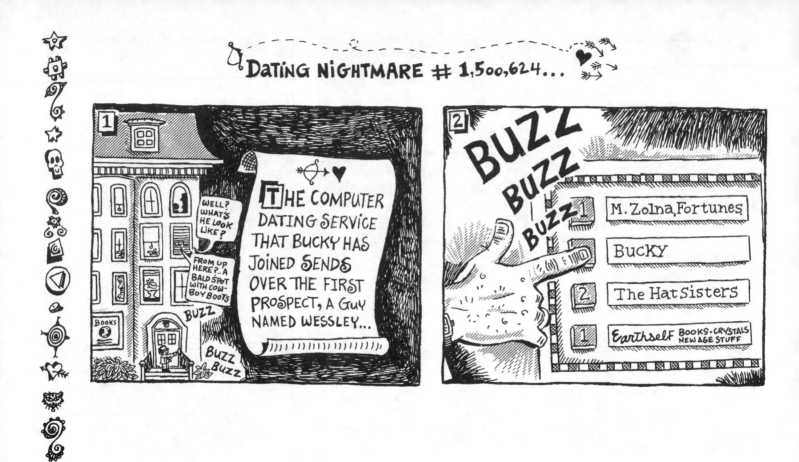

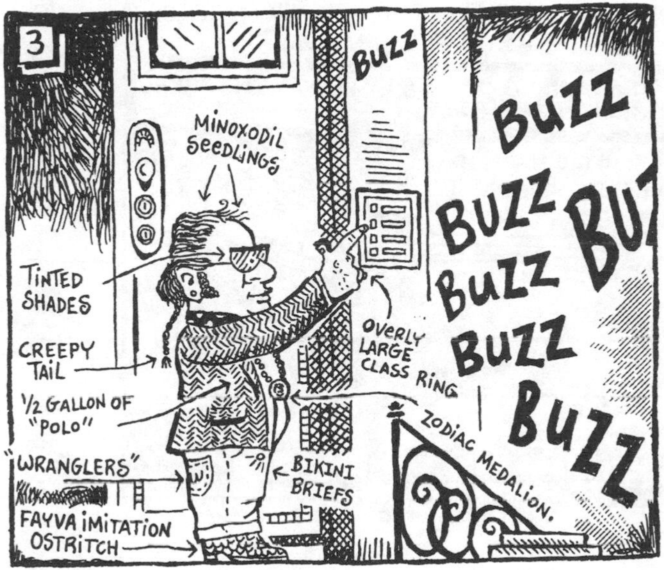
3
BUZZ
BUZZ
BUZZ
BUZZ
BUZZ
BUZZ
BUZZ
BU
MINOXODIL SEEDLINGS
TINTED SHADES
CREEPY TAIL
1/2 GALLON OF "POLO"
"WRANGLERS"
FAYVA IMITATION OSTRITCH
OVERLY LARGE CLASS RING
BIKINI BRIEFS
ZODIAC MEDALION.

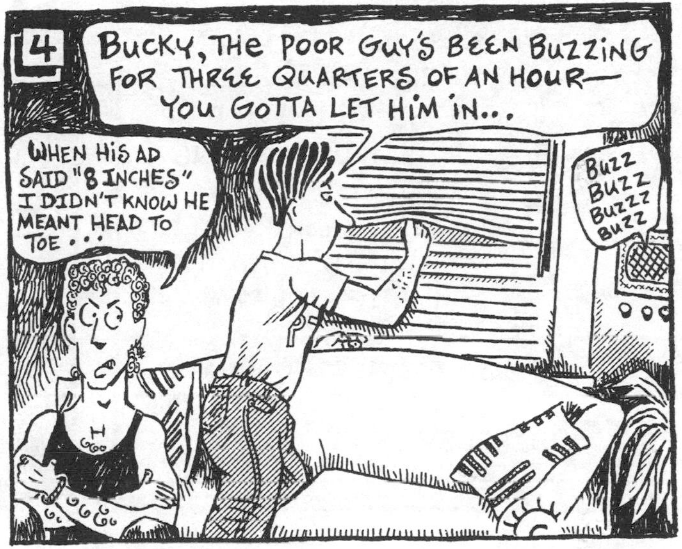
4
BUCKY, THE POOR GUY'S BEEN BUZZING FOR THREE QUARTERS OF AN HOUR— YOU GOTTA LET HIM IN...
WHEN HIS AD SAID "8 INCHES" I DIDN'T KNOW HE MEANT HEAD TO TOE...
BUZZ BUZZ BUZZZ BUZZ

CONTINUED →

5
LISTEN ETHAN, THE WAY I SEE IT, GETTING FIXED UP THROUGH A DATING SERVICE IS LIKE MAKING A CONTRACT THAT'S ONLY BINDING IF BOTH PARTIES ARE COMPLETELY HONEST.
BY DESCRIBING HIMSELF AS "TALL, BLOND, SURFER-DUDE" WESSLEY BROKE OUR CONTRACT. THEREFORE, I'M NOT LETTING HIM IN.
6
C'MON BUCKY.. DON'T YOU THINK YOU'RE BEING JUST A BIT SHALLOW?...
.. BESIDES "GQ" SAYS LAMBCHOP SIDEBURNS ARE COMING BACK...
ETHAN, HOW WOULD YOU LIKE TO BE DROPPED OUT OF A 3RD STORY WINDOW?
BUCKY?
BUZZZ
IT'S ME-WESSLEY
BUZZZ
YOUR DATE:
BUZZZ
I'M LOOKING FORWARD TO OUR DATE...
GQ

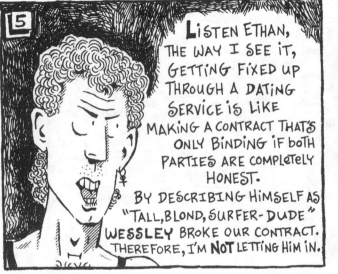

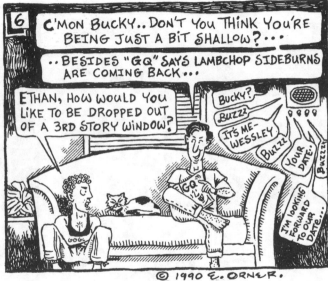

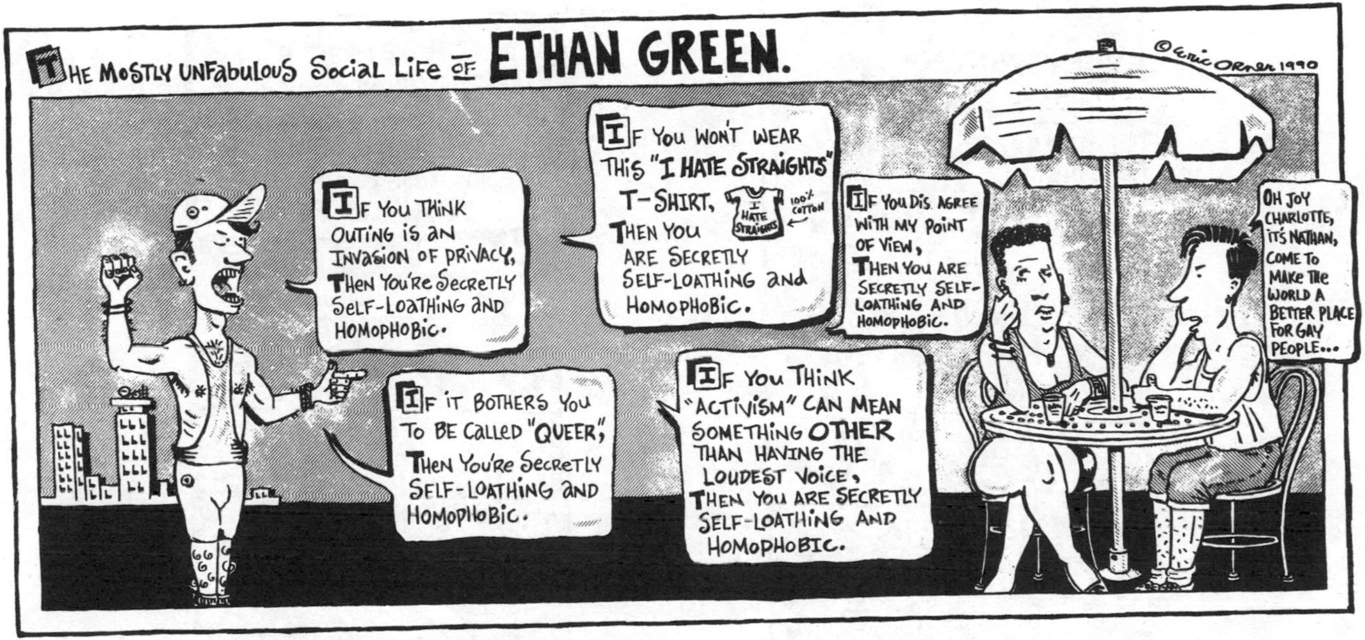
THE MOSTLY UNFABULOUS SOCIAL LIFE OF ETHAN GREEN.
©Eric Orner 1990
IF YOU THINK OUTING IS AN INVASION OF PRIVACY, THEN YOU'RE SECRETLY SELF-LOATHING AND HOMOPHOBIC.
IF IT BOTHERS YOU TO BE CALLED "QUEER", THEN YOU'RE SECRETLY SELF-LOATHING AND HOMOPHOBIC.
IF YOU WON'T WEAR THIS "I HATE STRAIGHTS" T-SHIRT, THEN YOU ARE SECRETLY SELF-LOATHING AND HOMOPHOBIC.
I HATE STRAIGHTS
100% COTTON
IF YOU THINK "ACTIVISM" CAN MEAN SOMETHING OTHER THAN HAVING THE LOUDEST VOICE, THEN YOU ARE SECRETLY SELF-LOATHING AND HOMOPHOBIC.
IF YOU DIS. AGREE WITH MY POINT OF VIEW, THEN YOU ARE SECRETLY SELF-LOATHING AND HOMOPHOBIC.
OH JOY CHARLOTTE, IT'S NATHAN, COME TO MAKE THE WORLD A BETTER PLACE FOR GAY PEOPLE...

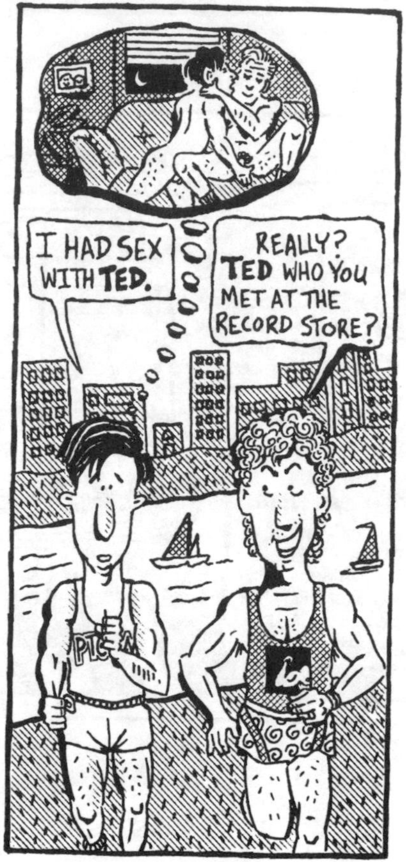

I HAD SEX WITH TED.
REALLY? TED WHO YOU MET AT THE RECORD STORE?

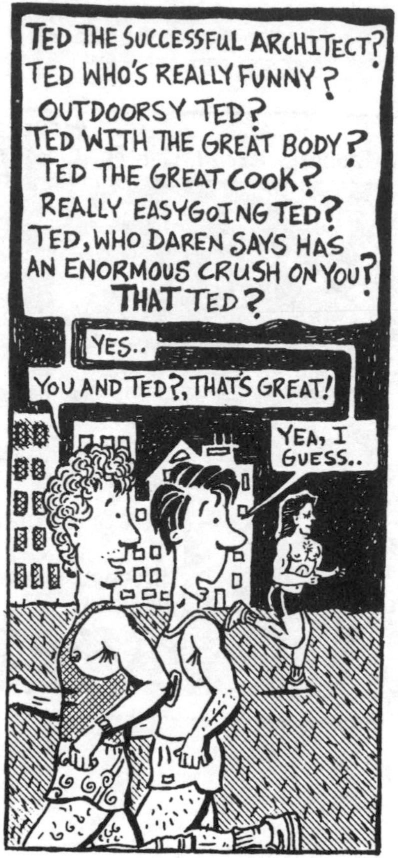

TED THE SUCCESSFUL ARCHITECT? TED WHO'S REALLY FUNNY? OUTDOORSY TED? TED WITH THE GREAT BODY? TED THE GREAT COOK? REALLY EASYGOING TED? TED, WHO DAREN SAYS HAS AN ENORMOUS CRUSH ON YOU? THAT TED?
YES..
YOU AND TED?, THAT'S GREAT!
YEA, I GUESS..

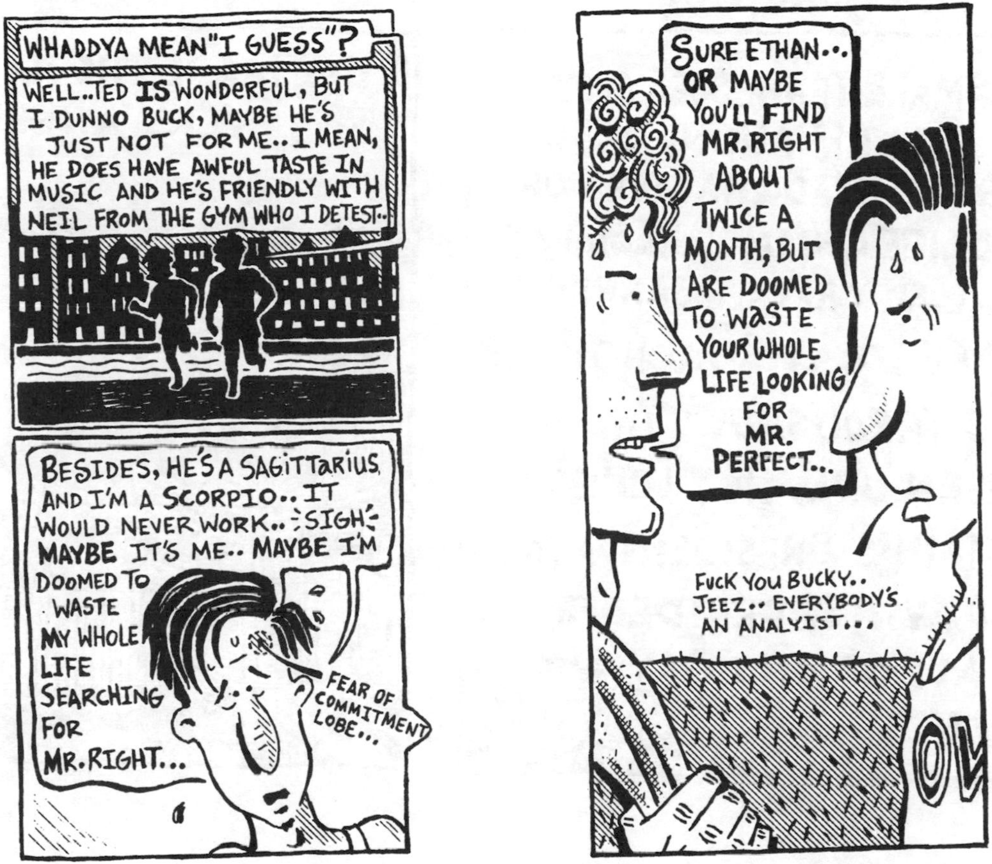
WHADDYA MEAN "I GUESS"?
WELL..TED IS WONDERFUL, BUT I DUNNO BUCK, MAYBE HE'S JUST NOT FOR ME.. I MEAN, HE DOES HAVE AWFUL TASTE IN MUSIC AND HE'S FRIENDLY WITH NEIL FROM THE GYM WHO I DETEST..
BESIDES, HE'S A SAGITTARIUS AND I'M A SCORPIO.. IT WOULD NEVER WORK.. SIGH MAYBE IT'S ME.. MAYBE I'M DOOMED TO WASTE MY WHOLE LIFE SEARCHING FOR MR.RIGHT...
FEAR OF COMMITMENT LOBE...
SURE ETHAN... OR MAYBE YOU'LL FIND MR.RIGHT ABOUT TWICE A MONTH, BUT ARE DOOMED TO WASTE YOUR WHOLE LIFE LOOKING FOR MR. PERFECT...
FUCK YOU BUCKY.. JEEZ.. EVERYBODY'S AN ANALYIST...

HAT SISTER ROAD TRIP.

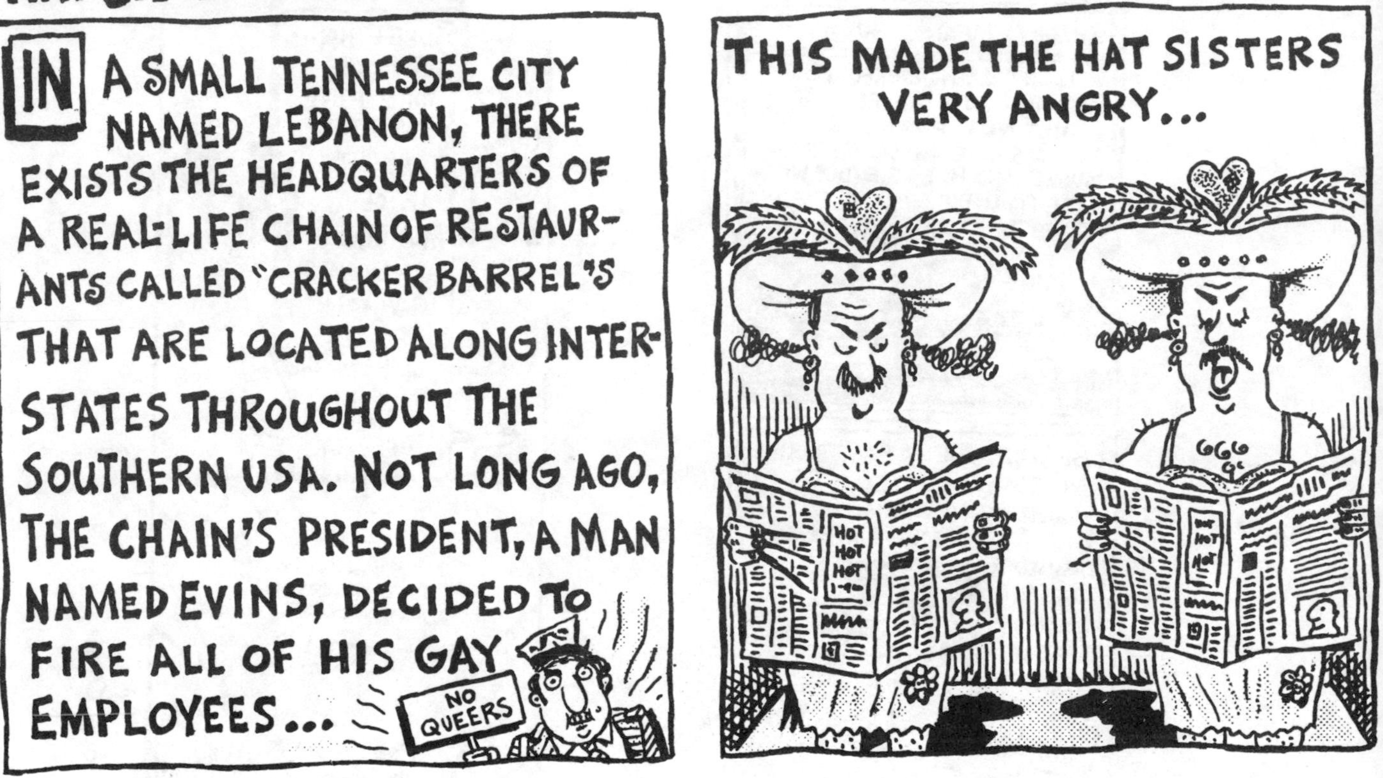
IN A SMALL TENNESSEE CITY NAMED LEBANON, THERE EXISTS THE HEADQUARTERS OF A REAL-LIFE CHAIN OF RESTAURANTS CALLED "CRACKER BARREL'S" THAT ARE LOCATED ALONG INTERSTATES THROUGHOUT THE SOUTHERN USA. NOT LONG AGO, THE CHAIN'S PRESIDENT, A MAN NAMED EVINS, DECIDED TO FIRE ALL OF HIS GAY EMPLOYEES...
NO QUEERS
THIS MADE THE HAT SISTERS VERY ANGRY...
HOT HOT HOT

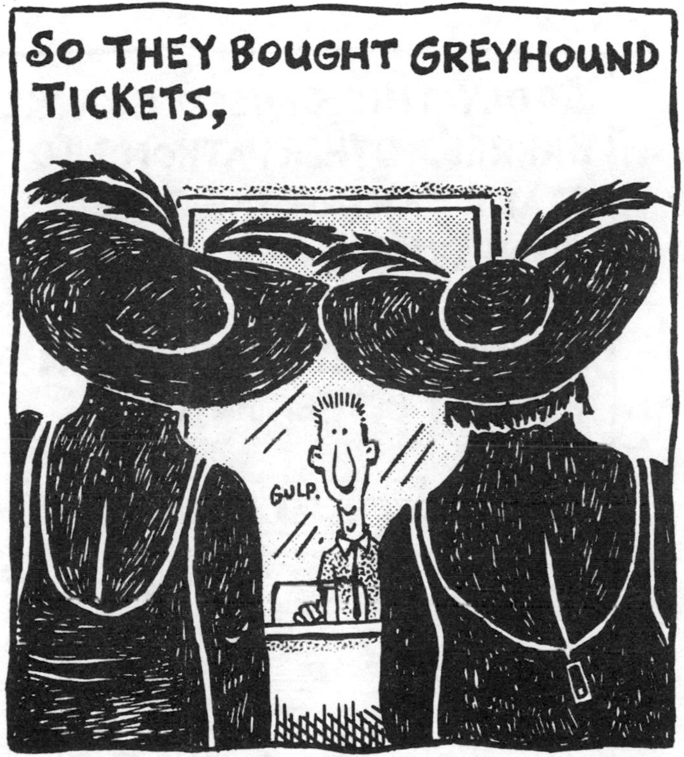
SO THEY BOUGHT GREYHOUND TICKETS,
GULP.

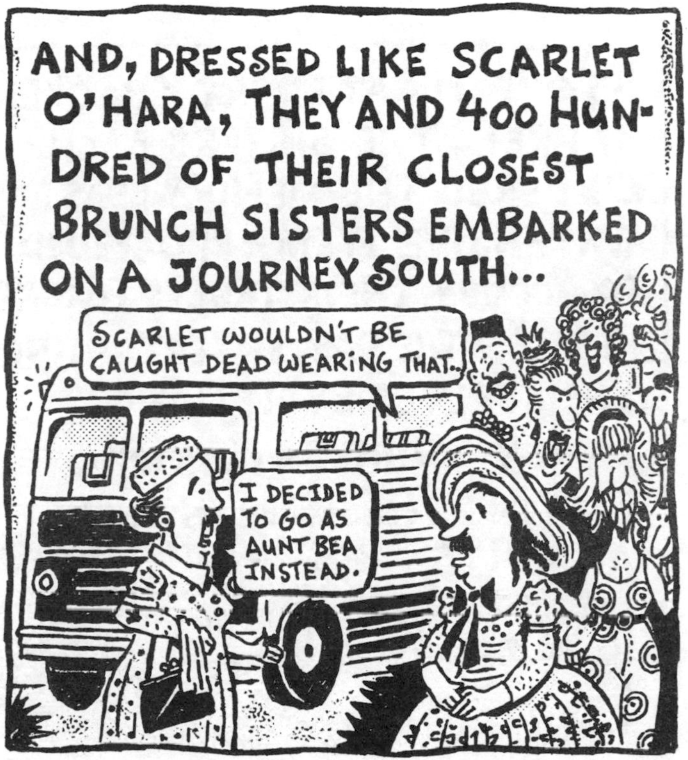
AND, DRESSED LIKE SCARLET O'HARA, THEY AND 400 HUN-DRED OF THEIR CLOSEST BRUNCH SISTERS EMBARKED ON A JOURNEY SOUTH...
SCARLET WOULDN'T BE CAUGHT DEAD WEARING THAT..
I DECIDED TO GO AS AUNT BEA INSTEAD.

CONTINUED →

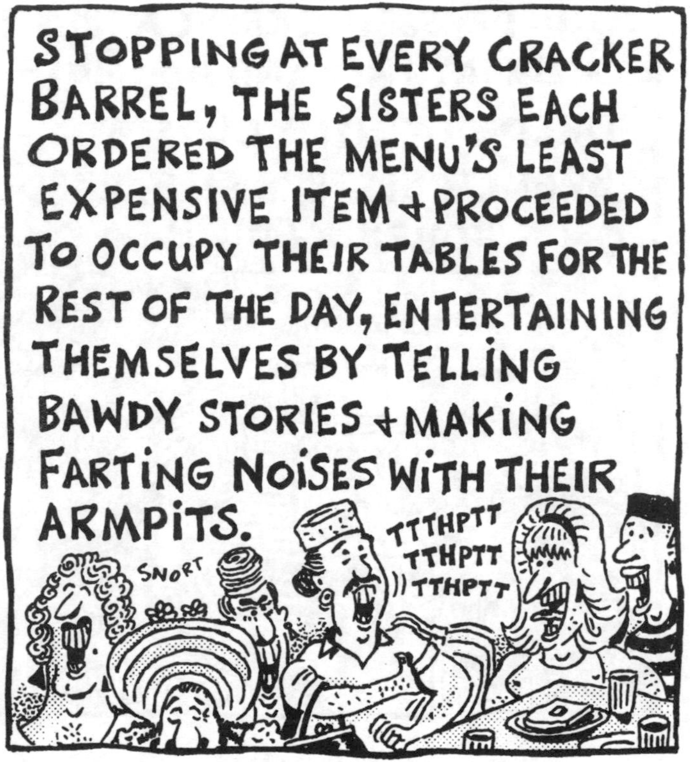
STOPPING AT EVERY CRACKER BARREL, THE SISTERS EACH ORDERED THE MENU'S LEAST EXPENSIVE ITEM + PROCEEDED TO OCCUPY THEIR TABLES FOR THE REST OF THE DAY, ENTERTAINING THEMSELVES BY TELLING BAWDY STORIES + MAKING FARTING NOISES WITH THEIR ARMPITS.
SNORT
TTTHPTT
TTHPTT
TTHPTT

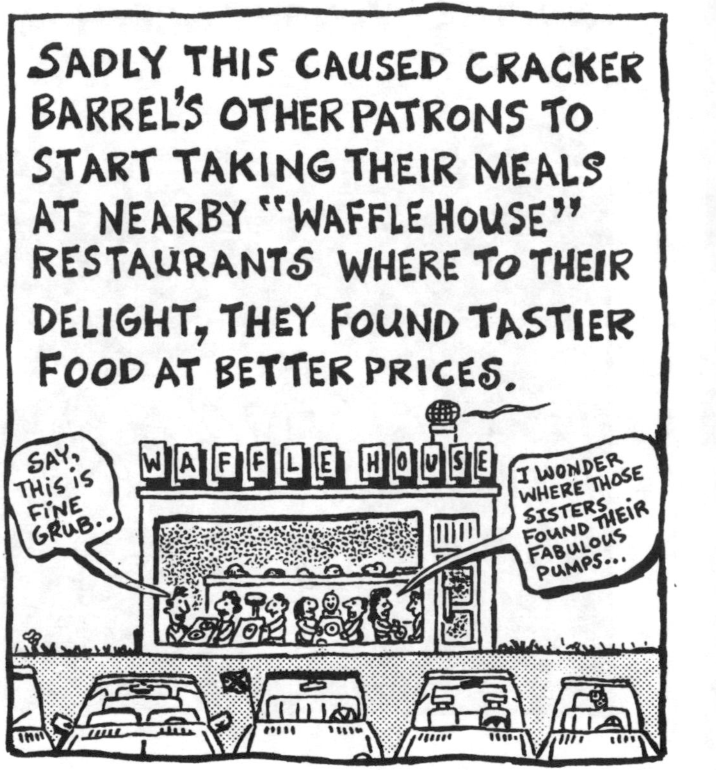
SADLY THIS CAUSED CRACKER BARREL'S OTHER PATRONS TO START TAKING THEIR MEALS AT NEARBY "WAFFLE HOUSE" RESTAURANTS WHERE TO THEIR DELIGHT, THEY FOUND TASTIER FOOD AT BETTER PRICES.
SAY, THIS IS FINE GRUB..
WAFFLE HOUSE
I WONDER WHERE THOSE SISTERS FOUND THEIR FABULOUS PUMPS...

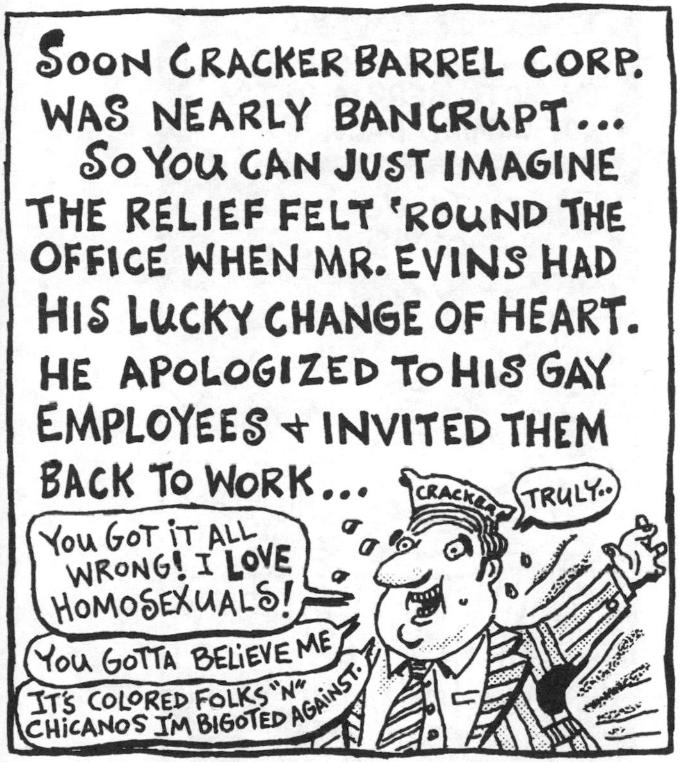
SOON CRACKER BARREL CORP. WAS NEARLY BANCRUPT...
SO YOU CAN JUST IMAGINE THE RELIEF FELT 'ROUND THE OFFICE WHEN MR. EVINS HAD HIS LUCKY CHANGE OF HEART. HE APOLOGIZED TO HIS GAY EMPLOYEES + INVITED THEM BACK TO WORK...
CRACKER
TRULY..
YOU GOT IT ALL WRONG! I LOVE HOMOSEXUALS!
YOU GOTTA BELIEVE ME
IT'S COLORED FOLKS "N" CHICANOS I'M BIGOTED AGAINST.

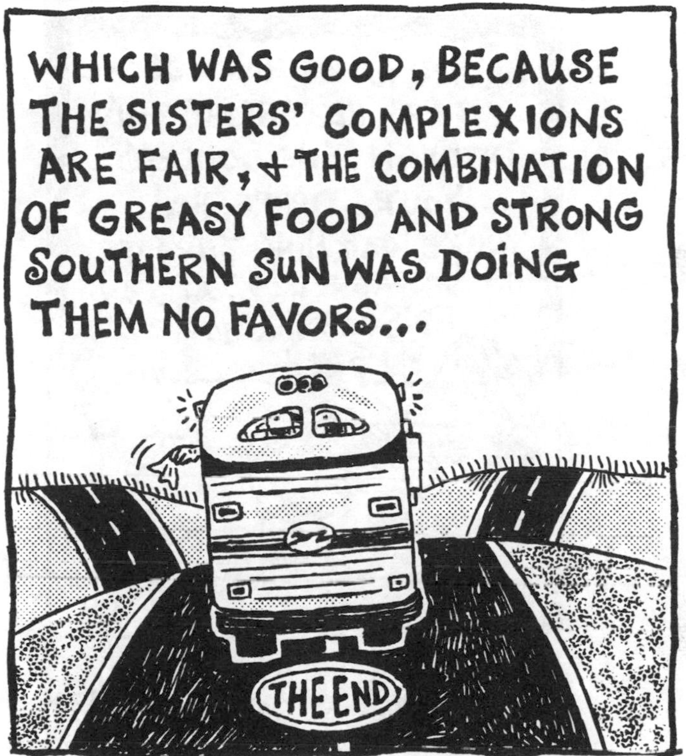
WHICH WAS GOOD, BECAUSE THE SISTERS' COMPLEXIONS ARE FAIR, + THE COMBINATION OF GREASY FOOD AND STRONG SOUTHERN SUN WAS DOING THEM NO FAVORS...
THE END

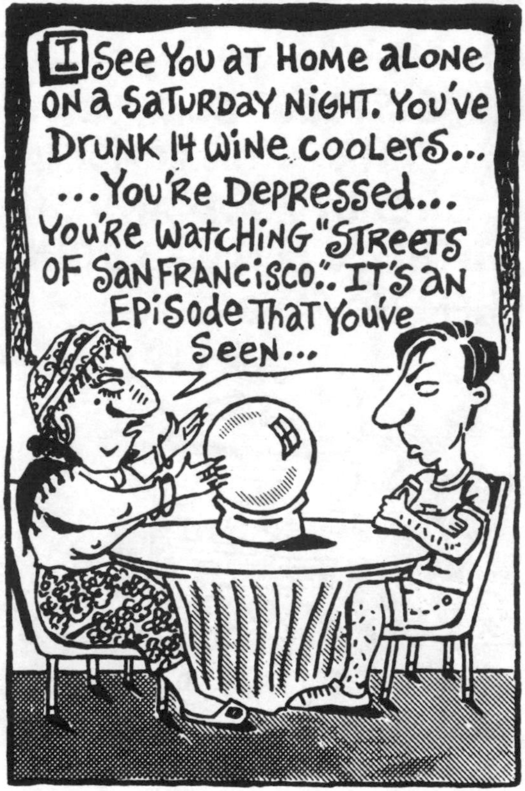
I SEE YOU AT HOME ALONE ON A SATURDAY NIGHT. YOU'VE DRUNK 14 WINE COOLERS... ...YOU'RE DEPRESSED... YOU'RE WATCHING "STREETS OF SAN FRANCISCO." IT'S AN EPISODE THAT YOU'VE SEEN...

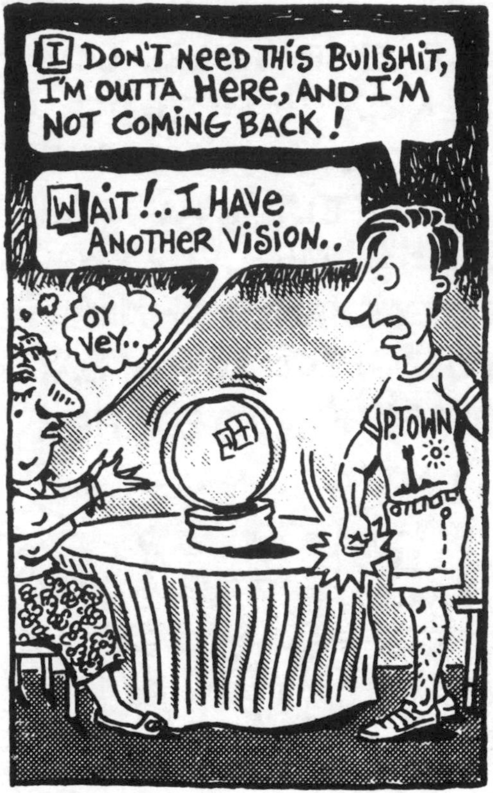
I DON'T NEED THIS BULLSHIT, I'M OUTTA HERE, AND I'M NOT COMING BACK!
WAIT!.. I HAVE ANOTHER VISION..
OY VEY..
P.TOWN

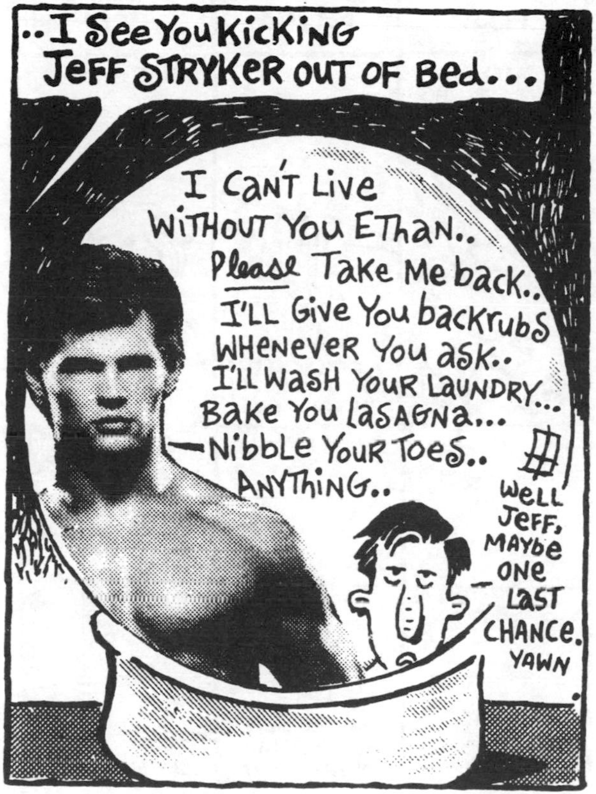
..I See You KicKing JeFF STRYKeR OUT OF Bed...
I CAN'T Live WiTHOUT You EThan.. Please Take Me back.. I'LL Give You backrubs WHenever You ask.. I'LL WASH YOUR LAUNDRY... Bake You lasagna... Nibble YouR Toes.. ANYThING..
WeLL JeFF, MAYbe ONE LAST CHANCE. YAWN

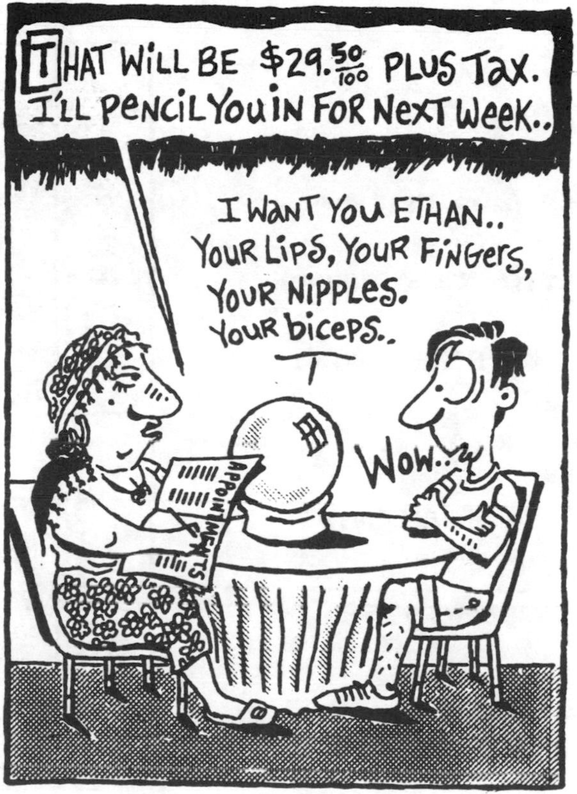
THAT WiLL BE $29.50/100 PLUS Tax. I'LL PenciL You iN FOR NeXT Week..
I WANT You ETHAN.. YOUR LiPS, YOUR FiNGers, YOUR NiPPLES. YOUR biceps..
APPOINTMENTS
Wow..

IMPRESS YOUR FRIENDS.

EXUDE WITTINESS AT BRUNCH.

ALWAYS BE IN THE KNOW,

with

THE ETHAN GREEN GUIDE

TO FABULOUSNESS

CHART.

FOODS
PLANS
POLITICS
PETS
FABULOUS.
LIME
LOW CAL
FROZEN FRUIT BARS
BELLY LOX
PASTA PRIMAVERA
2 DATES FOR SAME EVENING
YOU'RE SO MUCH MAN BUCKY.. TAKE ME NOW..
NO NO TAKE ME. TAKE ME
A DEMOCRATIC NOMINEE FOR PRES. WHO CAN WIN...
SHAR-PEIS.
GATSBY
REALLY NOT THAT FABULOUS.
BUGLES
BATMAN CEREAL
CANDY NECKLACES
NO DATES FOR SAME EVENING
THE PERSON THE DEMS WILL NOMINATE INSTEAD.
BETH.. THESE DONT LOOK LIKE MONKEYS... THEY LOOK LIKE BUGS..
SEA-MONKEYS.

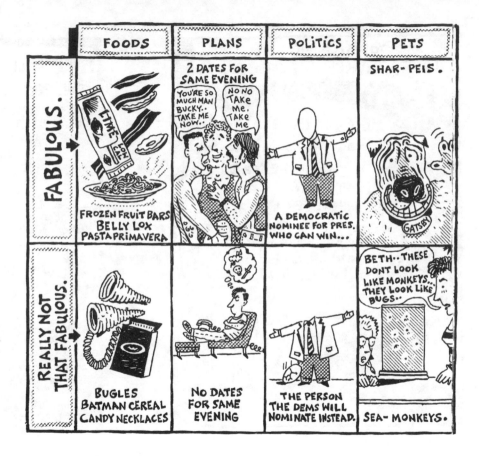

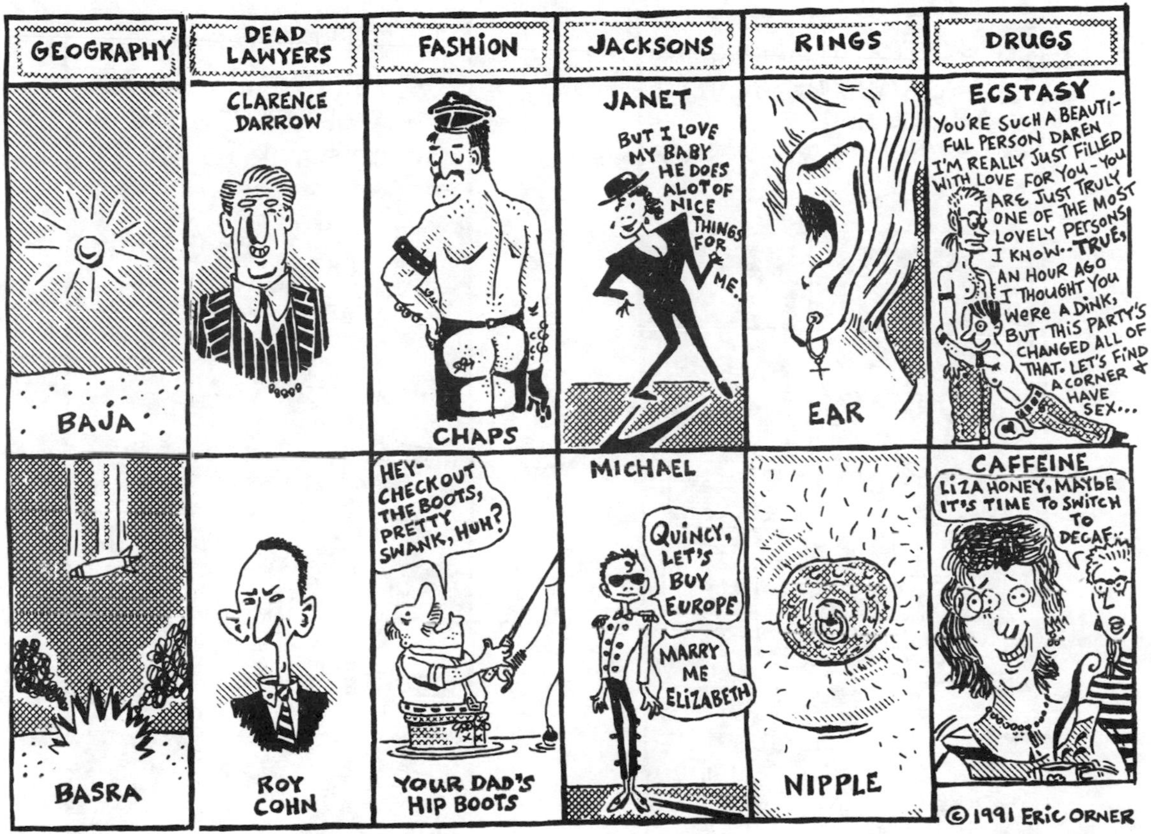

GEOGRAPHY
DEAD LAWYERS
FASHION
JACKSONS
RINGS
DRUGS
BAJA
CLARENCE DARROW
CHAPS
JANET
BUT I LOVE MY BABY HE DOES ALOT OF NICE THINGS FOR ME.
EAR
ECSTASY
YOU'RE SUCH A BEAUTIFUL PERSON DAREN I'M REALLY JUST FILLED WITH LOVE FOR YOU - YOU ARE JUST TRULY ONE OF THE MOST LOVELY PERSONS I KNOW.. TRUE, AN HOUR AGO I THOUGHT YOU WERE A DINK, BUT THIS PARTY'S CHANGED ALL OF THAT. LET'S FIND A CORNER & HAVE SEX...
BASRA
ROY COHN
HEY- CHECK OUT THE BOOTS, PRETTY SWANK, HUH?
YOUR DAD'S HIP BOOTS
MICHAEL
QUINCY, LET'S BUY EUROPE
MARRY ME ELIZABETH
NIPPLE
CAFFEINE
LIZA HONEY, MAYBE IT'S TIME TO SWITCH TO DECAF..
©1991 ERIC ORNER

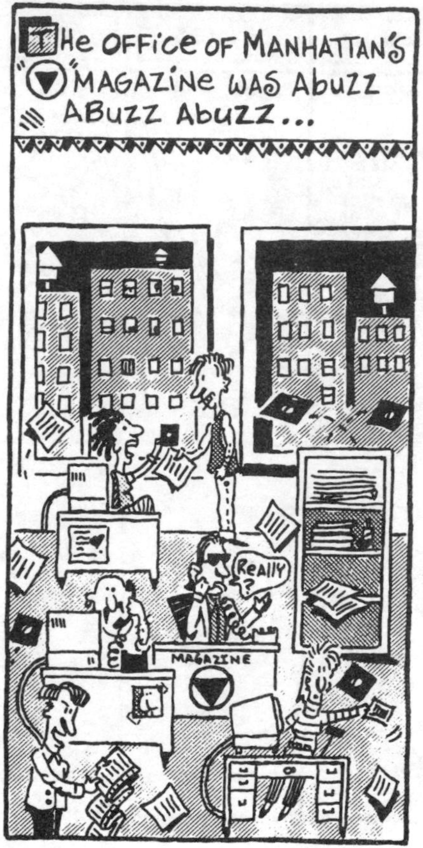
THE OFFICE OF MANHATTAN'S "▼" MAGAZINE WAS ABUZZ ABUZZ ABUZZ...
Really ?
MAGAZINE

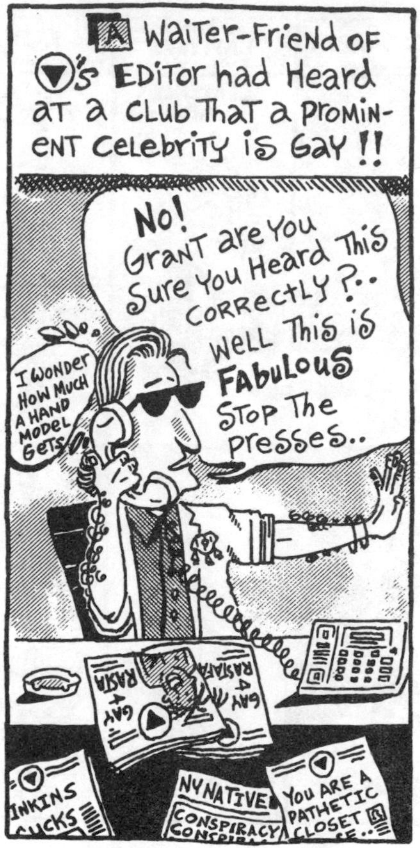
A WAITER-FRIEND OF ▼'S EDITOR HAD HEARD AT A CLUB THAT A PROMINENT CELEBRITY IS GAY !!
No! Grant are you sure you heard this correctly?.. Well this is FABULOUS Stop the presses..
I WONDER HOW MUCH A HAND MODEL GETS
GAY 4 RASTA
NY NATIVE
CONSPIRACY
YOU ARE A PATHETIC CLOSET

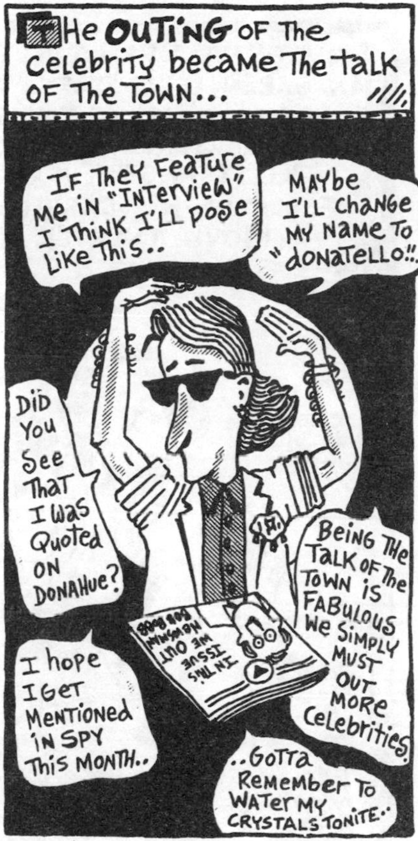
The OUTING of the celebrity became the talk of the town...
If they feature me in "Interview" I think I'll pose like this..
Maybe I'll change my name to "donatello"!!
Did you see that I was quoted on Donahue?
Being the talk of the town is fabulous we simply must out more celebrities.
I hope I get mentioned in SPY this month..
..Gotta remember to water my crystals tonite..

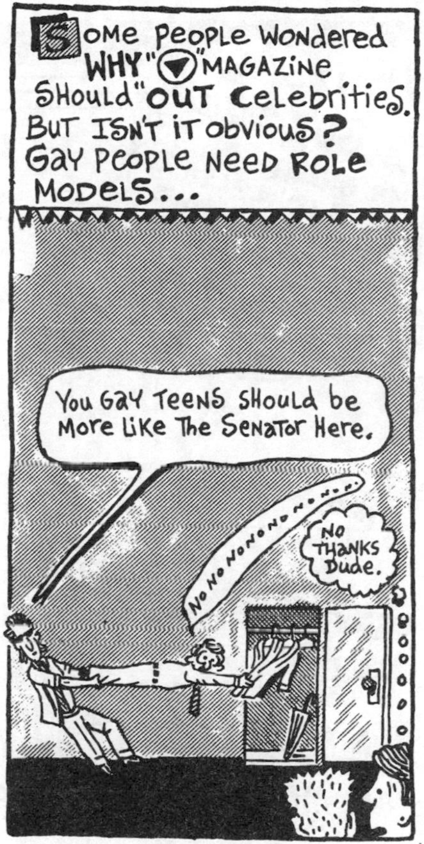
Some people wondered WHY "▼" magazine should "OUT" celebrities. But isn't it obvious? Gay people need ROLE MODELS...
You gay teens should be more like the Senator here.
No No No No No No No No No
No thanks dude.

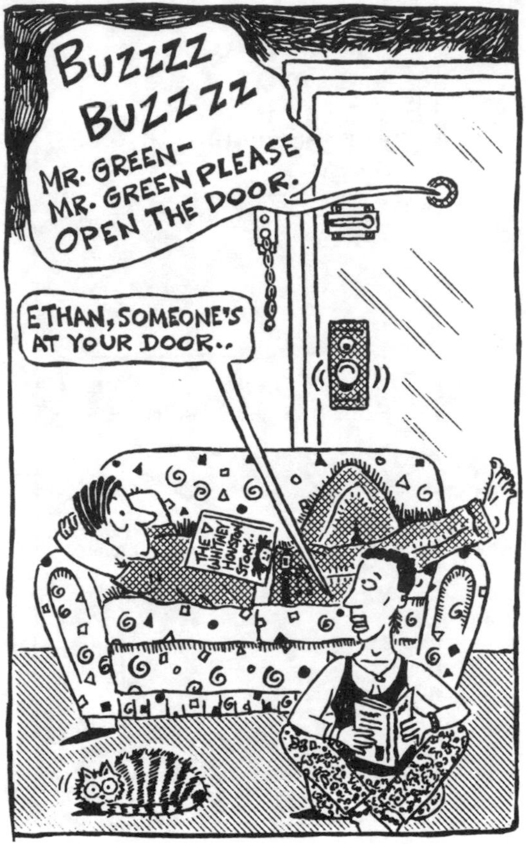
BUZZZZ
BUZZZZ
MR. GREEN-
MR. GREEN PLEASE
OPEN THE DOOR.
ETHAN, SOMEONE'S AT YOUR DOOR..
THE WHITNEY HOUSTON STORY

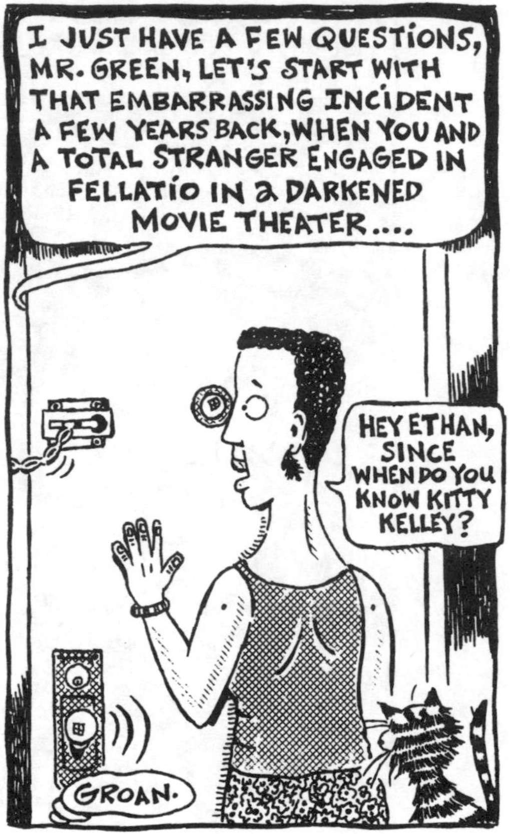
I JUST HAVE A FEW QUESTIONS, MR. GREEN, LET'S START WITH THAT EMBARRASSING INCIDENT A FEW YEARS BACK, WHEN YOU AND A TOTAL STRANGER ENGAGED IN FELLATIO IN A DARKENED MOVIE THEATER....
HEY ETHAN, SINCE WHEN DO YOU KNOW KITTY KELLEY?
GROAN.

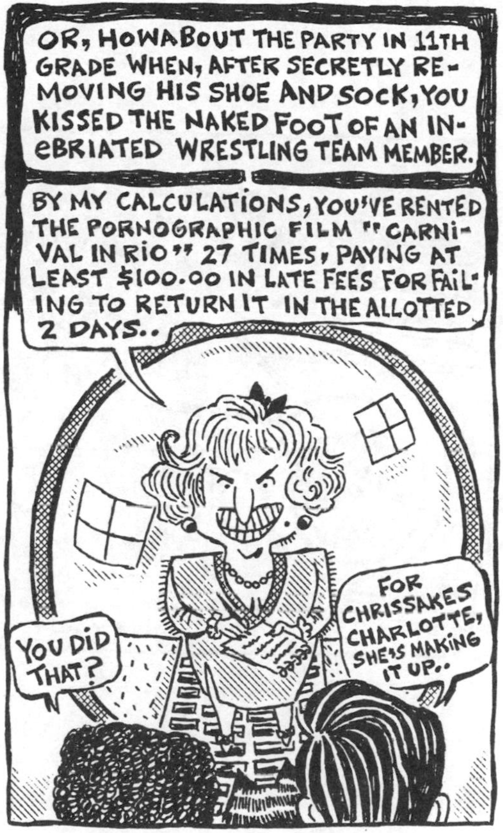
OR, HOWABOUT THE PARTY IN 11TH GRADE WHEN, AFTER SECRETLY RE-MOVING HIS SHOE AND SOCK, YOU KISSED THE NAKED FOOT OF AN IN-EBRIATED WRESTLING TEAM MEMBER.
BY MY CALCULATIONS, YOU'VE RENTED THE PORNOGRAPHIC FILM "CARNIVAL IN RIO" 27 TIMES, PAYING AT LEAST $100.00 IN LATE FEES FOR FAILING TO RETURN IT IN THE ALLOTTED 2 DAYS..
YOU DID THAT?
FOR CHRISSAKES CHARLOTTE, SHE'S MAKING IT UP..

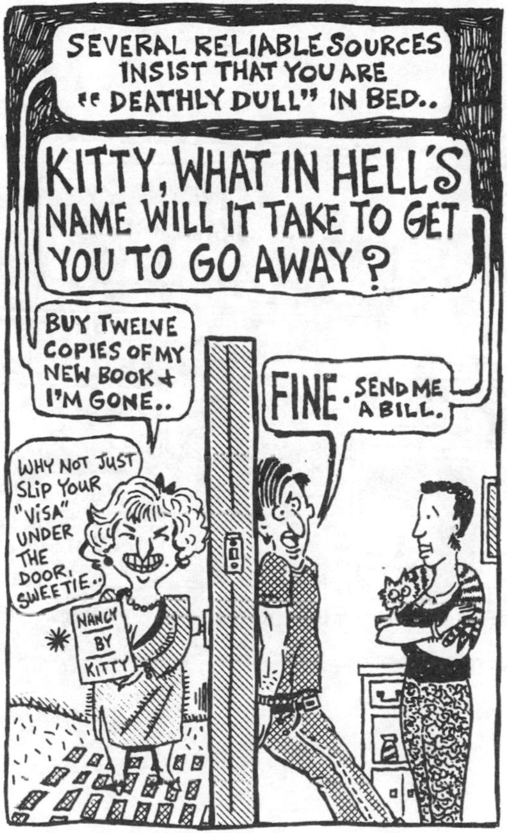
SEVERAL RELIABLE SOURCES INSIST THAT YOU ARE "DEATHLY DULL" IN BED..
KITTY, WHAT IN HELL'S NAME WILL IT TAKE TO GET YOU TO GO AWAY?
BUY TWELVE COPIES OF MY NEW BOOK + I'M GONE..
FINE. SEND ME A BILL.
WHY NOT JUST SLIP YOUR "VISA" UNDER THE DOOR, SWEETIE..
NANCY BY KITTY

* "NANCY" BOOK BONUS: "LATER, AFTER SHE AND GORBACHEV SHED THEIR LEATHER BONDAGE TOGS, NANCY LIT UP A SMOKE, "LET'S OFF MITTERAND" SHE SUGGESTED 'FRENCH GUYS BUG ME.'"

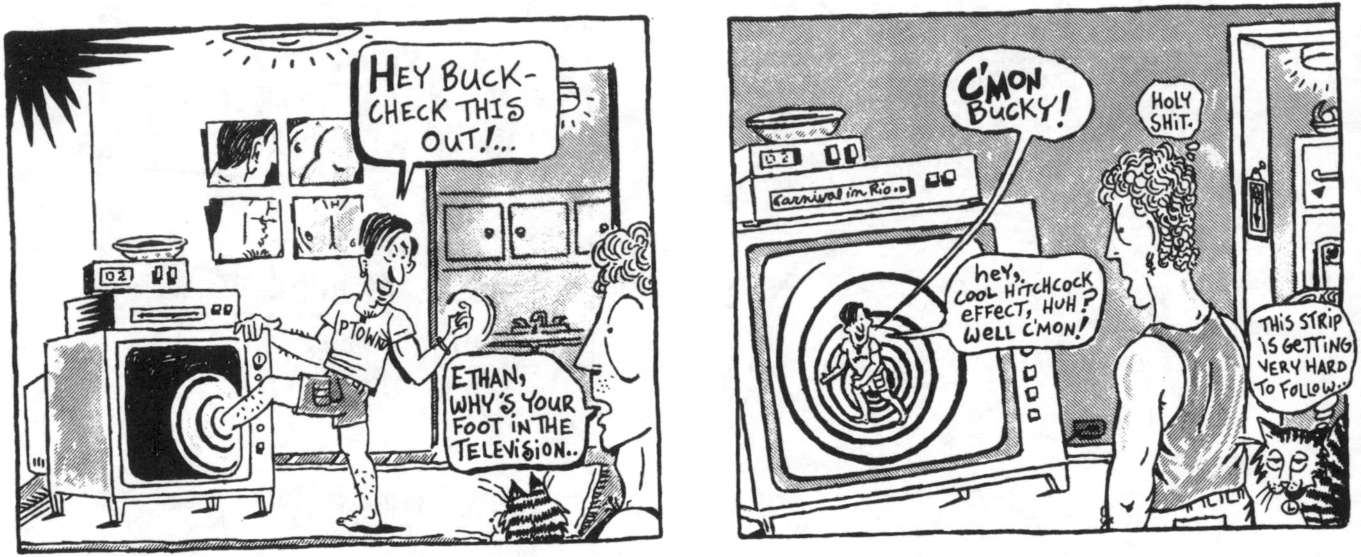
HEY BUCK-
CHECK THIS
OUT!...
PTOWN
ETHAN,
WHY'S YOUR
FOOT IN THE
TELEVISION..
Carnival in Rio
C'MON
BUCKY!
hey,
COOL HITCHCOCK
eFFECT, HUH?
WELL C'MON!
HOLY
SHIT.
THIS STRIP
IS GETTING
VERY HARD
TO FOLLOW..

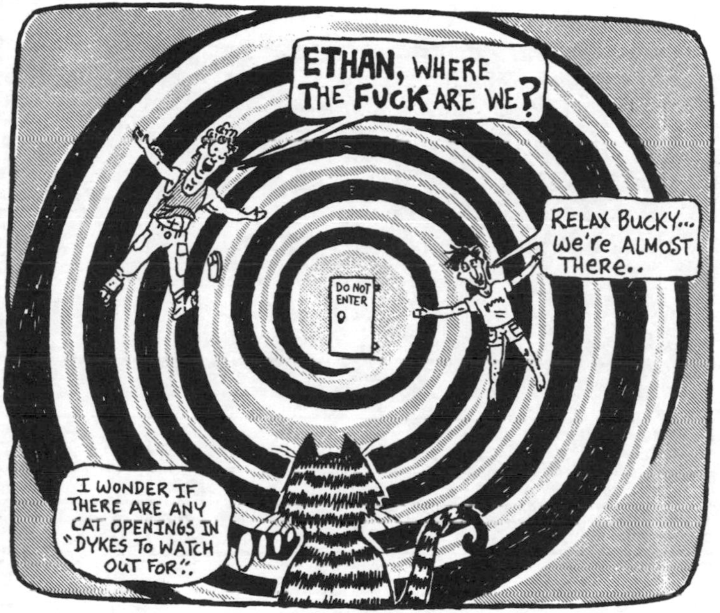
ETHAN, WHERE THE FUCK ARE WE?
RELAX BUCKY... WE'RE ALMOST THERE..
DO NOT ENTER
I WONDER IF THERE ARE ANY CAT OPENINGS IN "DYKES TO WATCH OUT FOR".

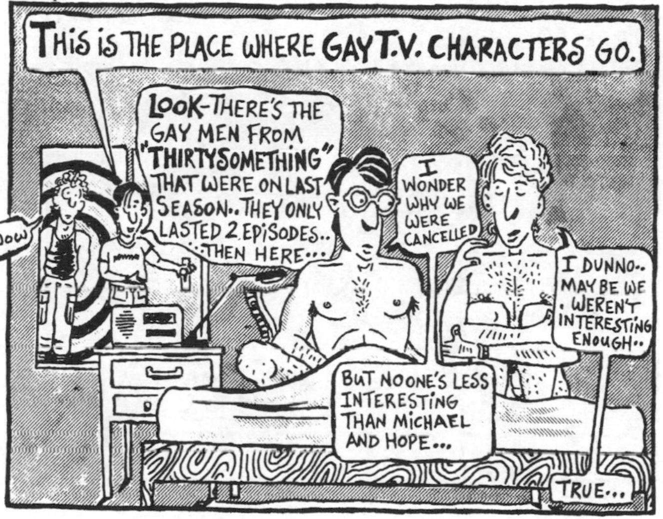
THIS IS THE PLACE WHERE GAY T.V. CHARACTERS GO.
LOOK-THERE'S THE GAY MEN FROM "THIRTYSOMETHING" THAT WERE ON LAST SEASON.. THEY ONLY LASTED 2 EPISODES.. ...THEN HERE...
WOW
I WONDER WHY WE WERE CANCELLED
I DUNNO.. MAYBE WE WEREN'T INTERESTING ENOUGH..
BUT NOONE'S LESS INTERESTING THAN MICHAEL AND HOPE...
TRUE...

CONTINUED →

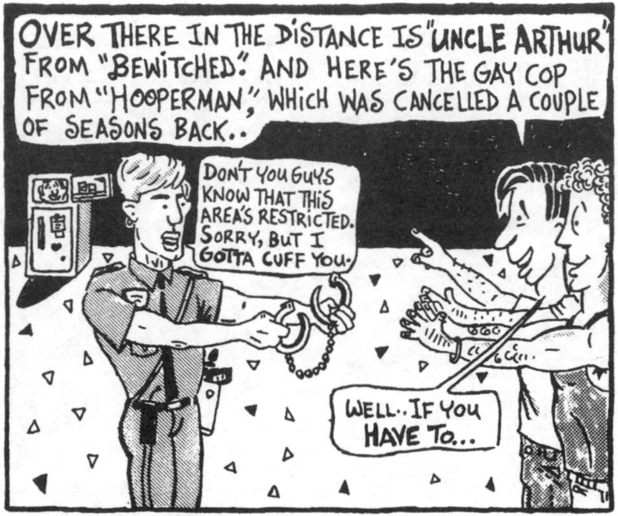
OVER THERE IN THE DISTANCE IS "UNCLE ARTHUR" FROM "BEWITCHED." AND HERE'S THE GAY COP FROM "HOOPERMAN," WHICH WAS CANCELLED A COUPLE OF SEASONS BACK..
DON'T YOU GUYS KNOW THAT THIS AREA'S RESTRICTED. SORRY, BUT I GOTTA CUFF YOU.
WELL.. IF YOU HAVE TO...

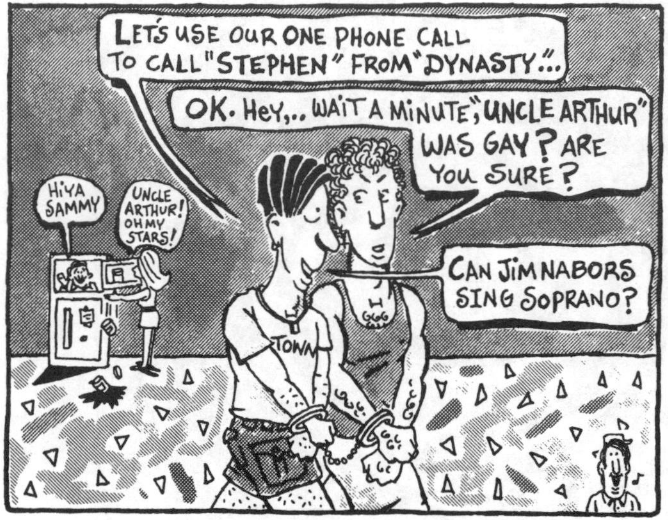
LET'S USE OUR ONE PHONE CALL TO CALL "STEPHEN" FROM "DYNASTY."...
OK. Hey,.. WAIT A MINUTE, "UNCLE ARTHUR" WAS GAY? ARE YOU SURE?
HiYA SAMMY
UNCLE ARTHUR! OH MY STARS!
CAN JIM NABORS SING SOPRANO?

THANKS TO A. SOUSA...

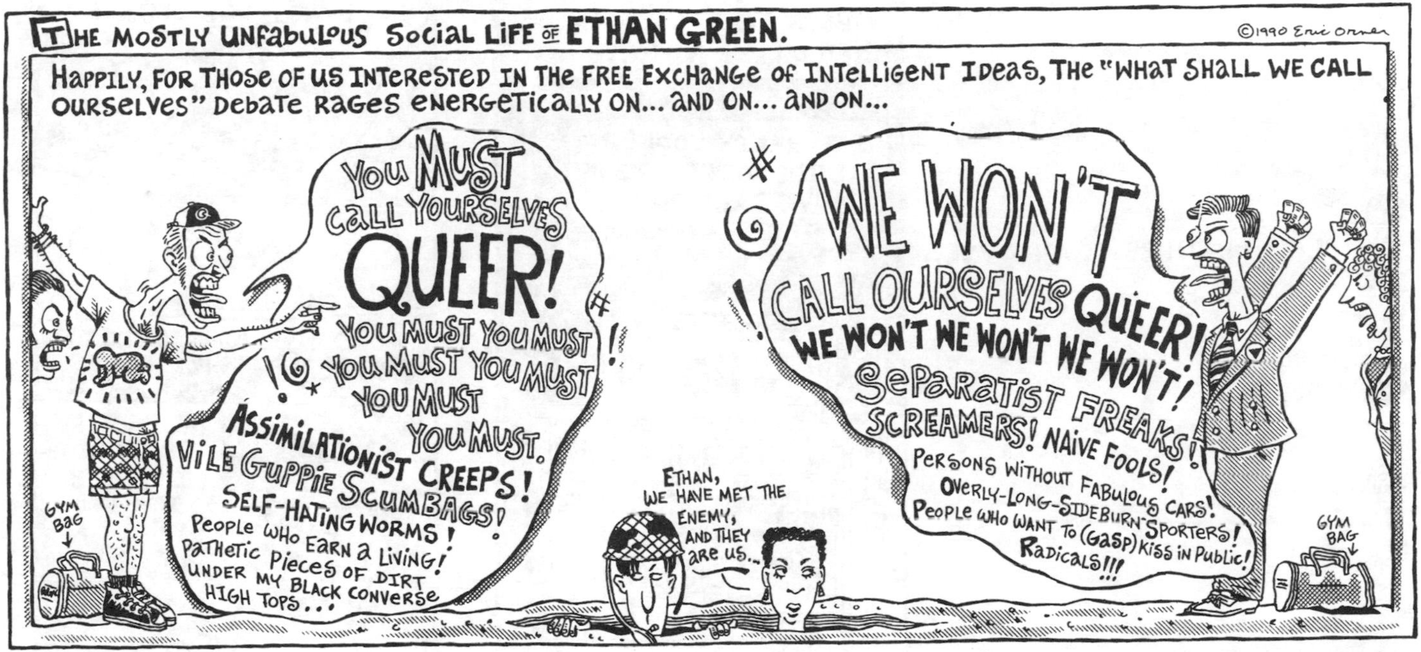
THE MOSTLY UNFABULOUS SOCIAL LIFE OF ETHAN GREEN.
©1990 Eric Orner
HAPPILY, FOR THOSE OF US INTERESTED IN THE FREE EXCHANGE OF INTELLIGENT IDEAS, THE "WHAT SHALL WE CALL OURSELVES" DEBATE RAGES ENERGETICALLY ON... AND ON... AND ON...
YOU MUST CALL YOURSELVES QUEER! YOU MUST YOU MUST YOU MUST YOU MUST YOU MUST YOU MUST. ASSIMILATIONIST CREEPS! VILE GUPPIE SCUMBAGS! SELF-HATING WORMS! PEOPLE WHO EARN A LIVING! PATHETIC PIECES OF DIRT UNDER MY BLACK CONVERSE HIGH TOPS...
GYM BAG
WE WON'T CALL OURSELVES QUEER! WE WON'T WE WON'T WE WON'T! SEPARATIST FREAKS! SCREAMERS! NAIVE FOOLS! PERSONS WITHOUT FABULOUS CARS! OVERLY-LONG-SIDEBURN-SPORTERS! PEOPLE WHO WANT TO (GASP) KISS IN PUBLIC! RADICALS!!!
GYM BAG
ETHAN, WE HAVE MET THE ENEMY, AND THEY ARE US...

LIZA + BETH RENT A MOVIE..

ETHAN SAID HE'S COMING OVER, SO TRY + PICK ONE HE'LL LIKE ALSO...
I ALREADY LOOKED- ALL THE ROBBIE BENSON MOVIES ARE OUT...
VIDEO
SOMEWHERE IN THE "RIDICULOUS FILMS OF THE 1970'S" SECTION, LIZA MAKES HER SELECTION
AIRPORT '77
PORT '77
SHOOT!!
AAAHH
GEO. KENNEDY DESERVES AN OSCAR...WOW!! -GENE SHALIT
BETH'LL NEVER GO FOR THIS....
OH HELL, CAN'T HURT TO ASK..
MEANWHILE, ACROSS THE STORE IN FOREIGN FILMS..
BABETTE'S Feast
DAS IST GUT!
C'EST BON!
THIS FOOD LOOKS REALLY GOOD!..WOW! -GENE SHALIT
THIS IS MY ALL TIME FAVORITE- I WONDER IF LIZA'LL GIVE IT A CHANCE..

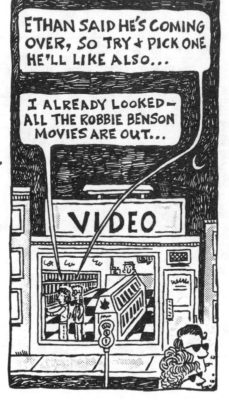

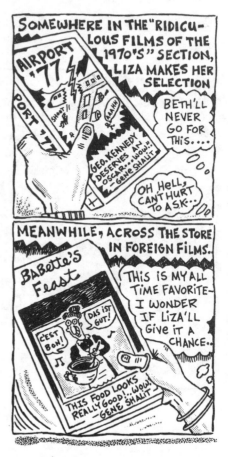

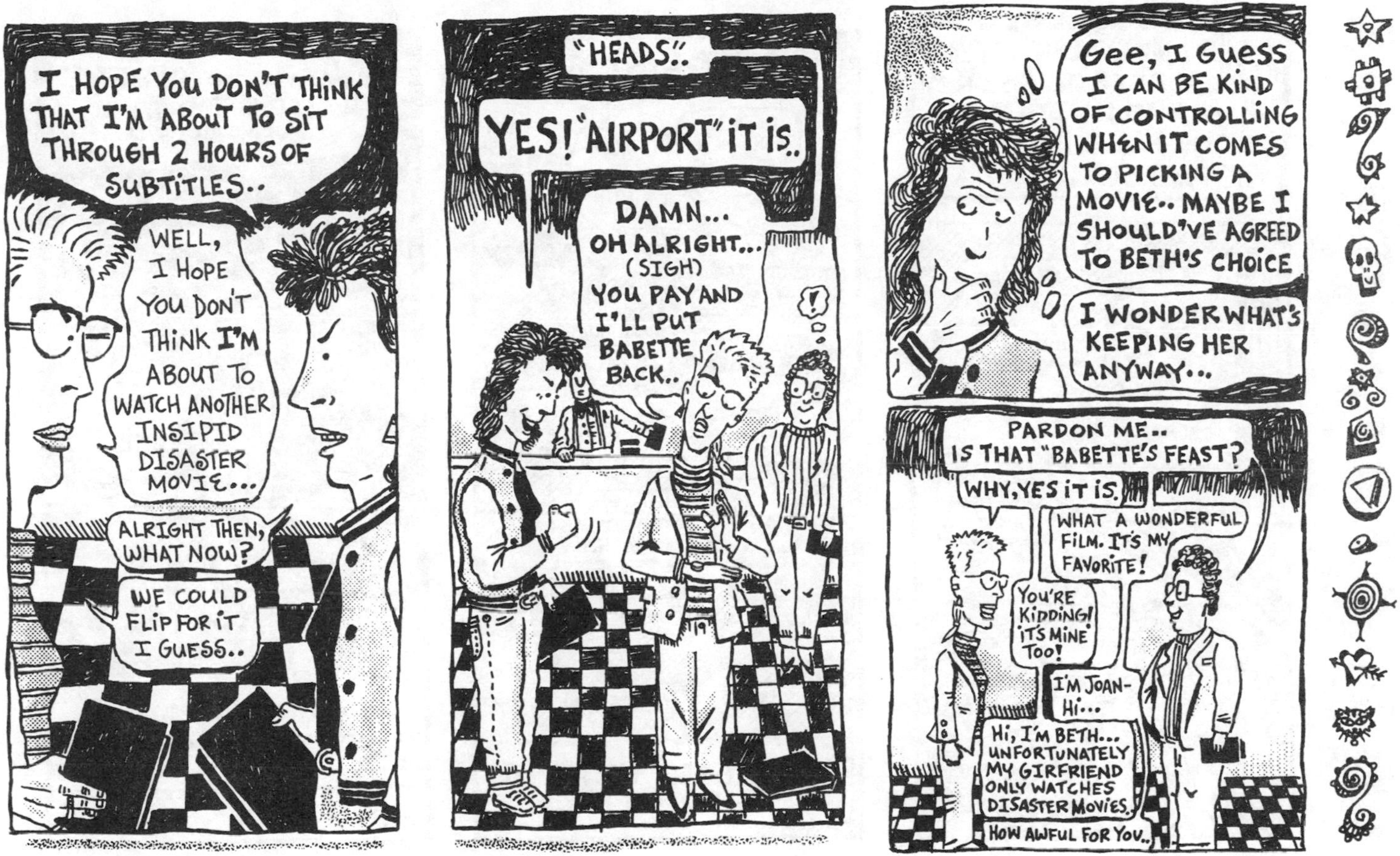
I HOPE YOU DON'T THINK THAT I'M ABOUT TO SIT THROUGH 2 HOURS OF SUBTITLES..
WELL, I HOPE YOU DON'T THINK I'M ABOUT TO WATCH ANOTHER INSIPID DISASTER MOVIE...
ALRIGHT THEN, WHAT NOW?
WE COULD FLIP FOR IT I GUESS..
"HEADS"..
YES! "AIRPORT" IT IS..
DAMN... OH ALRIGHT... (SIGH) YOU PAY AND I'LL PUT BABETTE BACK..
!
Gee, I GUESS I CAN BE KIND OF CONTROLLING WHEN IT COMES TO PICKING A MOVIE.. MAYBE I SHOULD'VE AGREED TO BETH'S CHOICE
I WONDER WHAT'S KEEPING HER ANYWAY...
PARDON ME.. IS THAT "BABETTE'S FEAST?
WHY, YES IT IS.
WHAT A WONDERFUL FILM. IT'S MY FAVORITE!
YOU'RE KIDDING! IT'S MINE TOO!
I'M JOAN-HI...
HI, I'M BETH... UNFORTUNATELY MY GIRFRIEND ONLY WATCHES DISASTER MOVIES.
HOW AWFUL FOR YOU..

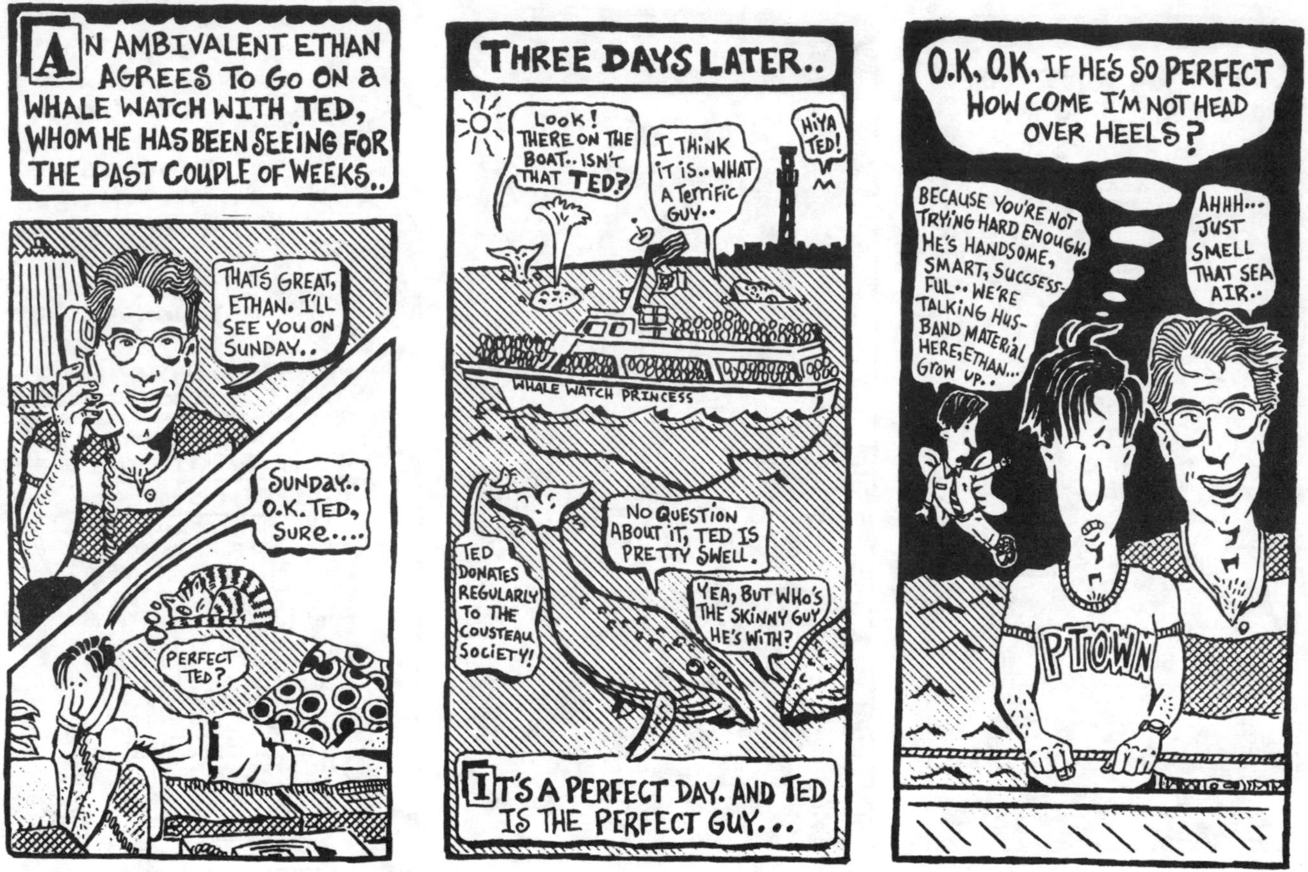
AN AMBIVALENT ETHAN AGREES TO GO ON A WHALE WATCH WITH TED, WHOM HE HAS BEEN SEEING FOR THE PAST COUPLE OF WEEKS..
THAT'S GREAT, ETHAN. I'LL SEE YOU ON SUNDAY..
SUNDAY.. O.K. TED, SURE....
PERFECT TED?
THREE DAYS LATER..
LOOK! THERE ON THE BOAT.. ISN'T THAT TED?
I THINK IT IS.. WHAT A TERRIFIC GUY..
HIYA TED!
WHALE WATCH PRINCESS
TED DONATES REGULARLY TO THE COUSTEAU SOCIETY!
NO QUESTION ABOUT IT, TED IS PRETTY SWELL.
YEA, BUT WHO'S THE SKINNY GUY HE'S WITH?
IT'S A PERFECT DAY. AND TED IS THE PERFECT GUY...
O.K, O.K, IF HE'S SO PERFECT HOW COME I'M NOT HEAD OVER HEELS?
BECAUSE YOU'RE NOT TRYING HARD ENOUGH. HE'S HANDSOME, SMART, SUCCESSFUL.. WE'RE TALKING HUSBAND MATERIAL HERE, ETHAN... GROW UP..
AHHH... JUST SMELL THAT SEA AIR..
PTOWN

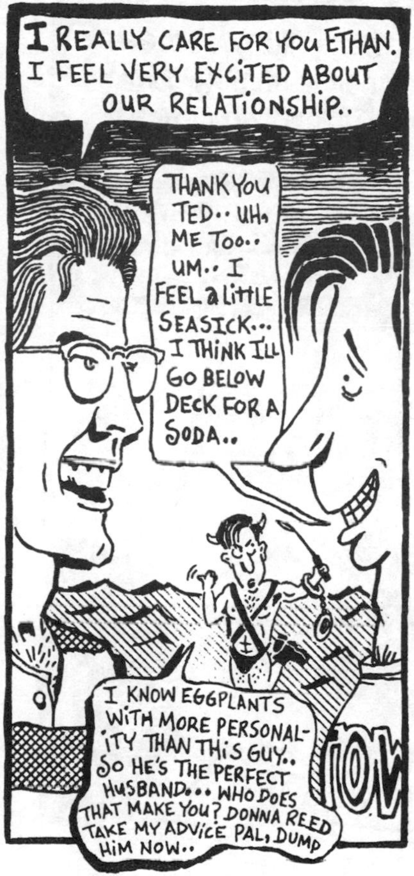
I REALLY CARE FOR YOU ETHAN. I FEEL VERY EXCITED ABOUT OUR RELATIONSHIP..
THANK YOU TED.. UH, ME TOO.. UM.. I FEEL A LITTLE SEASICK... I THINK I'LL GO BELOW DECK FOR A SODA..
I KNOW EGGPLANTS WITH MORE PERSONALITY THAN THIS GUY.. SO HE'S THE PERFECT HUSBAND... WHO DOES THAT MAKE YOU? DONNA REED TAKE MY ADVICE PAL, DUMP HIM NOW..

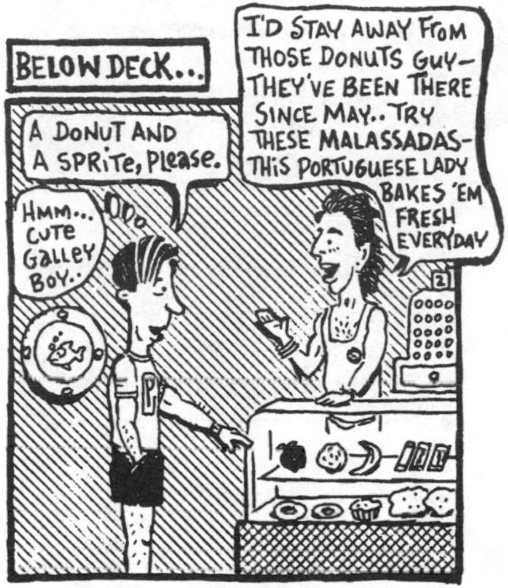
BELOW DECK...
A DONUT AND A SPRITE, PLEASE.
HMM... CUTE GALLEY BOY..
I'D STAY AWAY FROM THOSE DONUTS GUY– THEY'VE BEEN THERE SINCE MAY.. TRY THESE MALASSADAS– THIS PORTUGUESE LADY BAKES 'EM FRESH EVERYDAY

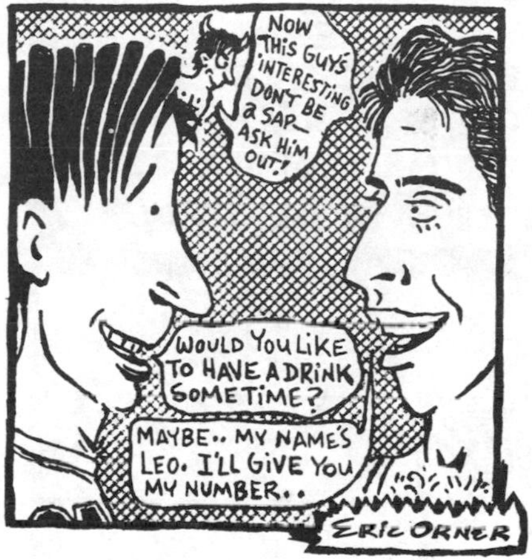
NOW THIS GUY'S INTERESTING DON'T BE A SAP– ASK HIM OUT!
WOULD YOU LIKE TO HAVE A DRINK SOMETIME?
MAYBE.. MY NAME'S LEO. I'LL GIVE YOU MY NUMBER..
ERIC ORNER

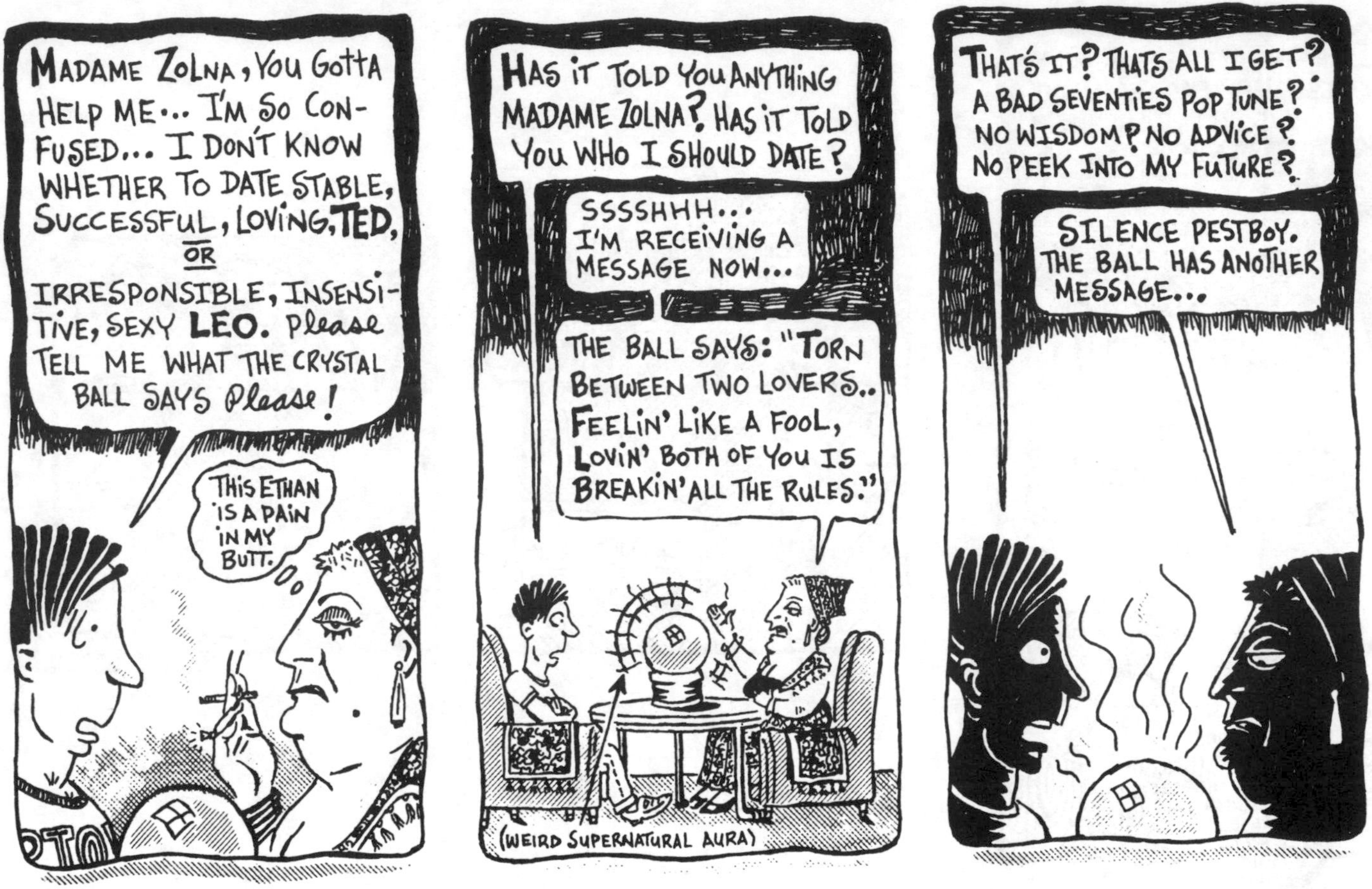
MADAME ZOLNA, YOU GOTTA HELP ME... I'M SO CONFUSED... I DON'T KNOW WHETHER TO DATE STABLE, SUCCESSFUL, LOVING, **TED**, OR IRRESPONSIBLE, INSENSITIVE, SEXY **LEO.** Please TELL ME WHAT THE CRYSTAL BALL SAYS Please!
THIS ETHAN IS A PAIN IN MY BUTT.
HAS IT TOLD YOU ANYTHING MADAME ZOLNA? HAS IT TOLD YOU WHO I SHOULD DATE?
SSSSHHH... I'M RECEIVING A MESSAGE NOW...
THE BALL SAYS: "TORN BETWEEN TWO LOVERS.. FEELIN' LIKE A FOOL, LOVIN' BOTH OF YOU IS BREAKIN' ALL THE RULES."
(WEIRD SUPERNATURAL AURA)
THAT'S IT? THATS ALL I GET? A BAD SEVENTIES POP TUNE? NO WISDOM? NO ADVICE? NO PEEK INTO MY FUTURE?
SILENCE PESTBOY. THE BALL HAS ANOTHER MESSAGE...

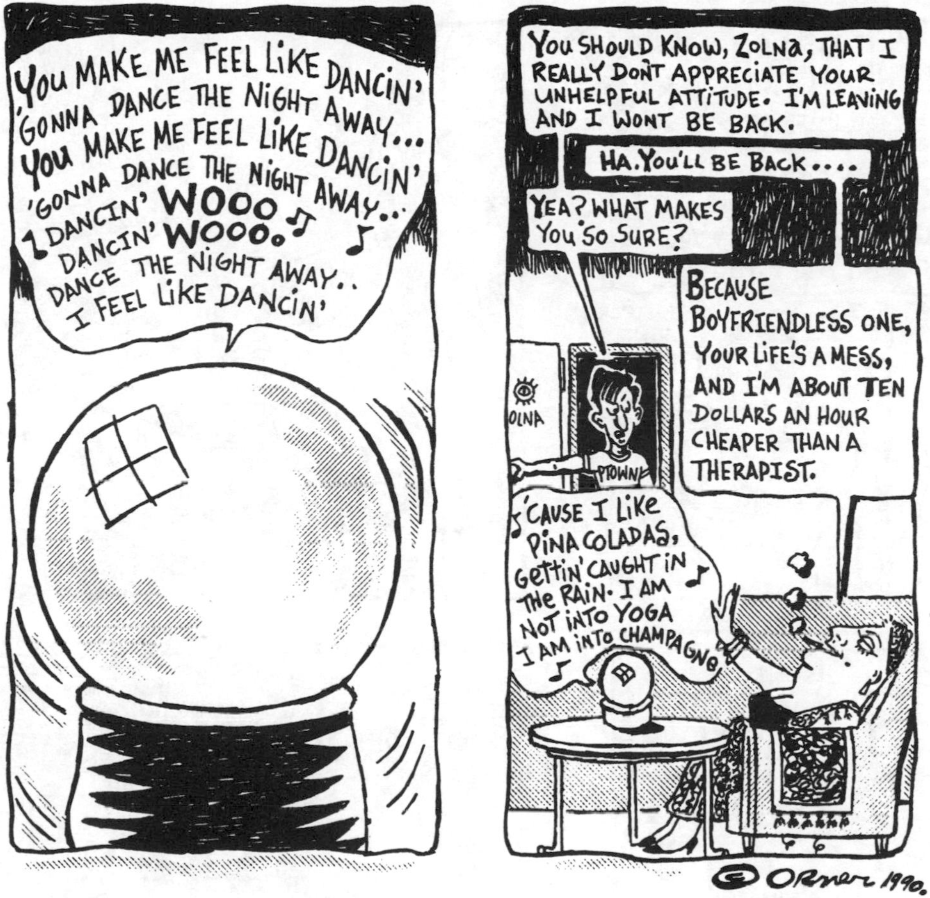
YOU MAKE ME FEEL LIKE DANCIN' 'GONNA DANCE THE NIGHT AWAY. YOU MAKE ME FEEL LIKE DANCIN' 'GONNA DANCE THE NIGHT AWAY... DANCIN' WOOO DANCIN' WOOO. DANCE THE NIGHT AWAY.. I FEEL LIKE DANCIN'
YOU SHOULD KNOW, ZOLNA, THAT I REALLY DON'T APPRECIATE YOUR UNHELPFUL ATTITUDE. I'M LEAVING AND I WONT BE BACK.
HA. YOU'LL BE BACK....
YEA? WHAT MAKES YOU SO SURE?
BECAUSE BOYFRIENDLESS ONE, YOUR LIFE'S A MESS, AND I'M ABOUT TEN DOLLARS AN HOUR CHEAPER THAN A THERAPIST.
'CAUSE I LIKE PINA COLADAS, GETTIN' CAUGHT IN THE RAIN. I AM NOT INTO YOGA I AM INTO CHAMPAGNE
OLNA
PTOWN
© ORNER 1990.

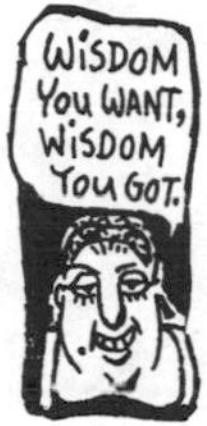
WISDOM YOU WANT, WISDOM YOU GOT.

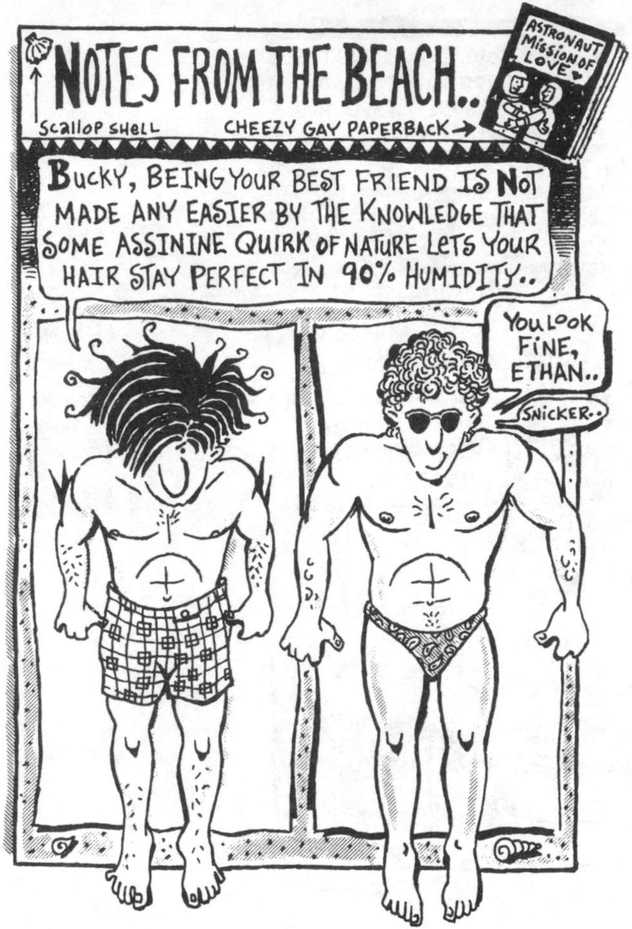
NOTES FROM THE BEACH..
ASTRONAUT MISSION OF LOVE
SCALLOP SHELL
CHEEZY GAY PAPERBACK
BUCKY, BEING YOUR BEST FRIEND IS NOT MADE ANY EASIER BY THE KNOWLEDGE THAT SOME ASSININE QUIRK OF NATURE LETS YOUR HAIR STAY PERFECT IN 90% HUMIDITY..
YOU LOOK FINE, ETHAN..
SNICKER..

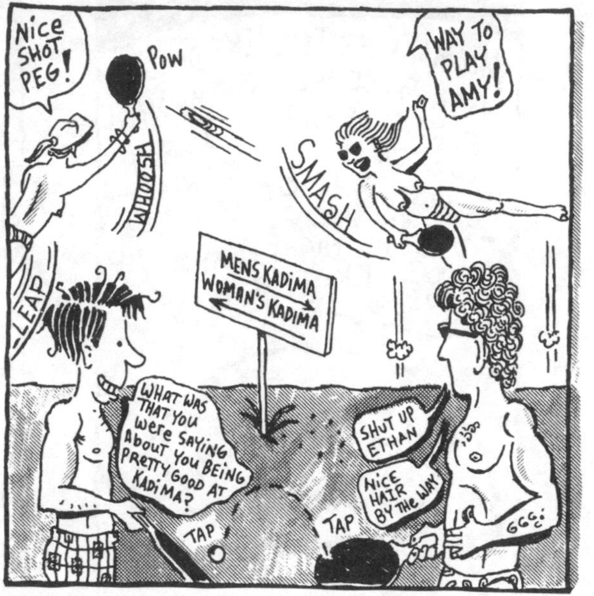
NICE SHOT PEG!
POW
WHOOSH
LEAP
SMASH
WAY TO PLAY AMY!
MENS KADIMA
WOMAN'S KADIMA
WHAT WAS THAT YOU WERE SAYING ABOUT YOU BEING PRETTY GOOD AT KADIMA?
SHUT UP ETHAN
NICE HAIR BY THE WAY
TAP
TAP

"ASTRONAUT MISSION OF LOVE" BONUS CARTOON.

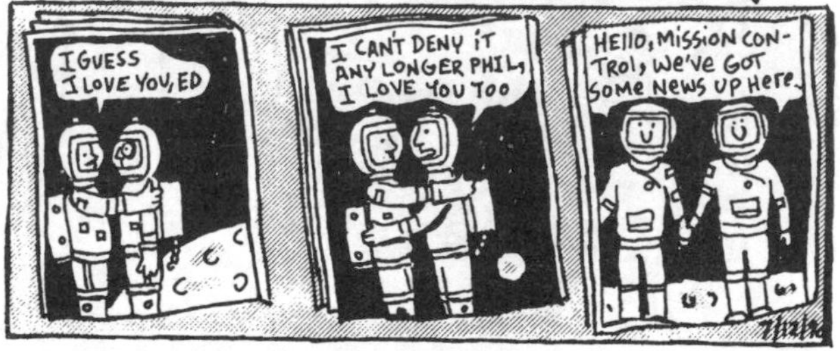
I GUESS I LOVE YOU, ED
I CAN'T DENY IT ANY LONGER PHIL, I LOVE YOU TOO
HELLO, MISSION CONTROL, WE'VE GOT SOME NEWS UP HERE.

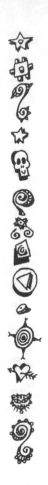

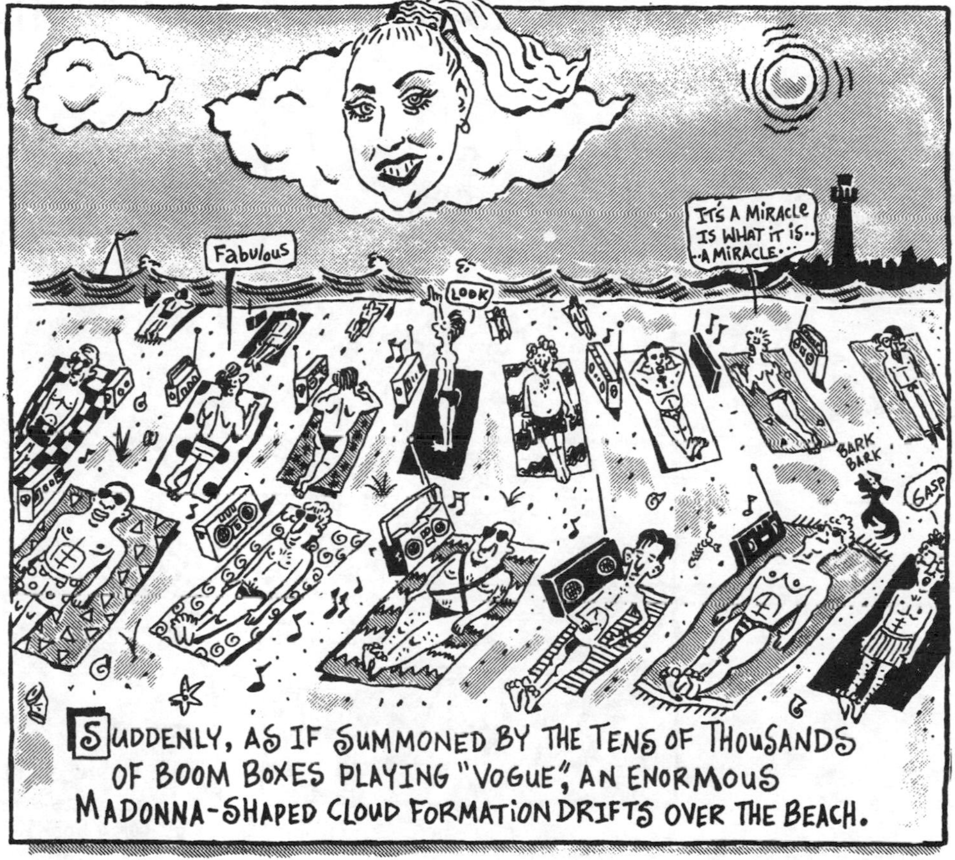
Fabulous
LOOK
IT'S A MIRACLE IS WHAT IT IS.. A MIRACLE...
BARK BARK
GASP
SUDDENLY, AS IF SUMMONED BY THE TENS OF THOUSANDS OF BOOM BOXES PLAYING "VOGUE", AN ENORMOUS MADONNA-SHAPED CLOUD FORMATION DRIFTS OVER THE BEACH.

THE 5 STAGES OF LEAVING YOUR FABULOUS WEEKEND AT THE BEACH.

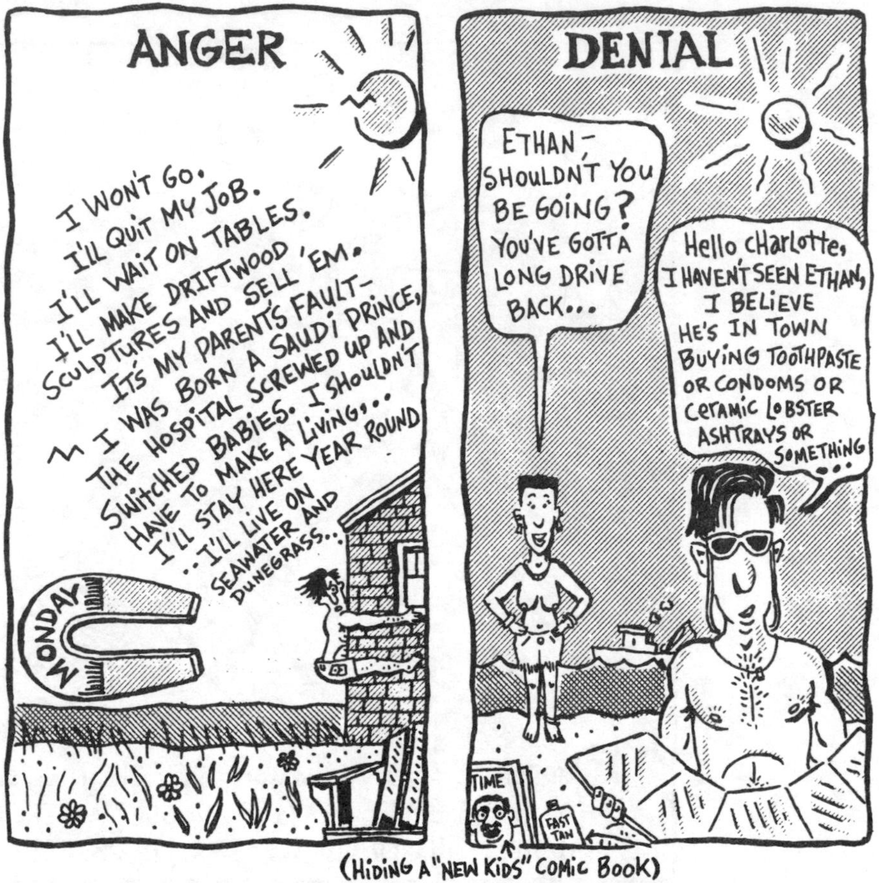

ANGER
I WON'T GO. I'LL QUIT MY JOB. I'LL WAIT ON TABLES. I'LL MAKE DRIFTWOOD SCULPTURES AND SELL 'EM. IT'S MY PARENTS' FAULT— I WAS BORN A SAUDI PRINCE, THE HOSPITAL SCREWED UP AND SWITCHED BABIES. I SHOULDN'T HAVE TO MAKE A LIVING... I'LL STAY HERE YEAR ROUND ..I'LL LIVE ON SEAWATER AND DUNEGRASS...
MONDAY
DENIAL
ETHAN,— SHOULDN'T YOU BE GOING? YOU'VE GOTTA LONG DRIVE BACK...
Hello Charlotte, I HAVEN'T SEEN ETHAN, I BELIEVE HE'S IN TOWN BUYING TOOTHPASTE OR CONDOMS OR CERAMIC LOBSTER ASHTRAYS OR SOMETHING...
TIME
FAST TAN
(HIDING A "NEW KIDS" COMIC BOOK)

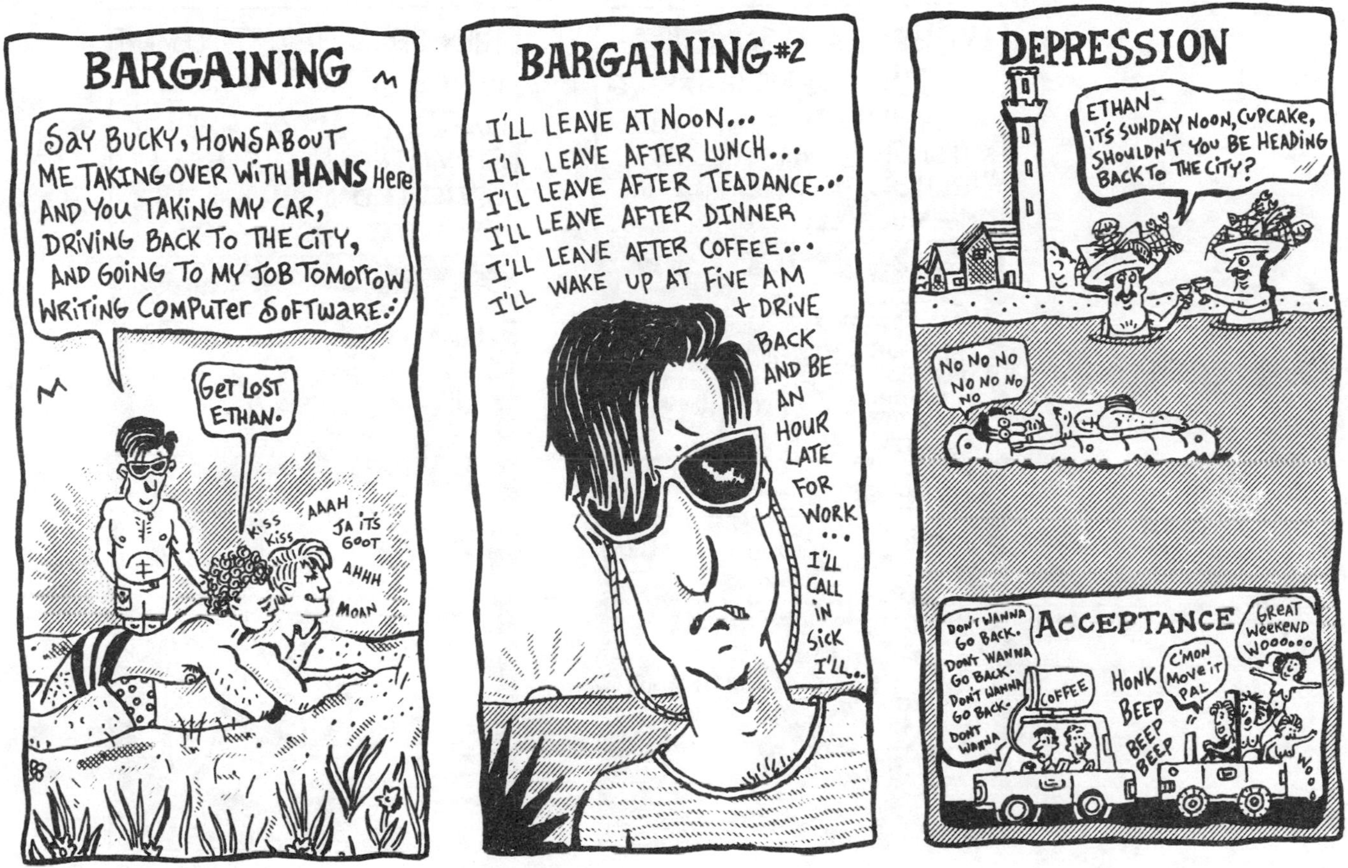
BARGAINING
Say BUCKY, HOWSABOUT ME TAKING OVER WITH HANS Here AND YOU TAKING MY CAR, DRIVING BACK TO THE CITY, AND GOING TO MY JOB TOMORROW WRITING COMPUTER SOFTWARE.
Get LOST ETHAN.
KISS KISS
AAAH
JA IT'S GOOT
AHHH
MOAN
BARGAINING #2
I'LL LEAVE AT NOON...
I'LL LEAVE AFTER LUNCH...
I'LL LEAVE AFTER TEADANCE...
I'LL LEAVE AFTER DINNER
I'LL LEAVE AFTER COFFEE...
I'LL WAKE UP AT FIVE AM & DRIVE BACK AND BE AN HOUR LATE FOR WORK... I'LL CALL IN SICK I'LL...
DEPRESSION
ETHAN- IT'S SUNDAY NOON, CUPCAKE, SHOULDN'T YOU BE HEADING BACK TO THE CITY?
NO NO NO NO NO NO NO
ACCEPTANCE
DON'T WANNA GO BACK. DON'T WANNA GO BACK. DON'T WANNA GO BACK. DON'T WANNA
COFFEE
HONK BEEP BEEP BEEP
C'MON MOVE IT PAL
GREAT WEEKEND WOOOOOO
WOOO

HATS VS HELMS

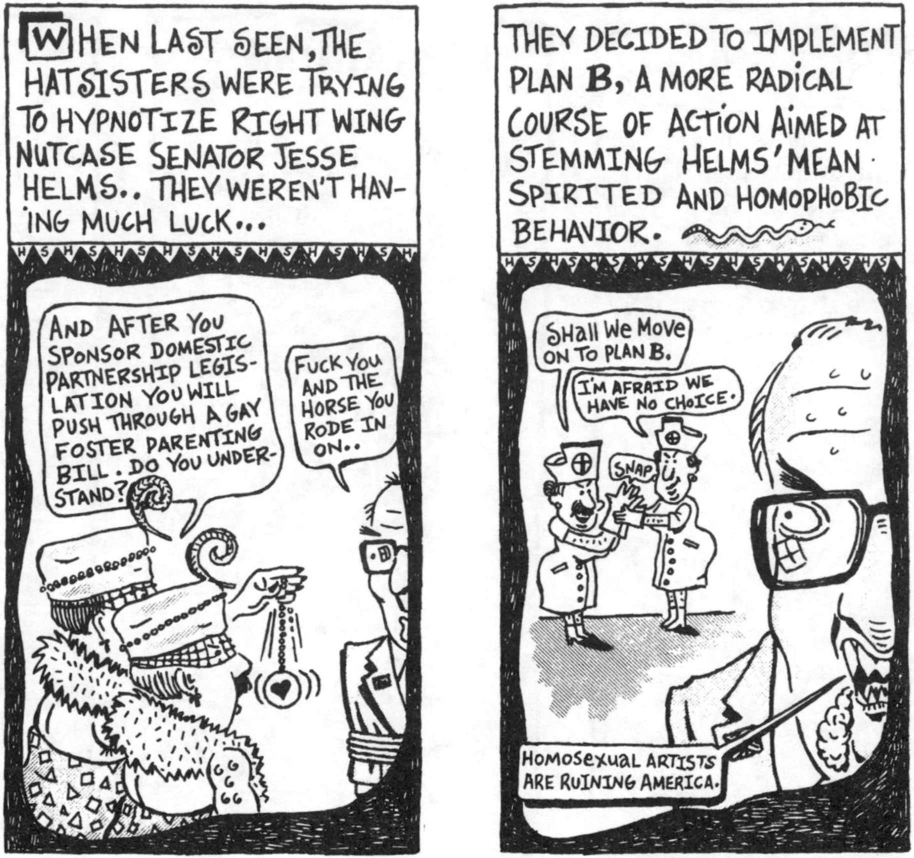
WHEN LAST SEEN, THE HATSISTERS WERE TRYING TO HYPNOTIZE RIGHT WING NUTCASE SENATOR JESSE HELMS.. THEY WEREN'T HAVING MUCH LUCK...
AND AFTER YOU SPONSOR DOMESTIC PARTNERSHIP LEGISLATION YOU WILL PUSH THROUGH A GAY FOSTER PARENTING BILL. DO YOU UNDERSTAND?
FUCK YOU AND THE HORSE YOU RODE IN ON..
THEY DECIDED TO IMPLEMENT PLAN B, A MORE RADICAL COURSE OF ACTION AIMED AT STEMMING HELMS' MEAN SPIRITED AND HOMOPHOBIC BEHAVIOR.
SHALL WE MOVE ON TO PLAN B.
I'M AFRAID WE HAVE NO CHOICE.
SNAP
HOMOSEXUAL ARTISTS ARE RUINING AMERICA.

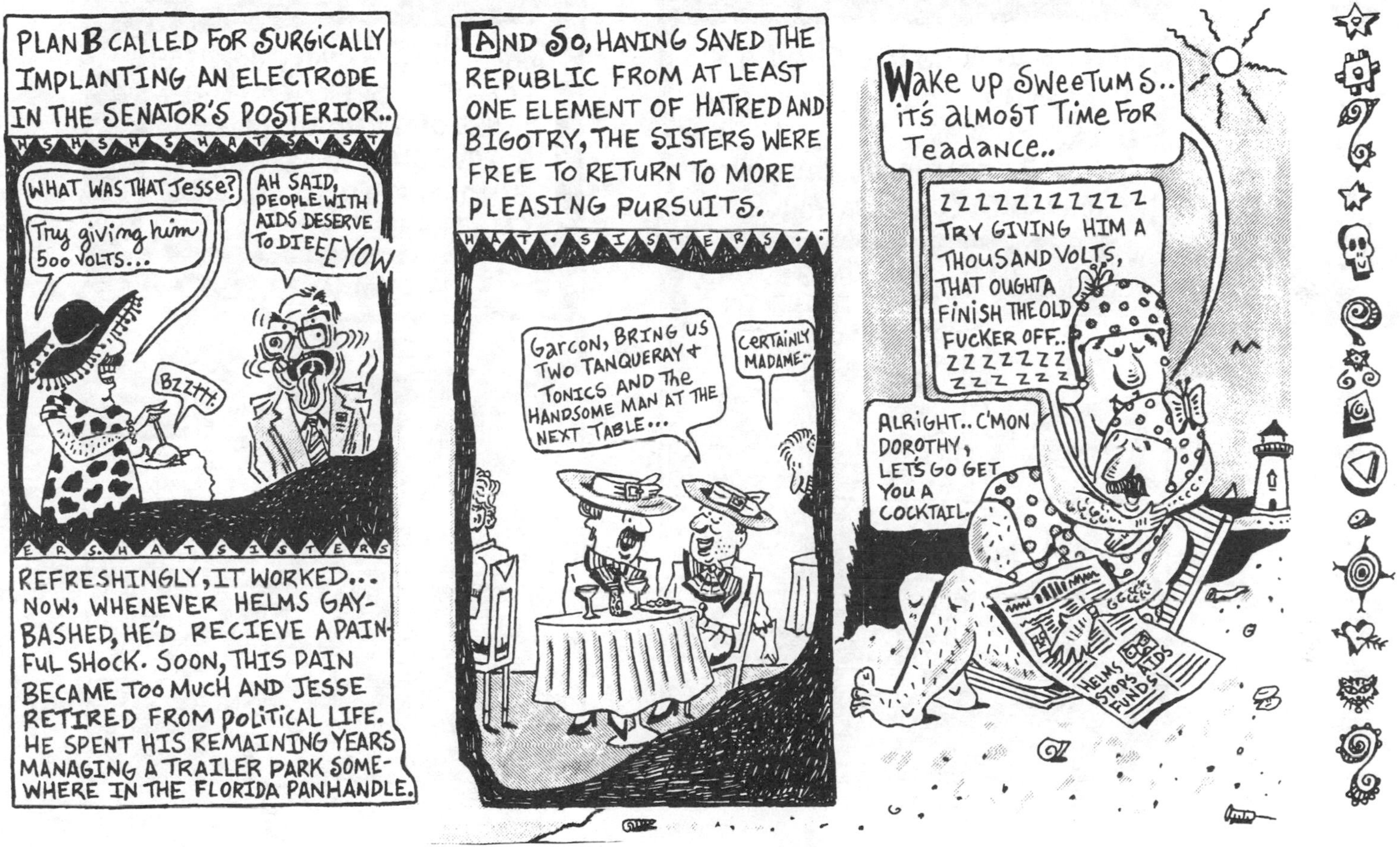
PLAN B CALLED FOR SURGICALLY IMPLANTING AN ELECTRODE IN THE SENATOR'S POSTERIOR..
WHAT WAS THAT Jesse?
AH SAID, PEOPLE WITH AIDS DESERVE TO DIEEEEYOW
Try giving him 500 VOLTS...
BZZttt.
REFRESHINGLY, IT WORKED... NOW, WHENEVER HELMS GAY-BASHED, HE'D RECIEVE A PAINFUL SHOCK. SOON, THIS PAIN BECAME TOO MUCH AND JESSE RETIRED FROM POLITICAL LIFE. HE SPENT HIS REMAINING YEARS MANAGING A TRAILER PARK SOMEWHERE IN THE FLORIDA PANHANDLE.
AND SO, HAVING SAVED THE REPUBLIC FROM AT LEAST ONE ELEMENT OF HATRED AND BIGOTRY, THE SISTERS WERE FREE TO RETURN TO MORE PLEASING PURSUITS.
Garcon, BRING US TWO TANQUERAY & TONICS AND The HANDSOME MAN AT THE NEXT TABLE...
CERTAINLY MADAME--
Wake up Sweetums.. it's almost Time For Teadance..
ZZZZZZZZZZZ Z
TRY GIVING HIM A THOUSAND VOLTS, THAT OUGHTA FINISH THE OLD FUCKER OFF.. ZZZZZZZ ZZZ ZZZ
ALRIGHT.. C'MON DOROTHY, LET'S GO GET YOU A COCKTAIL.
HELMS STOPS AIDS FUNDS

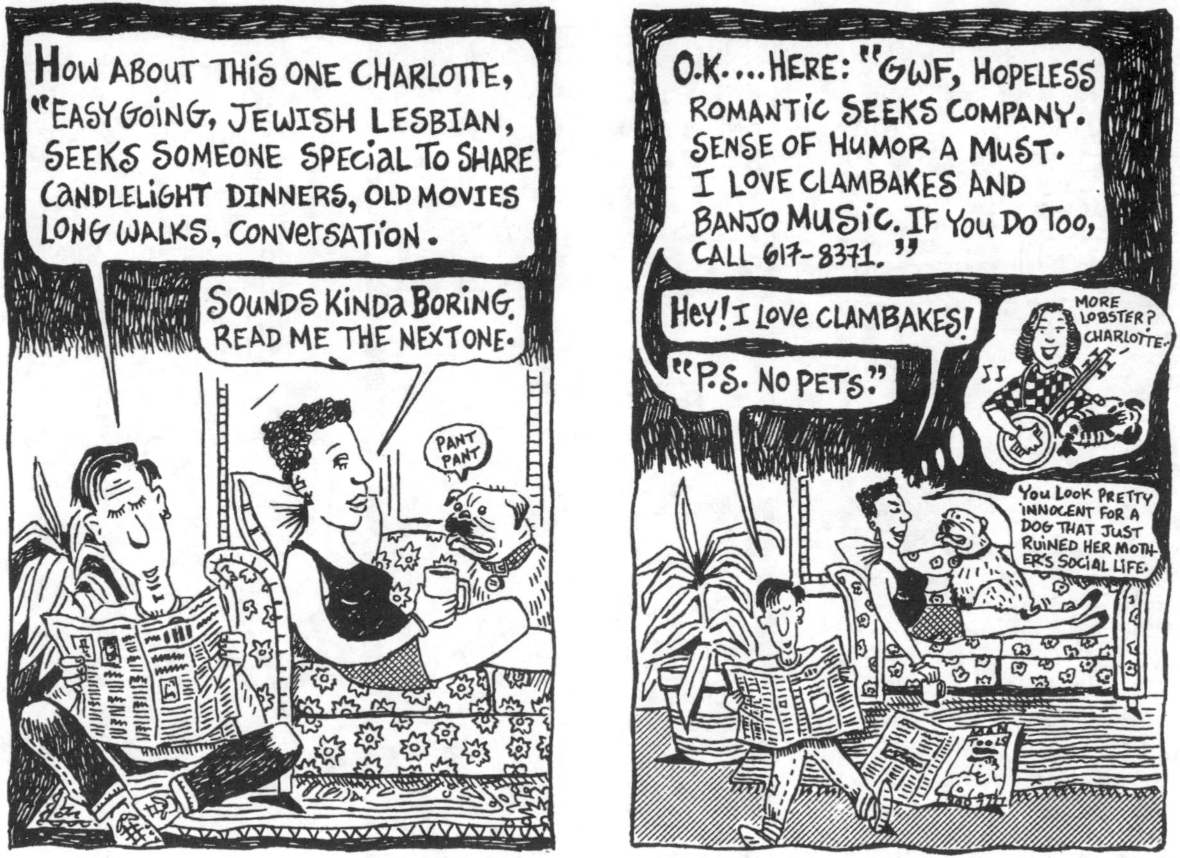
HOW ABOUT THIS ONE CHARLOTTE, "EASY GOING, JEWISH LESBIAN, SEEKS SOMEONE SPECIAL TO SHARE CANDLELIGHT DINNERS, OLD MOVIES LONG WALKS, CONVERSATION.
SOUNDS KINDA BORING. READ ME THE NEXT ONE.
PANT PANT
O.K.... HERE: "GWF, HOPELESS ROMANTIC SEEKS COMPANY. SENSE OF HUMOR A MUST. I LOVE CLAMBAKES AND BANJO MUSIC. IF YOU DO TOO, CALL 617-8371."
HEY! I LOVE CLAMBAKES!
MORE LOBSTER? CHARLOTTE-
"P.S. NO PETS."
YOU LOOK PRETTY INNOCENT FOR A DOG THAT JUST RUINED HER MOTHER'S SOCIAL LIFE.

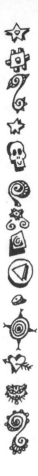

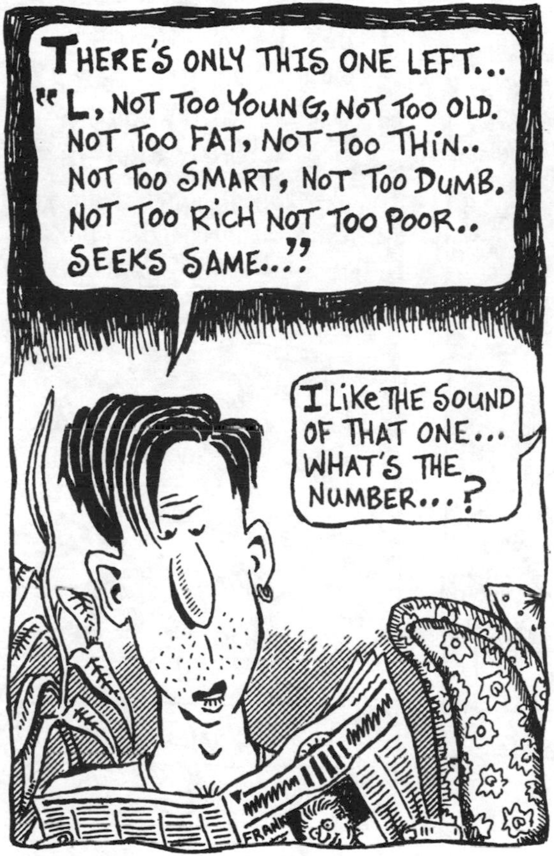
THERE'S ONLY THIS ONE LEFT... "L, NOT TOO YOUNG, NOT TOO OLD. NOT TOO FAT, NOT TOO THIN.. NOT TOO SMART, NOT TOO DUMB. NOT TOO RICH NOT TOO POOR.. SEEKS SAME..."
I LIKE THE SOUND OF THAT ONE... WHAT'S THE NUMBER...?

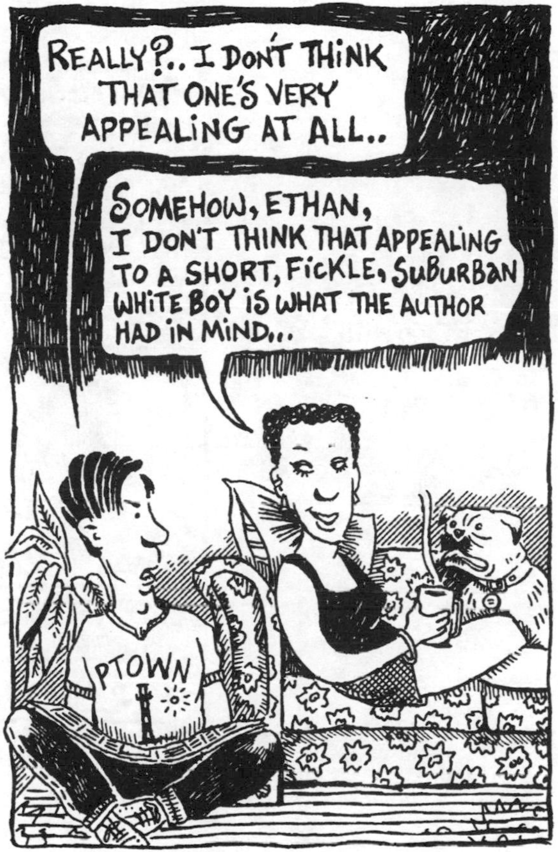
REALLY?.. I DON'T THINK THAT ONE'S VERY APPEALING AT ALL..
SOMEHOW, ETHAN, I DON'T THINK THAT APPEALING TO A SHORT, FICKLE, SUBURBAN WHITE BOY IS WHAT THE AUTHOR HAD IN MIND...
PTOWN

ETHAN SLEEPS WITH LEO FOR THE FIRST TIME.

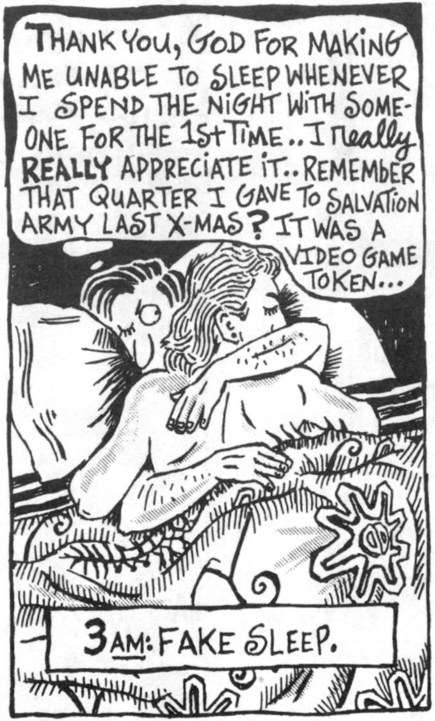
THANK YOU, GOD FOR MAKING ME UNABLE TO SLEEP WHENEVER I SPEND THE NIGHT WITH SOMEONE FOR THE 1st TIME.. I really REALLY APPRECIATE IT.. REMEMBER THAT QUARTER I GAVE TO SALVATION ARMY LAST X-MAS? IT WAS A VIDEO GAME TOKEN...
3AM: FAKE SLEEP.

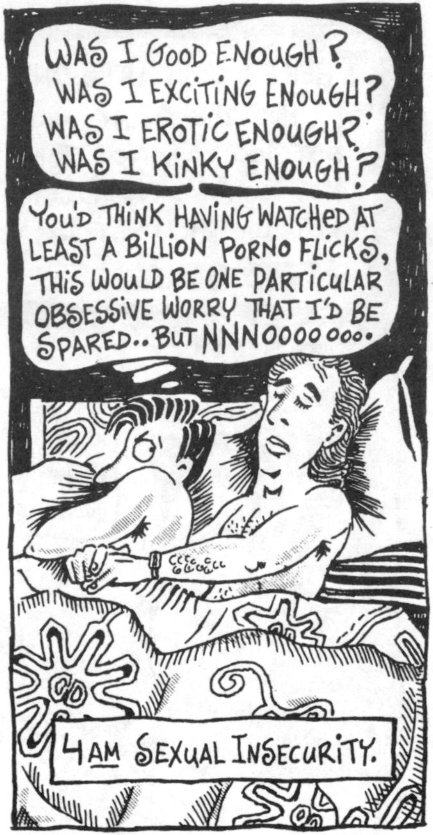
WAS I GOOD ENOUGH? WAS I EXCITING ENOUGH? WAS I EROTIC ENOUGH? WAS I KINKY ENOUGH?
YOU'D THINK HAVING WATCHED AT LEAST A BILLION PORNO FLICKS, THIS WOULD BE ONE PARTICULAR OBSESSIVE WORRY THAT I'D BE SPARED.. BUT NNNOOOOooo.
4AM SEXUAL INSECURITY.

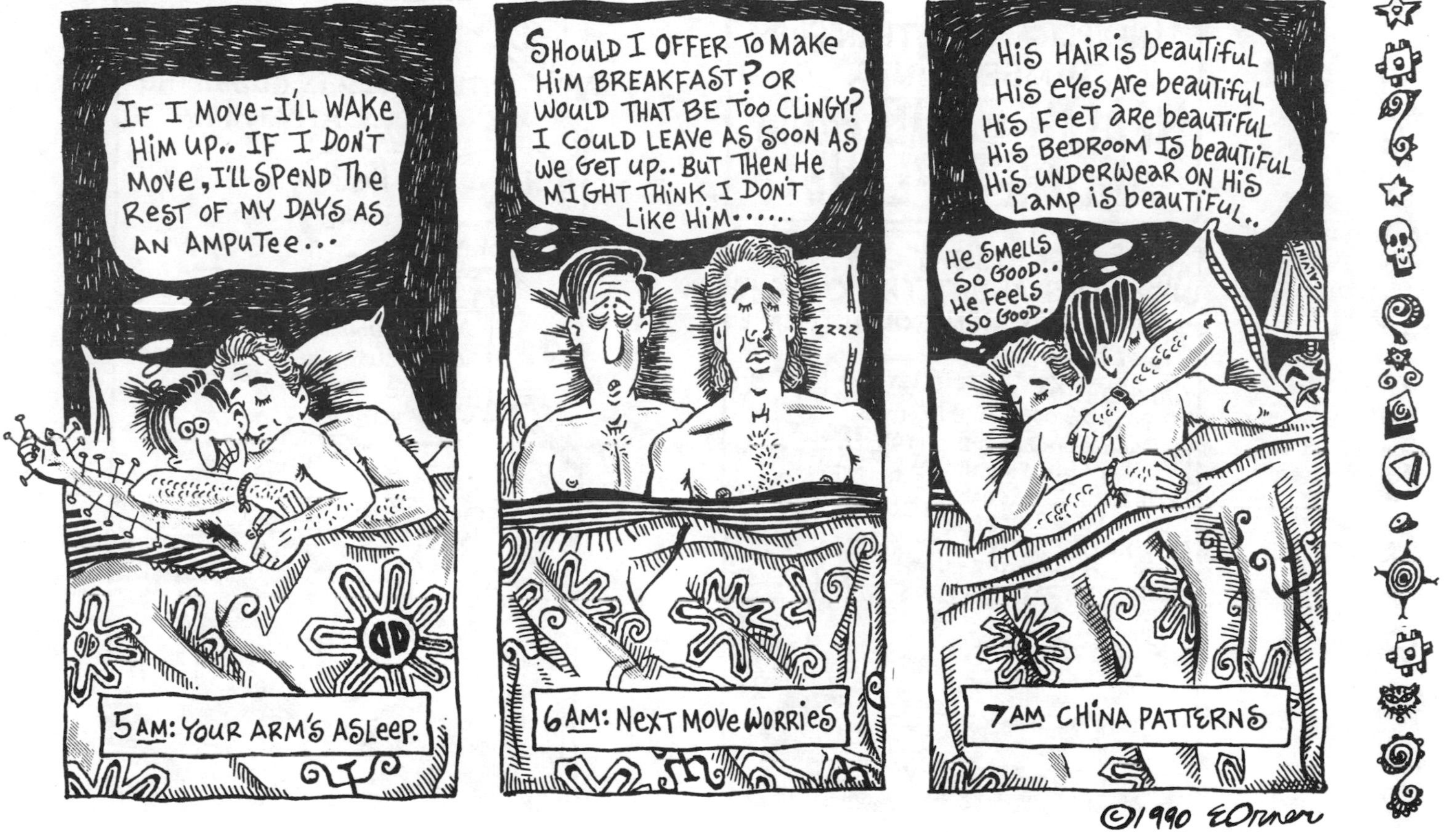
IF I MOVE-I'LL WAKE HIM UP.. IF I DON'T MOVE, I'LL SPEND THE REST OF MY DAYS AS AN AMPUTEE...
5AM: YOUR ARM'S ASLEEP.
SHOULD I OFFER TO MAKE HIM BREAKFAST? OR WOULD THAT BE TOO CLINGY? I COULD LEAVE AS SOON AS WE GET UP.. BUT THEN HE MIGHT THINK I DON'T LIKE HIM.....
ZZZZ
6AM: NEXT MOVE WORRIES
HIS HAIR IS BEAUTIFUL HIS EYES ARE BEAUTIFUL HIS FEET ARE BEAUTIFUL HIS BEDROOM IS BEAUTIFUL HIS UNDERWEAR ON HIS LAMP IS BEAUTIFUL..
HE SMELLS SO GOOD.. HE FEELS SO GOOD.
7AM CHINA PATTERNS
©1990 E Orner

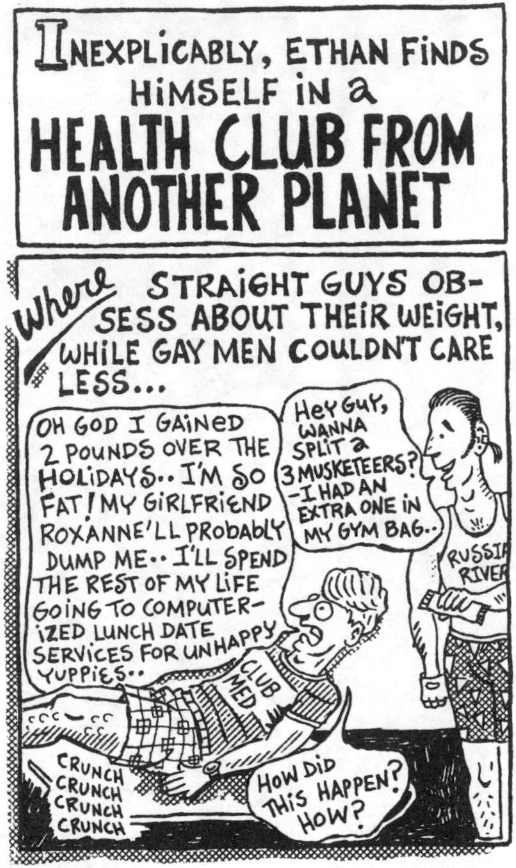
INEXPLICABLY, ETHAN FINDS HIMSELF IN A
HEALTH CLUB FROM ANOTHER PLANET
Where STRAIGHT GUYS OBSESS ABOUT THEIR WEIGHT, WHILE GAY MEN COULDN'T CARE LESS...
OH GOD I GAINED 2 POUNDS OVER THE HOLIDAYS.. I'M SO FAT! MY GIRLFRIEND ROXANNE'LL PROBABLY DUMP ME.. I'LL SPEND THE REST OF MY LIFE GOING TO COMPUTERIZED LUNCH DATE SERVICES FOR UNHAPPY YUPPIES..
Hey Guy, WANNA SPLIT a 3 MUSKETEERS? -I HAD AN EXTRA ONE IN MY GYM BAG..
RUSSIA RIVER
CLUB MED
CRUNCH CRUNCH CRUNCH CRUNCH
HOW DID THIS HAPPEN? HOW?

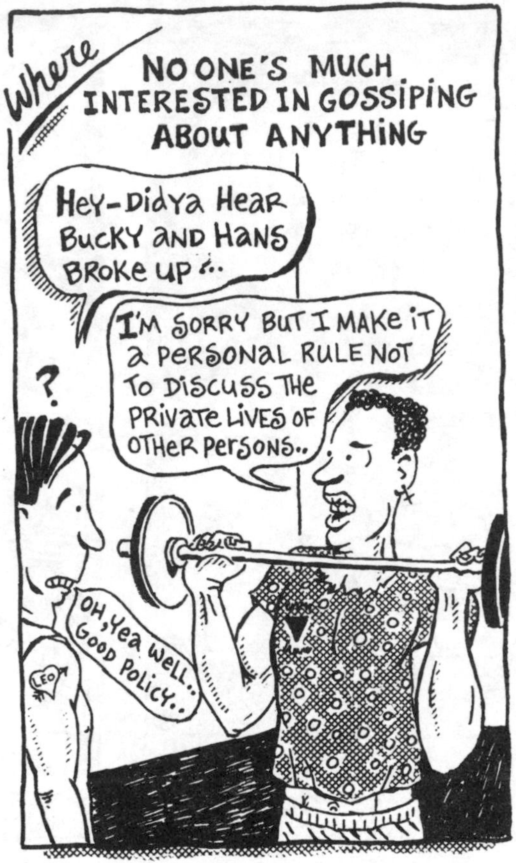
Where NO ONE'S MUCH INTERESTED IN GOSSIPING ABOUT ANYTHING
Hey-Didya Hear Bucky and Hans Broke up?..
I'M SORRY BUT I MAKE IT a PERSONAL RULE NOT TO DISCUSS THE PRIVATE LIVES OF OTHER PERSONS..
?
OH, Yea well.. Good Policy..
LEO

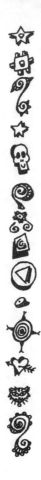

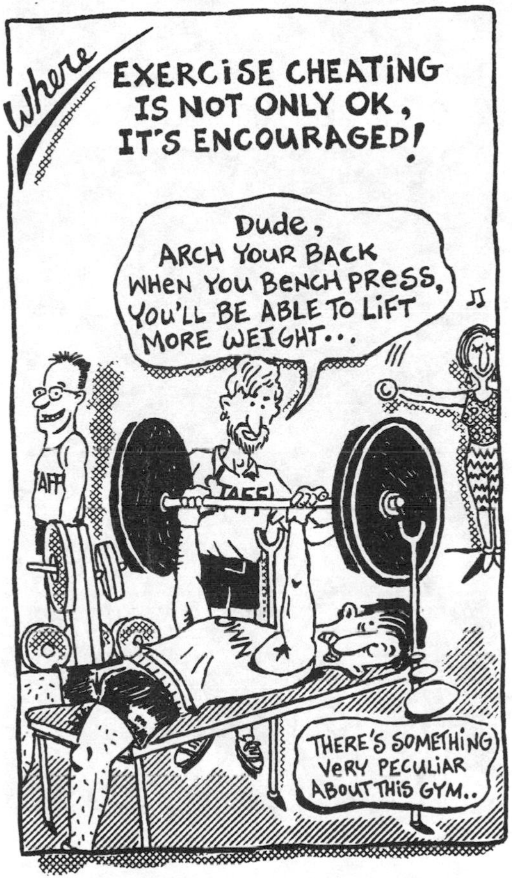
Where
EXERCISE CHEATING IS NOT ONLY OK, IT'S ENCOURAGED!
Dude, ARCH YOUR BACK WHEN YOU BENCH PRESS, YOU'LL BE ABLE TO LIFT MORE WEIGHT...
THERE'S SOMETHING VERY PECULIAR ABOUT THIS GYM..

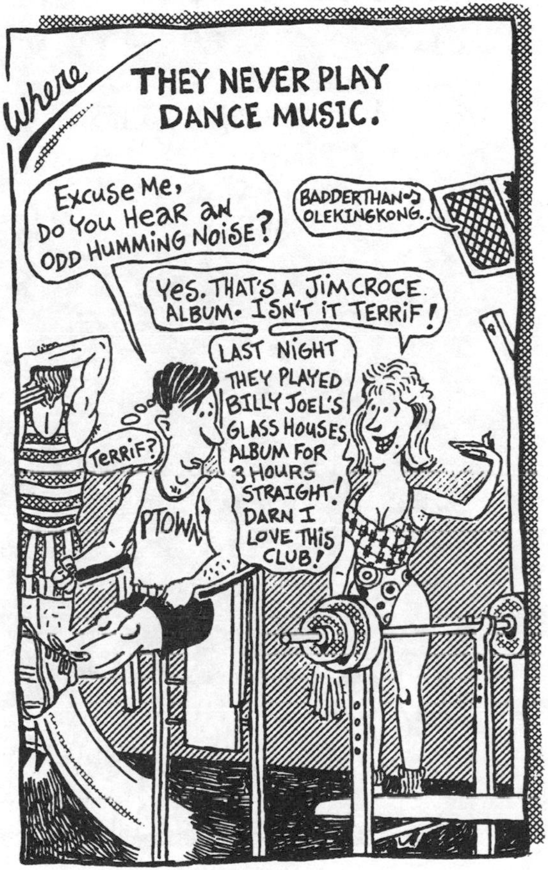
Where
THEY NEVER PLAY DANCE MUSIC.
Excuse Me, Do You Hear an ODD HUMMING NOISE?
BADDERTHAN OLEKINGKONG..
YES. THAT'S A JIM CROCE ALBUM. ISN'T IT TERRIF!
LAST NIGHT THEY PLAYED BILLY JOEL'S GLASS HOUSES ALBUM FOR 3 HOURS STRAIGHT! DARN I LOVE THIS CLUB!
TERRIF?
PTOWN

ASTRONAUT MISSION OF LOVE.

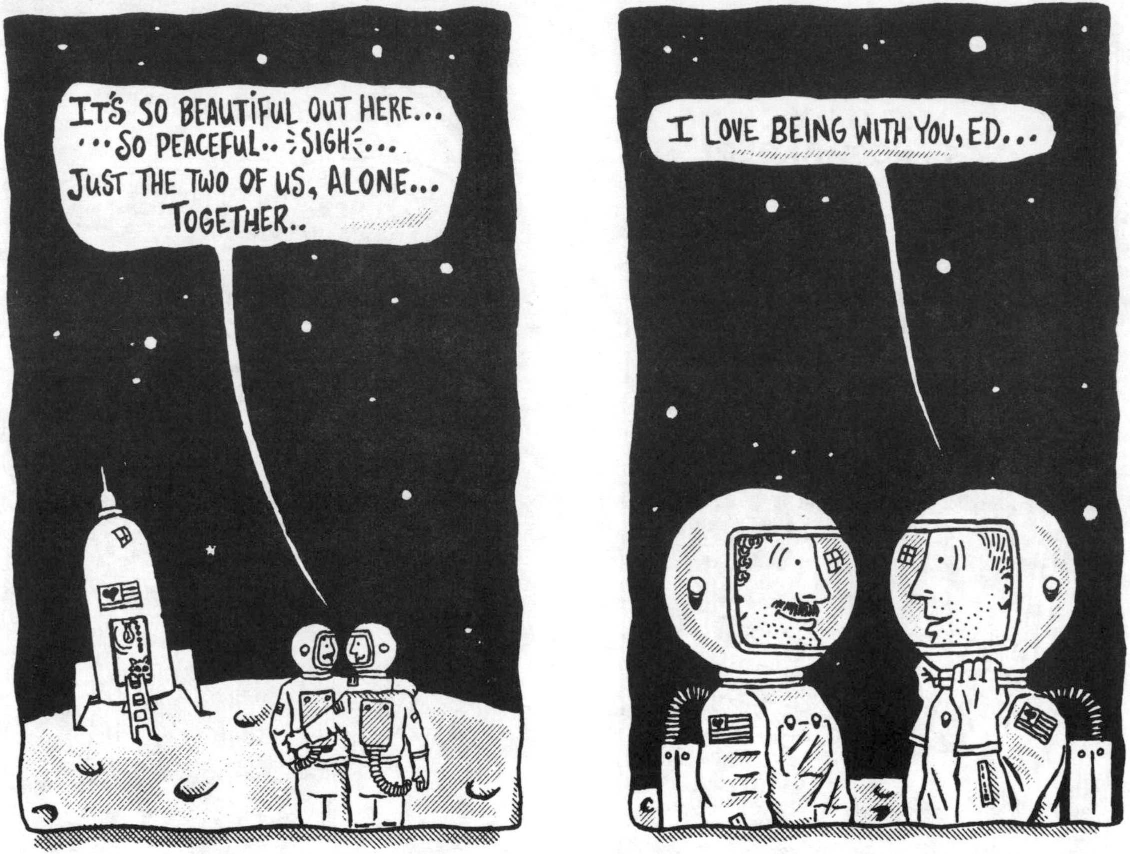

IT'S SO BEAUTIFUL OUT HERE... ...SO PEACEFUL.. SIGH... JUST THE TWO OF US, ALONE... TOGETHER..
I LOVE BEING WITH YOU, ED...

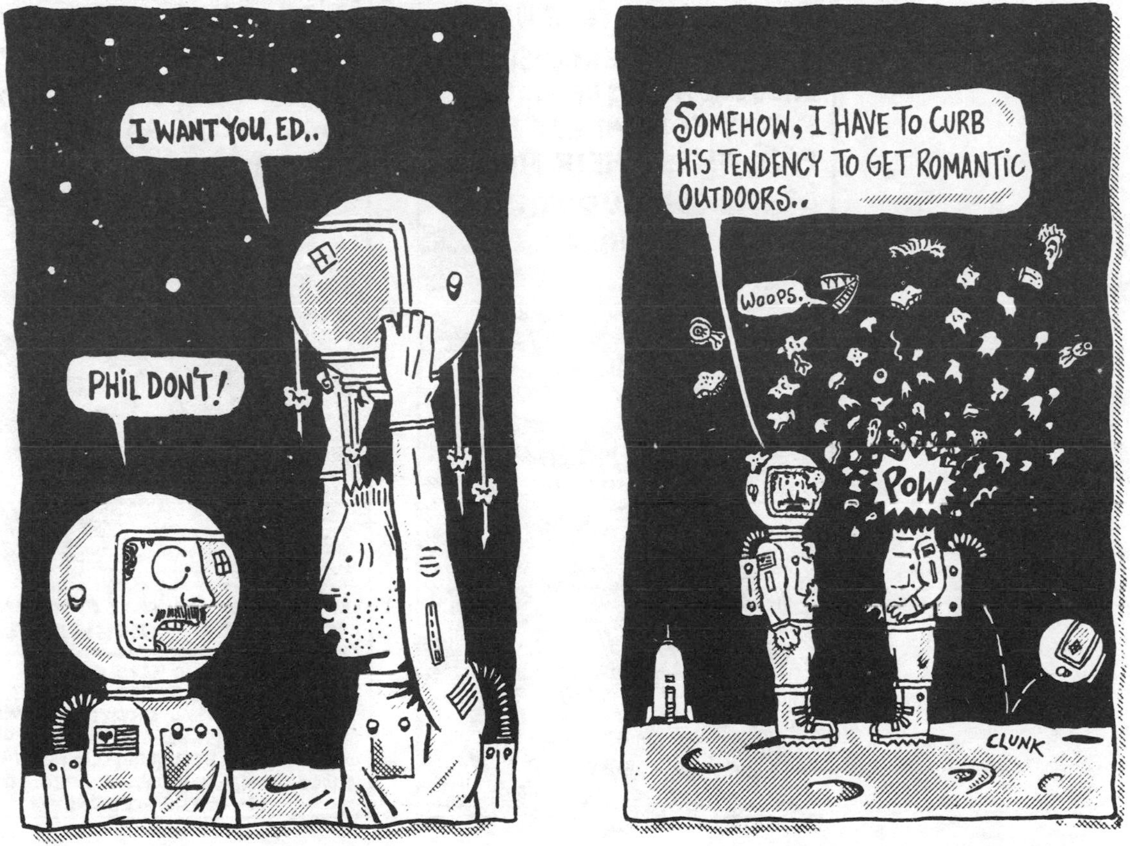
I WANT YOU, ED..
PHIL DON'T!
SOMEHOW, I HAVE TO CURB HIS TENDENCY TO GET ROMANTIC OUTDOORS..
WOOPS.
POW
CLUNK

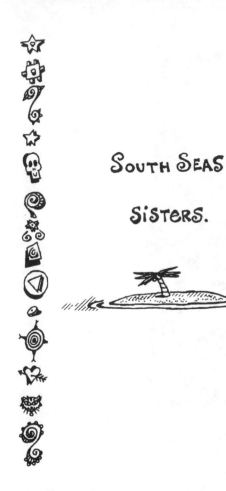

South Seas Sisters.

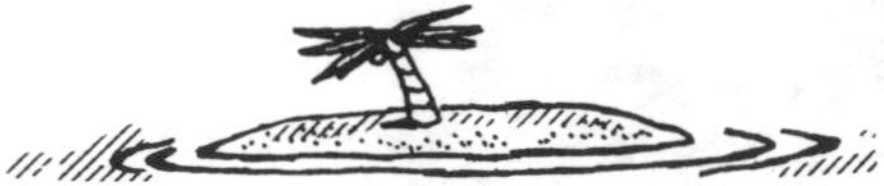

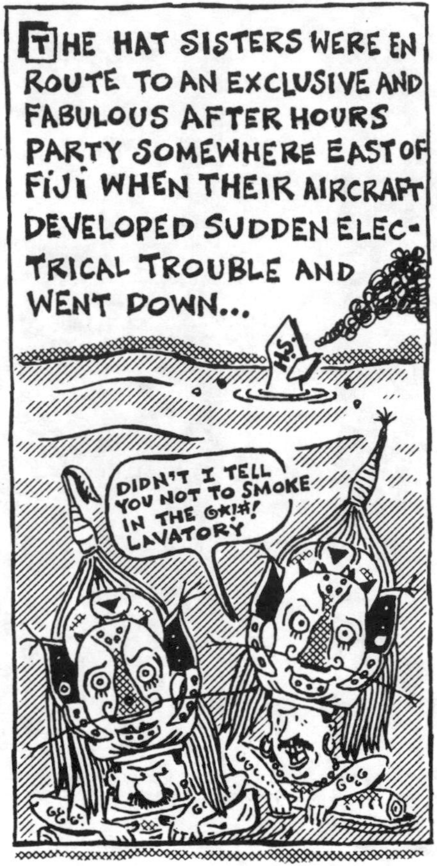

The Hat Sisters were en route to an exclusive and fabulous after hours party somewhere east of Fiji when their aircraft developed sudden electrical trouble and went down...
H.S.
Didn't I tell you not to smoke in the @*!#! lavatory

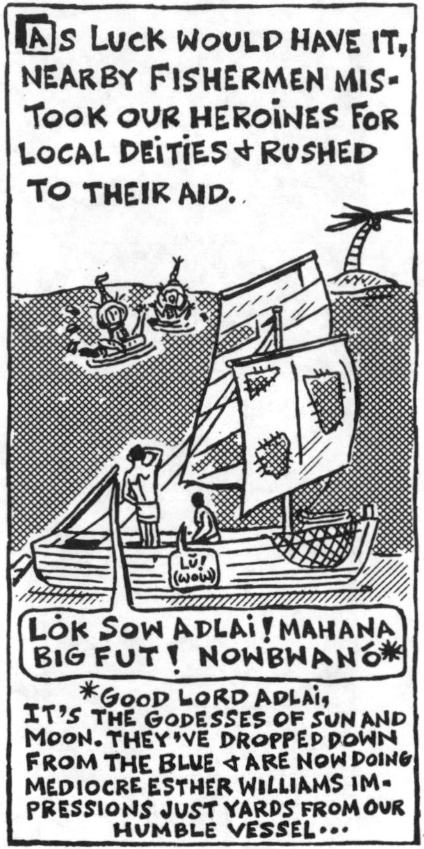

As luck would have it, nearby fishermen mistook our heroines for local deities & rushed to their aid.
LŪ! (WOW)
LÒK SOW ADLAI! MAHANA BIG FUT! NOWBWANÓ*
*Good Lord Adlai, it's the godesses of sun and moon. They've dropped down from the blue & are now doing mediocre Esther Williams impressions just yards from our humble vessel...

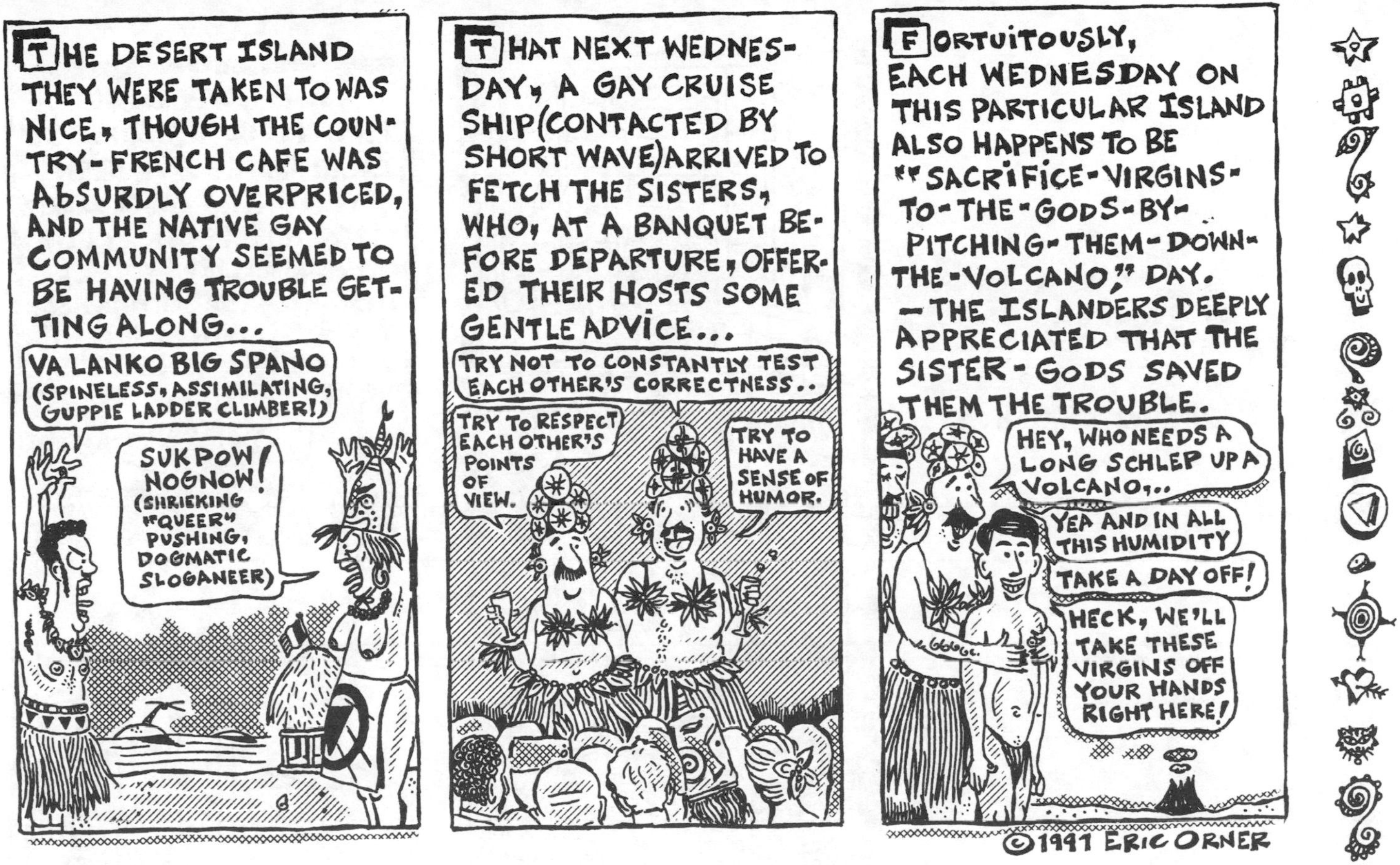
THE DESERT ISLAND THEY WERE TAKEN TO WAS NICE, THOUGH THE COUNTRY-FRENCH CAFE WAS ABSURDLY OVERPRICED, AND THE NATIVE GAY COMMUNITY SEEMED TO BE HAVING TROUBLE GETTING ALONG...
VA LANKO BIG SPANO (SPINELESS, ASSIMILATING, GUPPIE LADDER CLIMBER!)
SUK POW NOGNOW! (SHRIEKING "QUEER" PUSHING, DOGMATIC SLOGANEER)
THAT NEXT WEDNESDAY, A GAY CRUISE SHIP (CONTACTED BY SHORT WAVE) ARRIVED TO FETCH THE SISTERS, WHO, AT A BANQUET BEFORE DEPARTURE, OFFERED THEIR HOSTS SOME GENTLE ADVICE...
TRY NOT TO CONSTANTLY TEST EACH OTHER'S CORRECTNESS..
TRY TO RESPECT EACH OTHER'S POINTS OF VIEW.
TRY TO HAVE A SENSE OF HUMOR.
FORTUITOUSLY, EACH WEDNESDAY ON THIS PARTICULAR ISLAND ALSO HAPPENS TO BE "SACRIFICE-VIRGINS-TO-THE-GODS-BY-PITCHING-THEM-DOWN-THE-VOLCANO," DAY. — THE ISLANDERS DEEPLY APPRECIATED THAT THE SISTER-GODS SAVED THEM THE TROUBLE.
HEY, WHO NEEDS A LONG SCHLEP UP A VOLCANO,..
YEA AND IN ALL THIS HUMIDITY
TAKE A DAY OFF!
HECK, WE'LL TAKE THESE VIRGINS OFF YOUR HANDS RIGHT HERE!
©1991 ERIC ORNER

Audra's

New Age Stuff..

CHIME CHIME
Audra's New Age Stuff
HI AUDRA!
BUCKY! CHARLOTTE! COME ON IN...
I CAN'T BELIEVE THESE TWO BUY INTO THIS HOCUS POCUS
I'M SO PLEASED THAT YOU BOTH STOPPED BY! CHARLOTTE, I'VE BEEN SAVING THIS ROSE QUARTZ MARBLE ESPECIALLY FOR YOU.. I BELIEVE YOU'LL DISCOVER THAT IT WILL HELP YOU TO REMAIN AS ONE WITH YOUR WHOLE EARTHSELF..
OH AUDRA IT'S SO BEAUTIFUL I'LL TAKE IT!
I CAN FEEL ITS ENERGY!

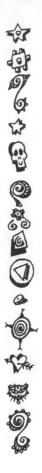

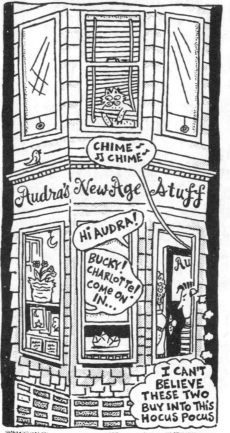

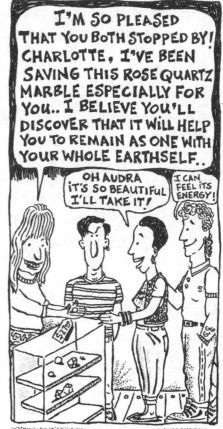

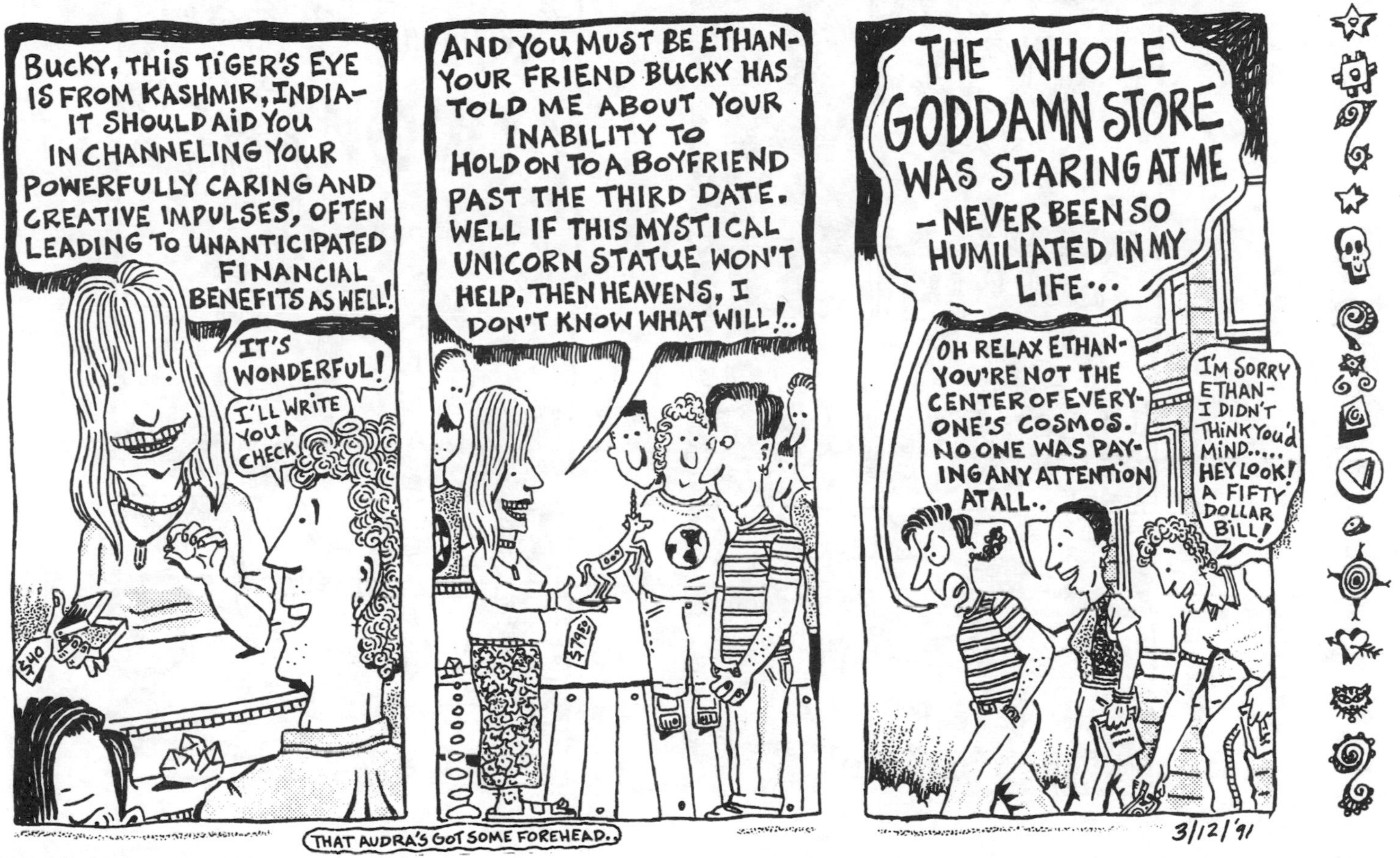
BUCKY, THIS TIGER'S EYE IS FROM KASHMIR, INDIA- IT SHOULD AID YOU IN CHANNELING YOUR POWERFULLY CARING AND CREATIVE IMPULSES, OFTEN LEADING TO UNANTICIPATED FINANCIAL BENEFITS AS WELL!
IT'S WONDERFUL!
I'LL WRITE YOU A CHECK
$40
AND YOU MUST BE ETHAN- YOUR FRIEND BUCKY HAS TOLD ME ABOUT YOUR INABILITY TO HOLD ON TO A BOYFRIEND PAST THE THIRD DATE. WELL IF THIS MYSTICAL UNICORN STATUE WON'T HELP, THEN HEAVENS, I DON'T KNOW WHAT WILL!..
$79.50
THE WHOLE GODDAMN STORE WAS STARING AT ME - NEVER BEEN SO HUMILIATED IN MY LIFE...
OH RELAX ETHAN- YOU'RE NOT THE CENTER OF EVERY- ONE'S COSMOS. NO ONE WAS PAY- ING ANY ATTENTION AT ALL..
I'M SORRY ETHAN- I DIDN'T THINK YOU'D MIND..... HEY LOOK! A FIFTY DOLLAR BILL!
THAT AUDRA'S GOT SOME FOREHEAD..
3/12/'91

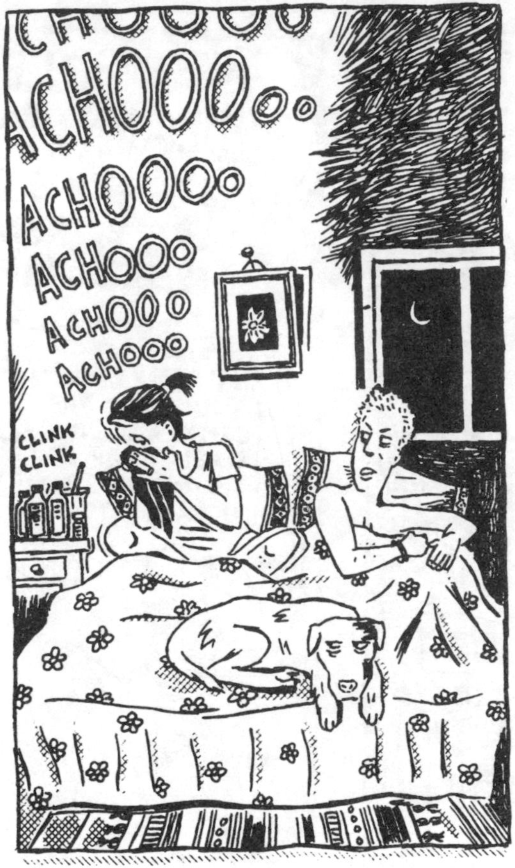
ACHOOOOoo
ACHOOOOo
ACHOOOO
ACHOOO
ACHOOO
CLINK CLINK

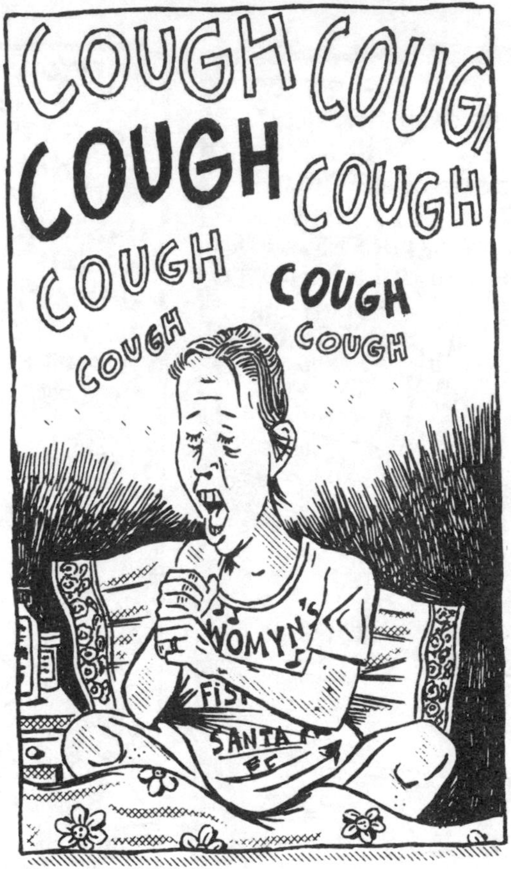
COUGH
COUGH
COUGH
COUGH
COUGH
COUGH
COUGH
WOMYN'S
FIST
SANTA

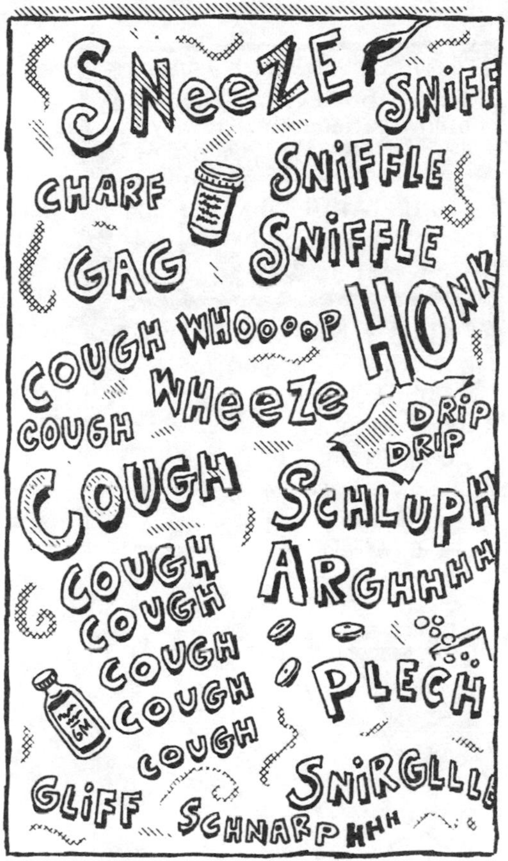
SNEEZE
SNIFF
CHARF
SNIFFLE
GAG
SNIFFLE
COUGH
WHOOOOP
HONK
WHEEZE
COUGH
DRIP
DRIP
COUGH
SCHLUPH
COUGH
COUGH
ARGHHHH
COUGH
COUGH
PLECH
COUGH
GLIFF
SCHNARPHHH
SNIRGLLLE

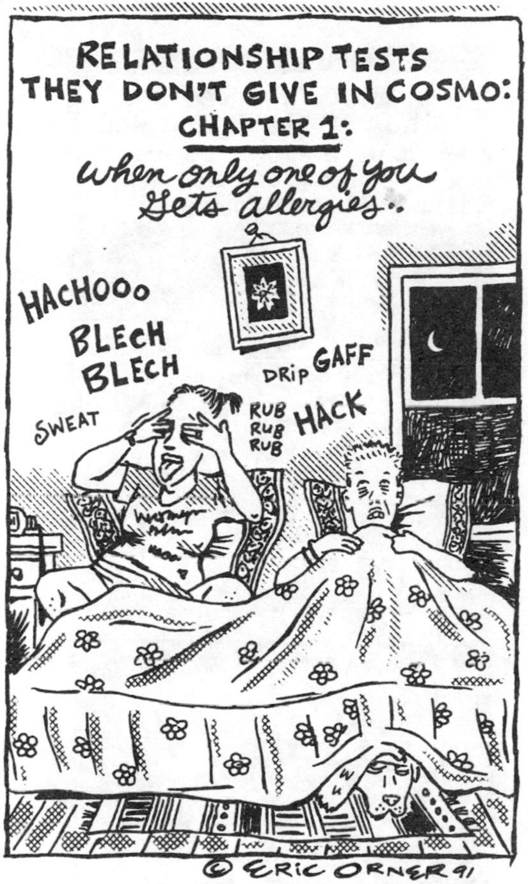
RELATIONSHIP TESTS
THEY DON'T GIVE IN COSMO:
CHAPTER 1:
when only one of you
Gets allergies..
HACHOOO
BLECH
BLECH
DRIP
GAFF
SWEAT
RUB
RUB
RUB
HACK
© ERIC ORNER 91

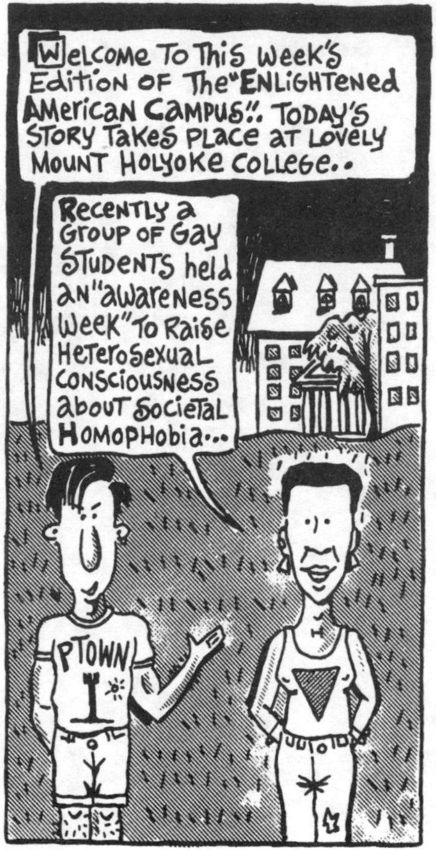
Welcome To This Week's Edition of The "ENLIGHTENED AMERICAN CAMPUS". TODAY'S STORY TAKES PLACE AT LOVELY MOUNT HOLYOKE COLLEGE..
RECENTLY a Group OF Gay STUDENTS held an "awareness Week" To Raise HeteroSexual CONSCIOUSNESS about Societal HOMOPHobia...
PTOWN

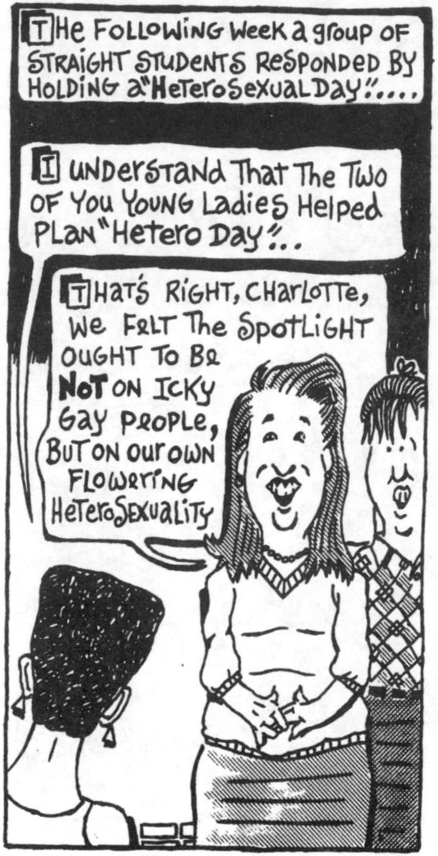
THE FOLLOWING Week a group OF STRAIGHT STUDENTS RESPONDED BY HOLDING a "HeteroSexual Day"....
I UNDERSTAND That The Two OF You YOUNG Ladies Helped PLan "Hetero Day"...
THAT'S RIGHT, CHARLOTTE, We FELT The SpotLiGHT OUGHT To Be NOT ON ICKY Gay PeOPLE, BUT ON our OWN FLOWeriNG HeteroSEXUALITY

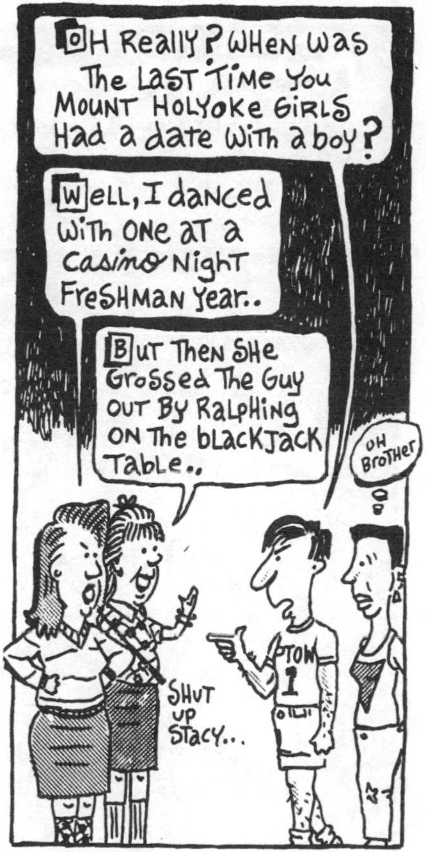
OH Really? WHEN WAS The LAST TIME You MOUNT HOLYOKE GIRLS Had a date With a boy?
WELL, I danced With ONE AT a casino Night FreSHMAN Year..
BUT Then SHE Grossed The Guy OUT By RalpHing ON The blackjack Table..
OH BroTHer
SHUT up STACY...

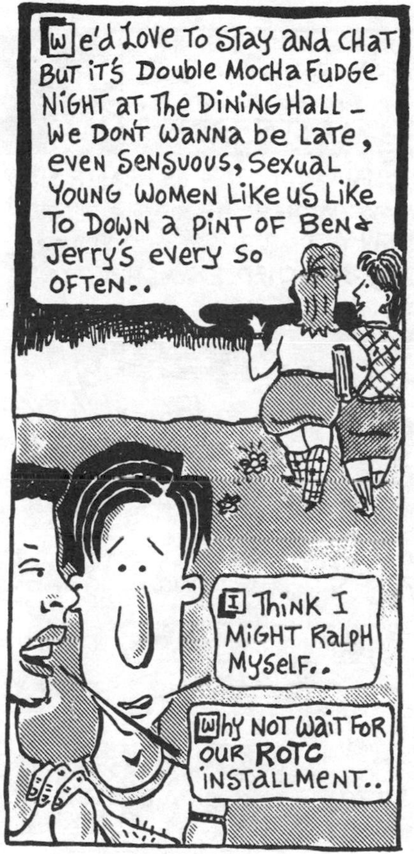
We'd Love To STAY and CHAT BUT IT'S Double MocHa FudGe NiGHT at The DiniNG HaLL - We DON'T WaNNa be LaTe, even SenSuous, SeXuaL YOUNG WOMEN Like US Like To DOWN a PINT OF Ben & Jerry's every So OFTeN..
I Think I MiGHT RalpH MySelF..
WHY NOT WaiT FOR OUR ROTC INSTALLMENT..

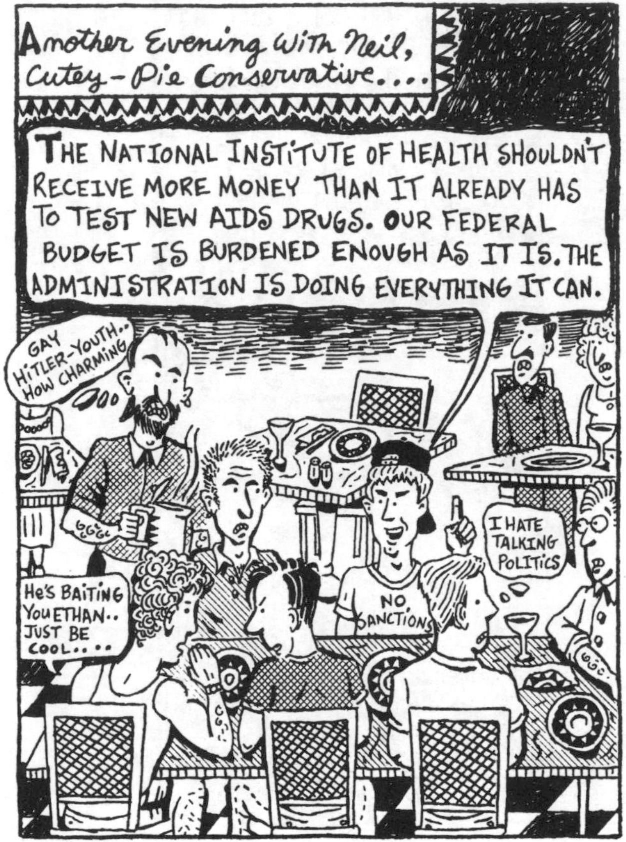
Another Evening With Neil, Cutey-Pie Conservative....
THE NATIONAL INSTITUTE OF HEALTH SHOULDN'T RECEIVE MORE MONEY THAN IT ALREADY HAS TO TEST NEW AIDS DRUGS. OUR FEDERAL BUDGET IS BURDENED ENOUGH AS IT IS. THE ADMINISTRATION IS DOING EVERYTHING IT CAN.
GAY HITLER-YOUTH.. HOW CHARMING
He's BAITING YOU ETHAN.. JUST BE COOL.....
I HATE TALKING POLITICS
NO SANCTIONS

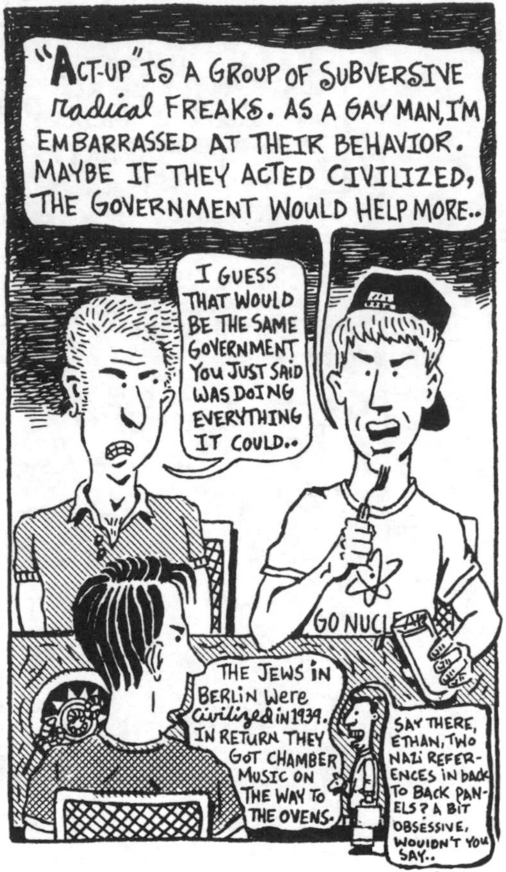
"ACT-UP" IS A GROUP OF SUBVERSIVE radical FREAKS. AS A GAY MAN, I'M EMBARRASSED AT THEIR BEHAVIOR. MAYBE IF THEY ACTED CIVILIZED, THE GOVERNMENT WOULD HELP MORE..
I GUESS THAT WOULD BE THE SAME GOVERNMENT YOU JUST SAID WAS DOING EVERYTHING IT COULD..
GO NUCLE
THE JEWS IN BERLIN WERE civilized in 1939. IN RETURN THEY GOT CHAMBER MUSIC ON THE WAY TO THE OVENS.
SAY THERE, ETHAN, TWO NAZI REFERENCES IN BACK TO BACK PANELS? A BIT OBSESSIVE, WOULDN'T YOU SAY..

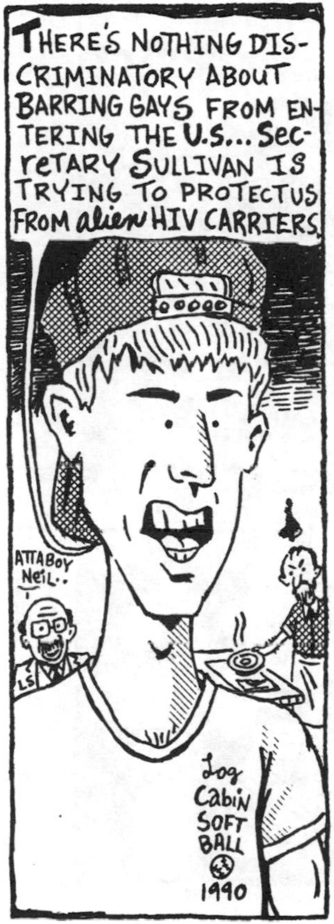
THERE'S NOTHING DISCRIMINATORY ABOUT BARRING GAYS FROM ENTERING THE U.S... SECretary SULLIVAN IS TRYING TO PROTECT US FROM alien HIV CARRIERS.
ATTABOY NEIL..
LS
Log Cabin SOFT BALL 1990

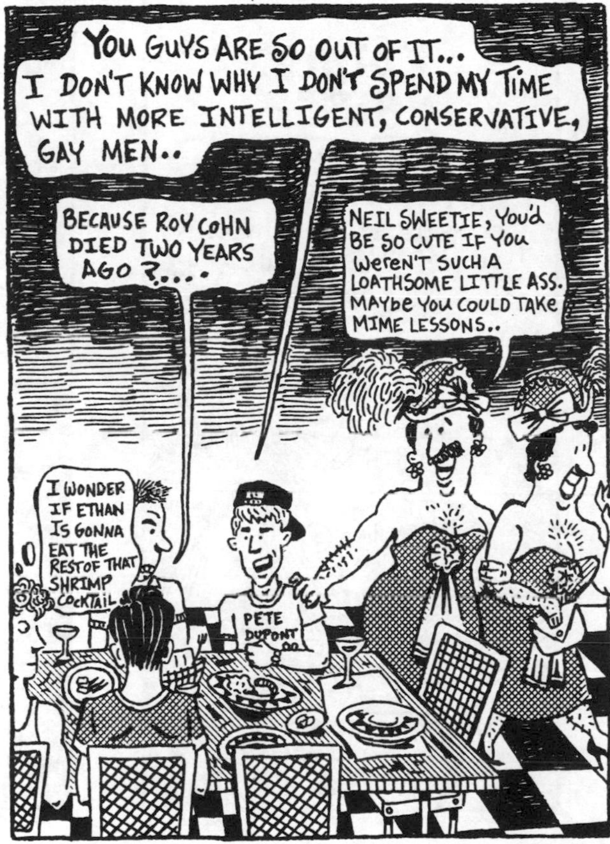
YOU GUYS ARE SO OUT OF IT... I DON'T KNOW WHY I DON'T SPEND MY TIME WITH MORE INTELLIGENT, CONSERVATIVE, GAY MEN..
BECAUSE ROY COHN DIED TWO YEARS AGO ?....
NEIL SWEETIE, You'd BE SO CUTE IF YOU weren'T SUCH A LOATHSOME LITTLE ASS. MAYbe YOU COULD TAKE MIME LESSONS..
I WONDER IF ETHAN IS GONNA EAT THE REST OF THAT SHRIMP COCKTAIL..
PETE DUPONT

Please return to
Kaleidoscope Youth Center
P.O. Box 8104
Columbus, OH 43201

HOLIDAY GIFT EXTRAVA-GANZA

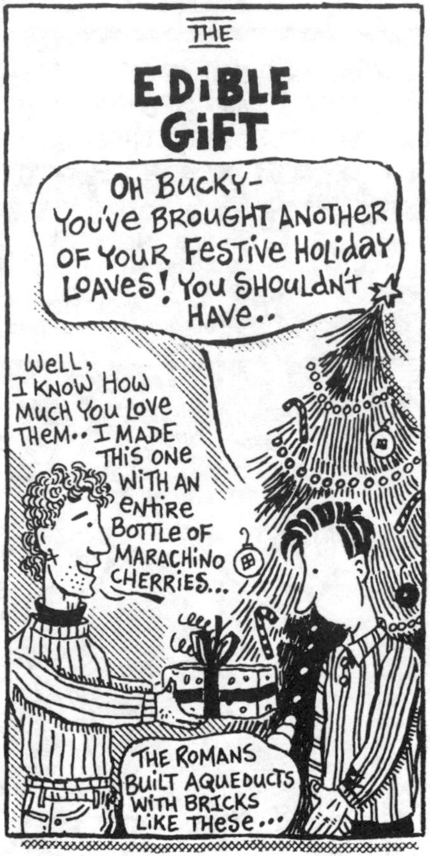

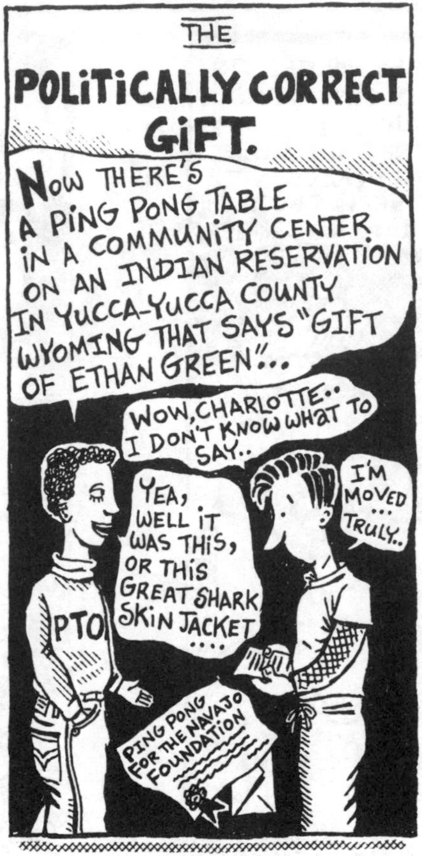

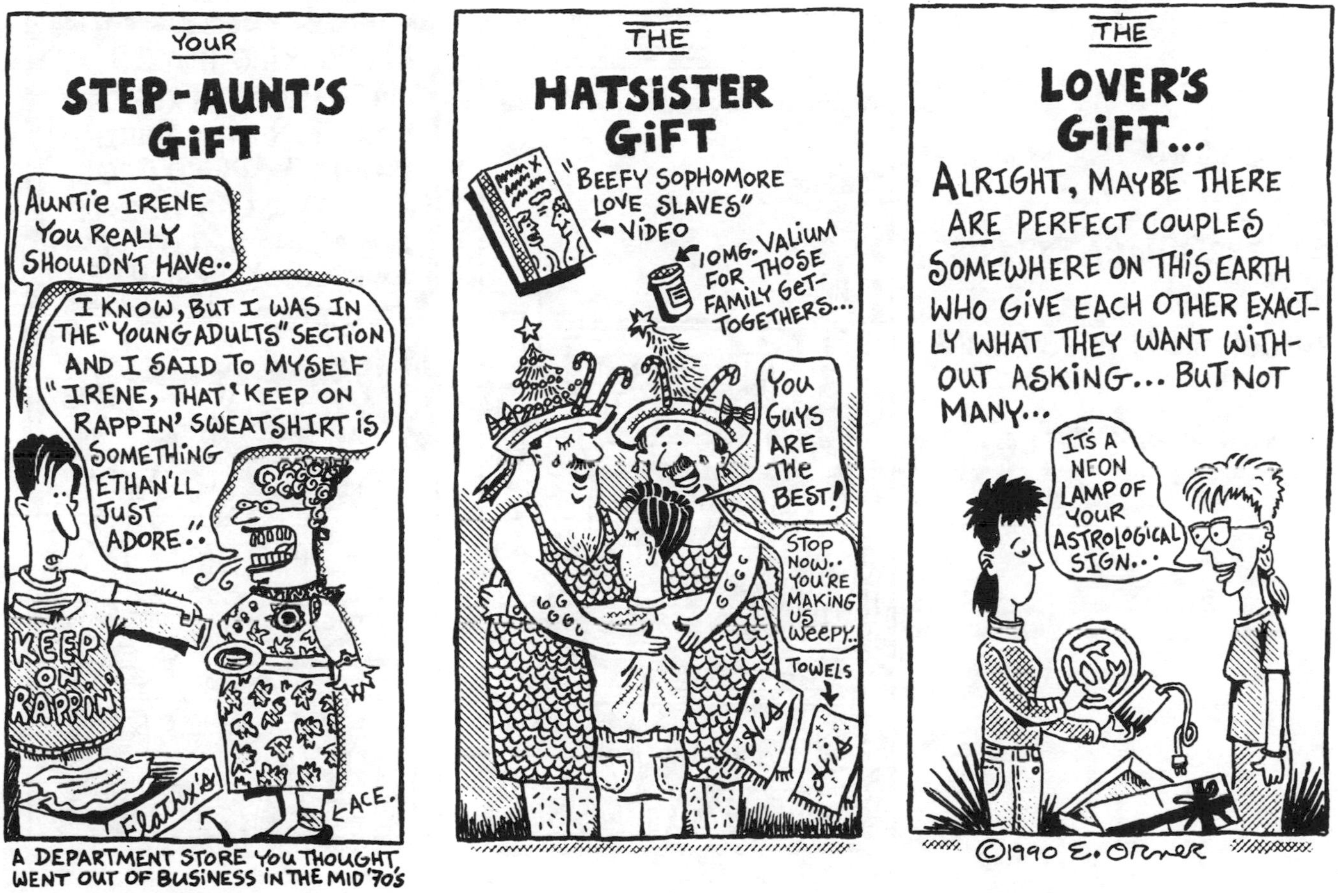
YOUR
STEP-AUNT'S GIFT
AUNTIE IRENE YOU REALLY SHOULDN'T HAVE..
I KNOW, BUT I WAS IN THE "YOUNG ADULTS" SECTION AND I SAID TO MYSELF "IRENE, THAT 'KEEP ON RAPPIN' SWEATSHIRT IS SOMETHING ETHAN'LL JUST ADORE!"
KEEP ON RAPPIN'
Flathx's
ACE.
A DEPARTMENT STORE YOU THOUGHT WENT OUT OF BUSINESS IN THE MID '70'S
THE
HATSISTER GIFT
"BEEFY SOPHOMORE LOVE SLAVES" ← VIDEO
10MG. VALIUM FOR THOSE FAMILY GET-TOGETHERS...
YOU GUYS ARE THE BEST!
STOP NOW.. YOU'RE MAKING US WEEPY..
TOWELS
His
His
THE
LOVER'S GIFT...
ALRIGHT, MAYBE THERE ARE PERFECT COUPLES SOMEWHERE ON THIS EARTH WHO GIVE EACH OTHER EXACTLY WHAT THEY WANT WITHOUT ASKING... BUT NOT MANY...
IT'S A NEON LAMP OF YOUR ASTROLOGICAL SIGN...
©1990 E. ORNER

SURPRISINGLY, ETHAN'S ROMANCE WITH LEO SEEMS TO BE GOING WELL...

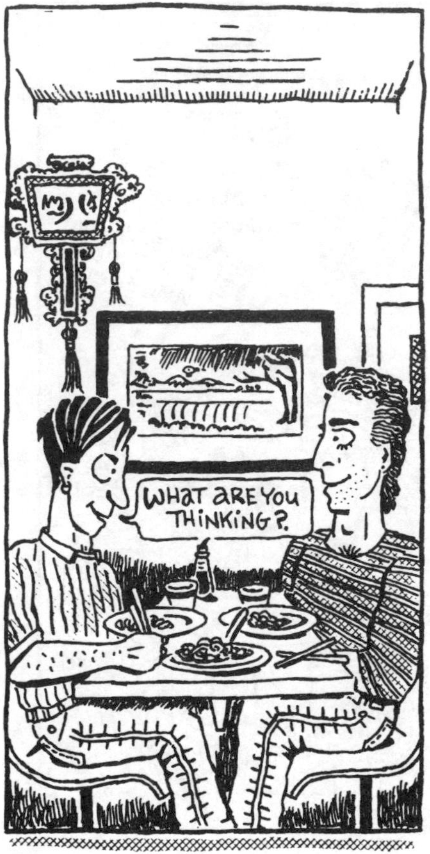
WHAT ARE YOU THINKING?

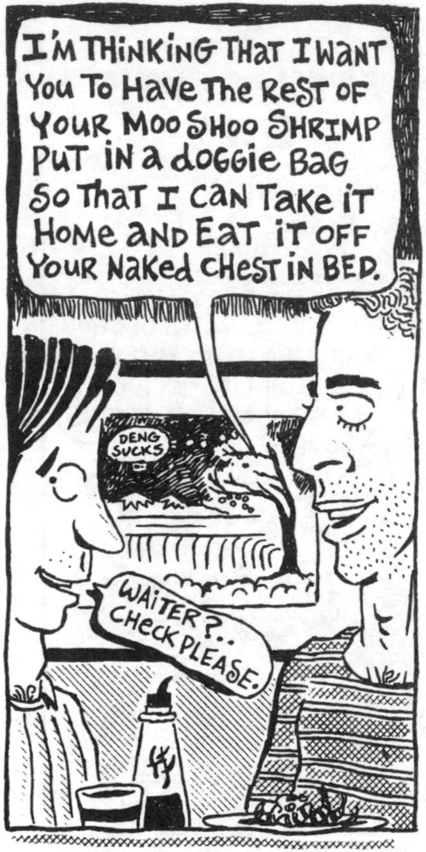
I'M THINKING THAT I WANT YOU TO HAVE THE REST OF YOUR MOO SHOO SHRIMP PUT IN A DOGGIE BAG SO THAT I CAN TAKE IT HOME AND EAT IT OFF YOUR NAKED CHEST IN BED.
DENG SUCKS
WAITER?.. CHECK PLEASE.

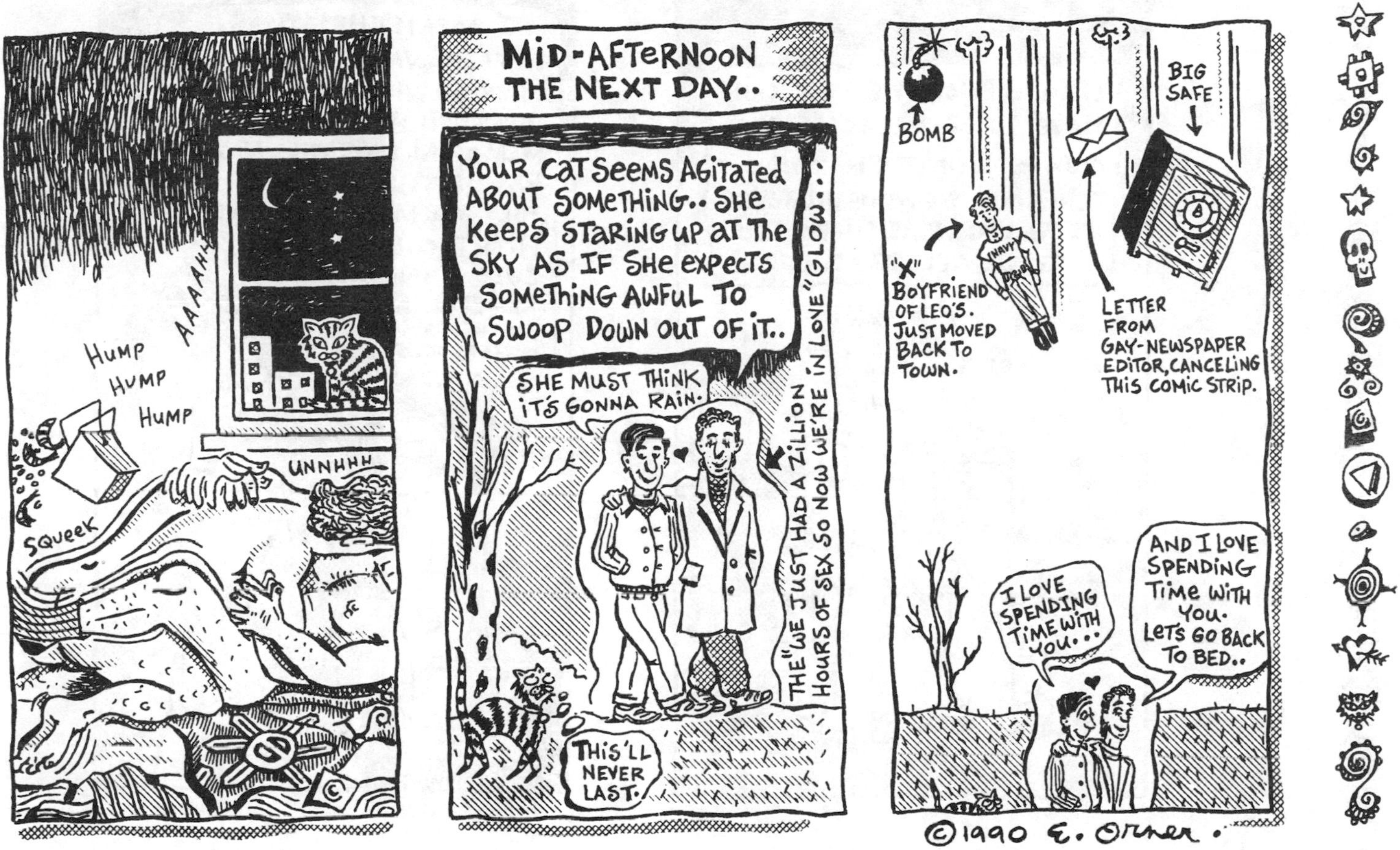

HUMP
HUMP
HUMP
AAAAHH
UNNHHH
SQUEEK
MID-AFTERNOON THE NEXT DAY..
YOUR CAT SEEMS AGITATED ABOUT SOMETHING.. SHE KEEPS STARING UP AT THE SKY AS IF SHE EXPECTS SOMETHING AWFUL TO SWOOP DOWN OUT OF IT..
SHE MUST THINK IT'S GONNA RAIN.
THE "WE JUST HAD A ZILLION HOURS OF SEX SO NOW WE'RE IN LOVE" GLOW...
THIS'LL NEVER LAST.
BOMB
"X" BOYFRIEND OF LEO'S. JUST MOVED BACK TO TOWN.
NAVY
BIG SAFE
LETTER FROM GAY-NEWSPAPER EDITOR, CANCELING THIS COMIC STRIP.
I LOVE SPENDING TIME WITH YOU...
AND I LOVE SPENDING TIME WITH YOU. LET'S GO BACK TO BED..
©1990 E. Orner.

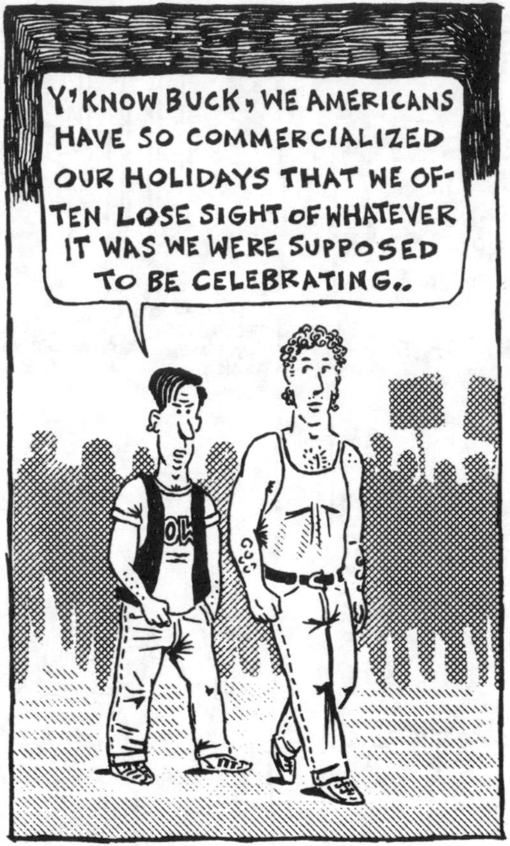
Y'KNOW BUCK, WE AMERICANS HAVE SO COMMERCIALIZED OUR HOLIDAYS THAT WE OFTEN LOSE SIGHT OF WHATEVER IT WAS WE WERE SUPPOSED TO BE CELEBRATING..
IOW

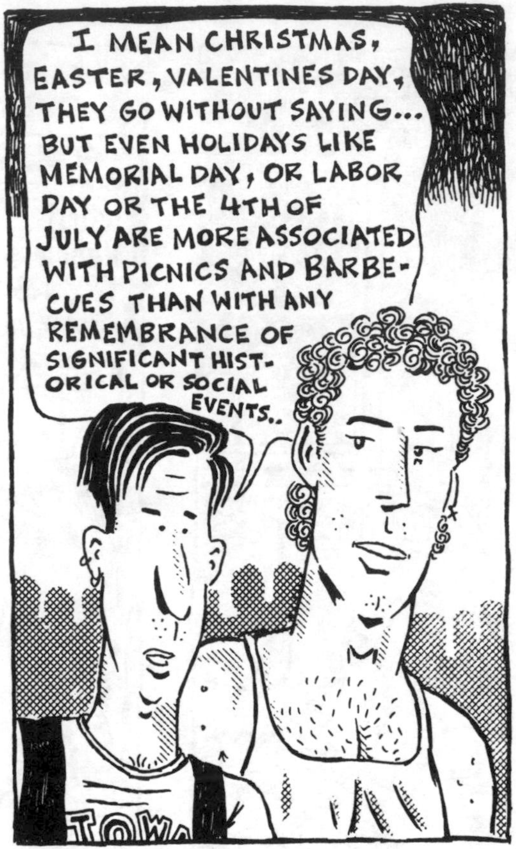
I MEAN CHRISTMAS, EASTER, VALENTINES DAY, THEY GO WITHOUT SAYING... BUT EVEN HOLIDAYS LIKE MEMORIAL DAY, OR LABOR DAY OR THE 4TH OF JULY ARE MORE ASSOCIATED WITH PICNICS AND BARBECUES THAN WITH ANY REMEMBRANCE OF SIGNIFICANT HISTORICAL OR SOCIAL EVENTS..
IOWA

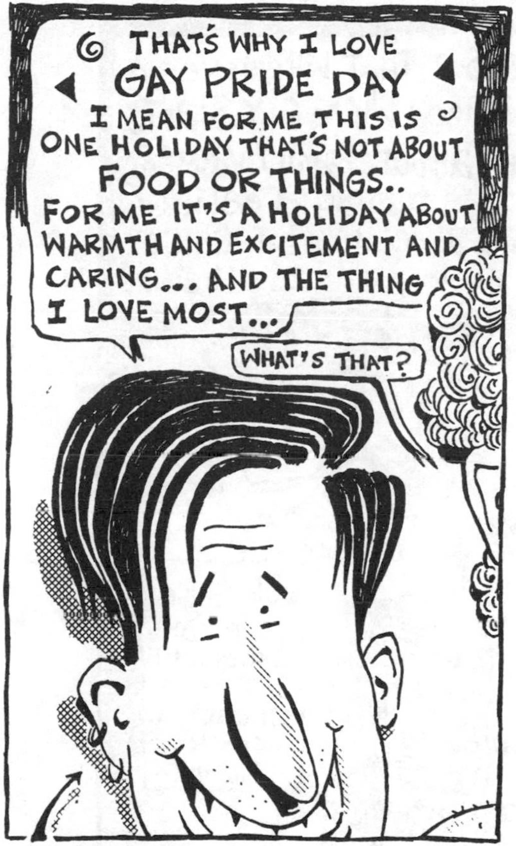
THAT'S WHY I LOVE GAY PRIDE DAY
I MEAN FOR ME THIS IS ONE HOLIDAY THAT'S NOT ABOUT FOOD OR THINGS.. FOR ME IT'S A HOLIDAY ABOUT WARMTH AND EXCITEMENT AND CARING... AND THE THING I LOVE MOST...
WHAT'S THAT?

HIP PRIDE DAY, DOUBLE EARRING THANG.

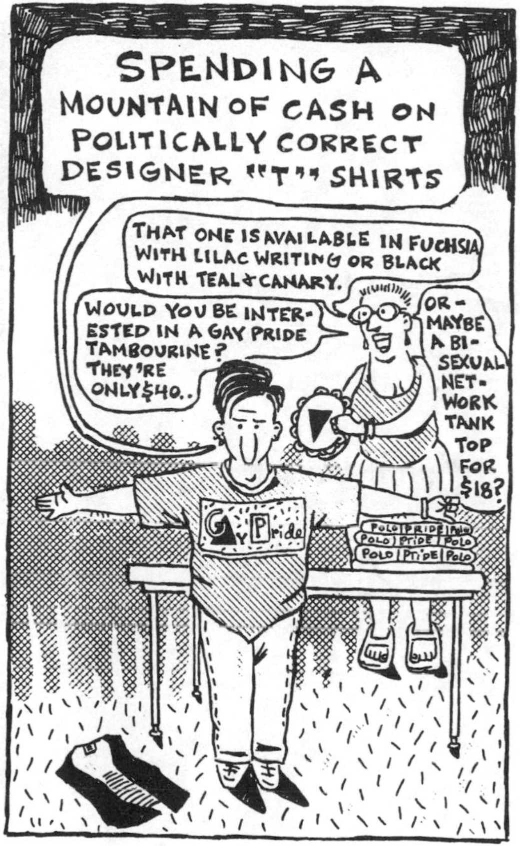
SPENDING A MOUNTAIN OF CASH ON POLITICALLY CORRECT DESIGNER "T" SHIRTS
THAT ONE IS AVAILABLE IN FUCHSIA WITH LILAC WRITING OR BLACK WITH TEAL & CANARY.
WOULD YOU BE INTER-ESTED IN A GAY PRIDE TAMBOURINE? THEY'RE ONLY $40..
OR - MAYBE A BI-SEXUAL NET-WORK TANK TOP FOR $18?
GAY Pride
POLO PRIDE POLO

Late one night

in

Cincinnati..

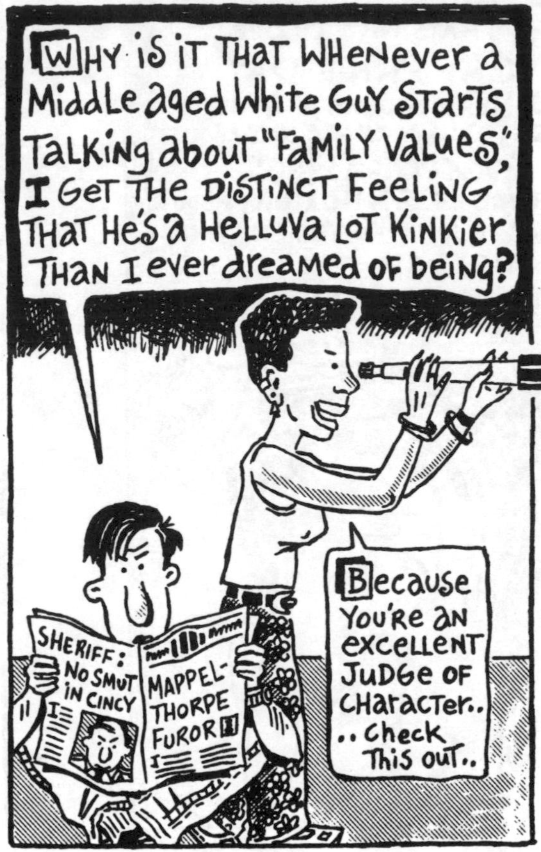
Why is it that whenever a Middle aged White Guy starts talking about "Family Values", I get the distinct feeling that he's a helluva lot kinkier than I ever dreamed of being?
Sheriff: No Smut in Cincy
Mappelthorpe Furor
Because you're an excellent judge of character.. ..Check this out..

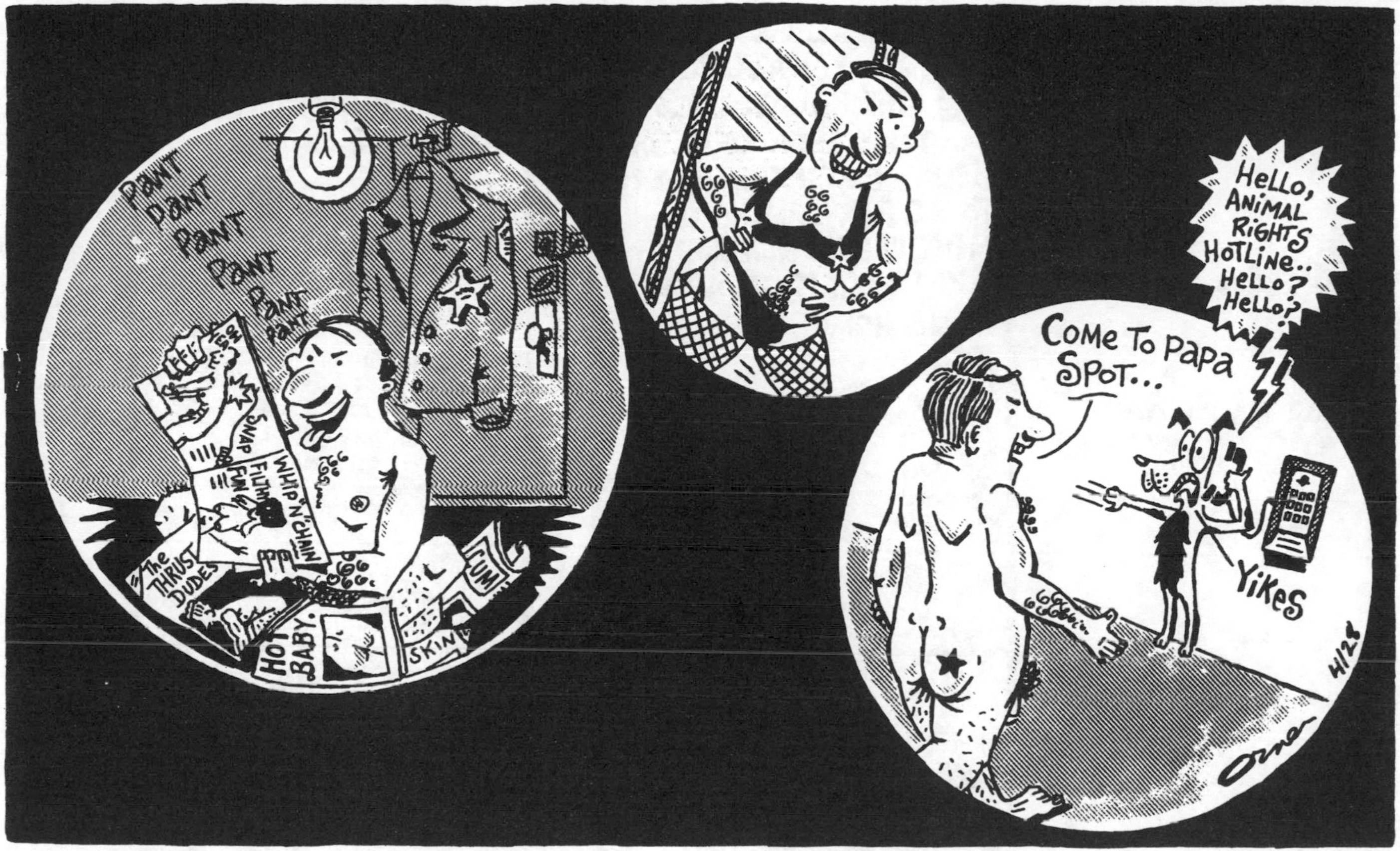
PANT
PANT
PANT
PANT
PANT
pant
SNAP
WHIP'N'CHAIN
FILTH FUN
The THRUST DUDES
CUM
HOT BABY.
SKIN
COME TO PAPA SPOT...
HELLO, ANIMAL RIGHTS HOTLINE.. HELLO? HELLO?
YIKES
4/28
Orner

Hat Sister Revenge

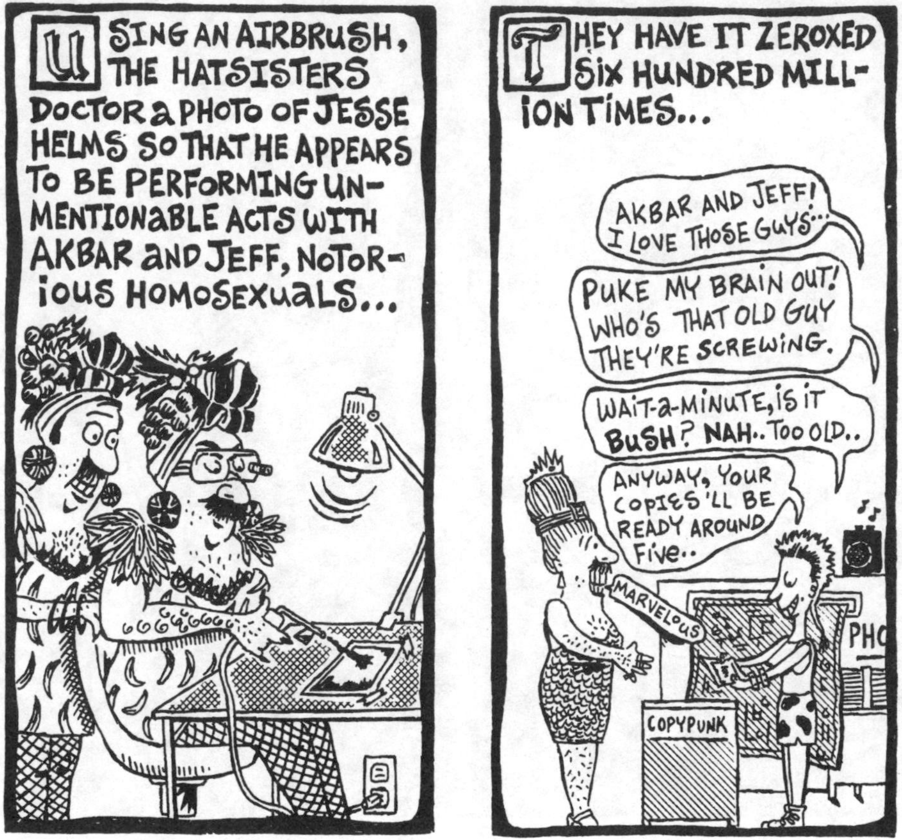
USING AN AIRBRUSH, THE HATSISTERS DOCTOR a PHOTO OF JESSE HELMS SO THAT HE APPEARS TO BE PERFORMING UN-MENTIONABLE ACTS WITH AKBAR and JEFF, NOTOR-ious HOMOSEXUaLS...
THEY HAVE IT ZEROXED SIX HUNDRED MILL-ION TIMES...
AKBAR AND JEFF! I LOVE THOSE GUYS...
PUKE MY BRAIN OUT! WHO'S THAT OLD GUY THEY'RE SCREWING.
WAIT-a-MINUTE, IS IT BUSH? NAH.. TOO OLD..
ANYWAY, YOUR COPIES'LL BE READY AROUND FIVE..
MARVELOUS
COPYPUNK
PHO

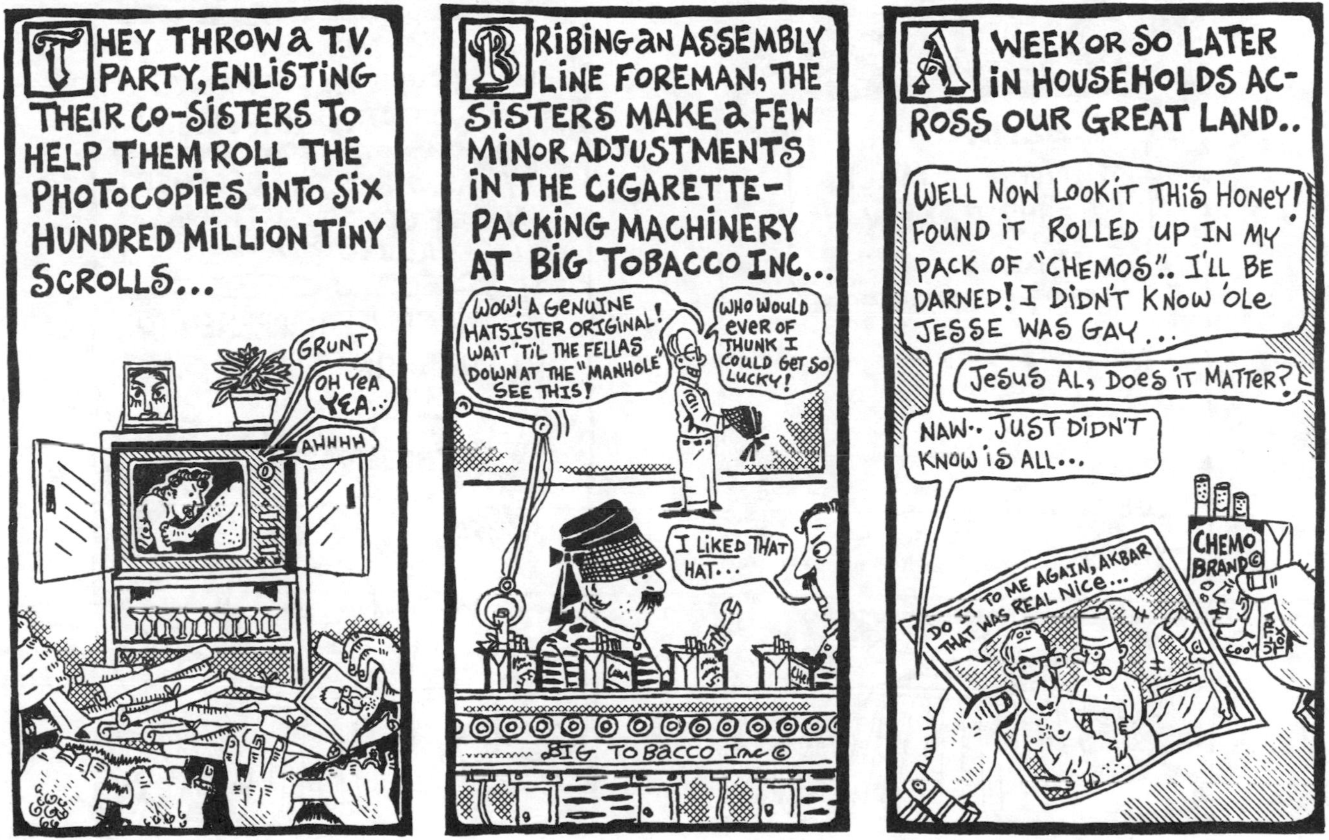
THEY THROW a T.V. PARTY, ENLISTING THEIR CO-SISTERS TO HELP THEM ROLL THE PHOTOCOPIES INTO SIX HUNDRED MILLION TINY SCROLLS...
GRUNT
OH YEA YEA...
AHHHH
BRIBING an ASSEMBLY LINE FOREMAN, THE SISTERS MAKE a FEW MINOR ADJUSTMENTS IN THE CIGARETTE-PACKING MACHINERY AT BIG TOBACCO INC...
WOW! A GENUINE HATSISTER ORIGINAL! WAIT 'TIL THE FELLAS DOWN AT THE "MANHOLE" SEE THIS!
WHO WOULD EVER OF THUNK I COULD GET SO LUCKY!
I LIKED THAT HAT...
BIG TOBACCO INC©
A WEEK OR SO LATER IN HOUSEHOLDS ACROSS OUR GREAT LAND..
WELL NOW LOOKIT THIS HONEY! FOUND IT ROLLED UP IN MY PACK OF "CHEMOS".. I'LL BE DARNED! I DIDN'T KNOW 'OLE JESSE WAS GAY...
JESUS AL, DOES IT MATTER?
NAW.. JUST DIDN'T KNOW IS ALL...
DO IT TO ME AGAIN, AKBAR THAT WAS REAL NICE...
CHEMO BRAND©

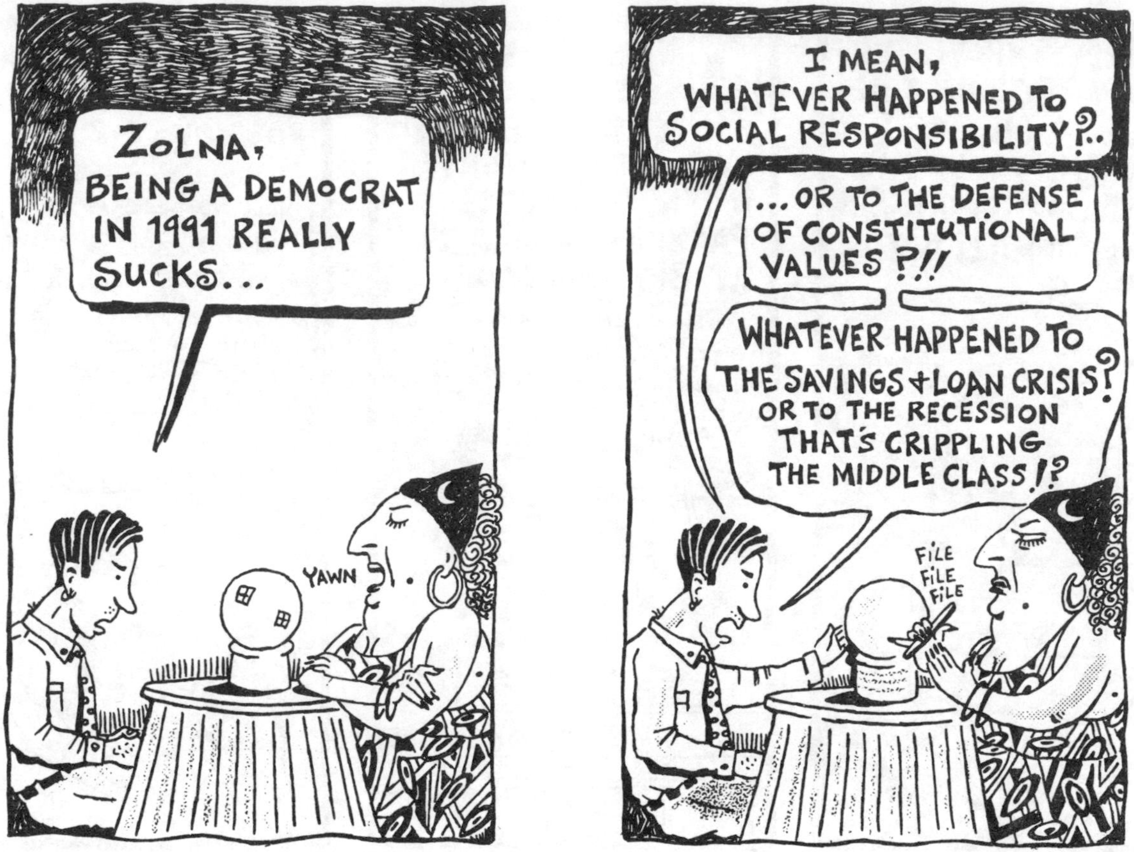
ZOLNA, BEING A DEMOCRAT IN 1991 REALLY SUCKS...
YAWN
I MEAN, WHATEVER HAPPENED TO SOCIAL RESPONSIBILITY?..
...OR TO THE DEFENSE OF CONSTITUTIONAL VALUES?!!
WHATEVER HAPPENED TO THE SAVINGS + LOAN CRISIS? OR TO THE RECESSION THAT'S CRIPPLING THE MIDDLE CLASS!?
FILE FILE FILE

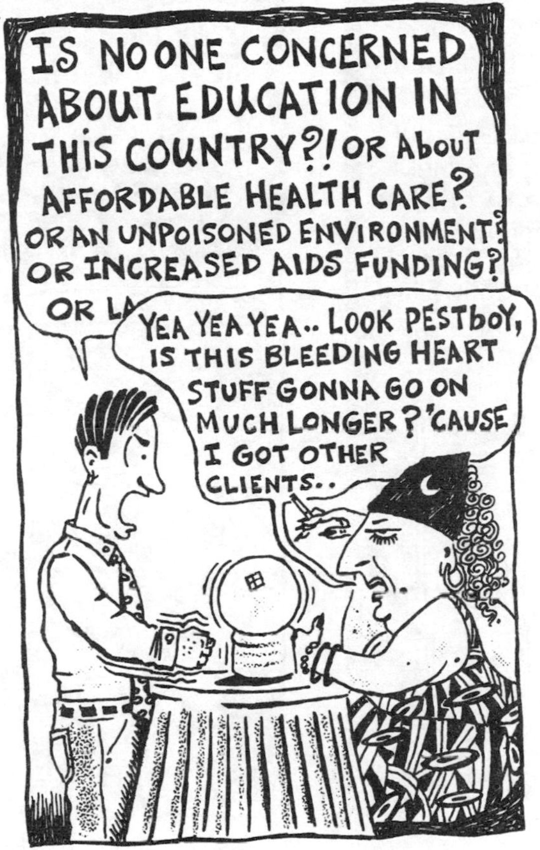
IS NO ONE CONCERNED ABOUT EDUCATION IN THIS COUNTRY?! OR About AFFORDABLE HEALTH CARE? OR AN UNPOISONED ENVIRONMENT? OR INCREASED AIDS FUNDING? OR LA
YEA YEA YEA.. LOOK PESTBOY, IS THIS BLEEDING HEART STUFF GONNA GO ON MUCH LONGER? 'CAUSE I GOT OTHER CLIENTS..

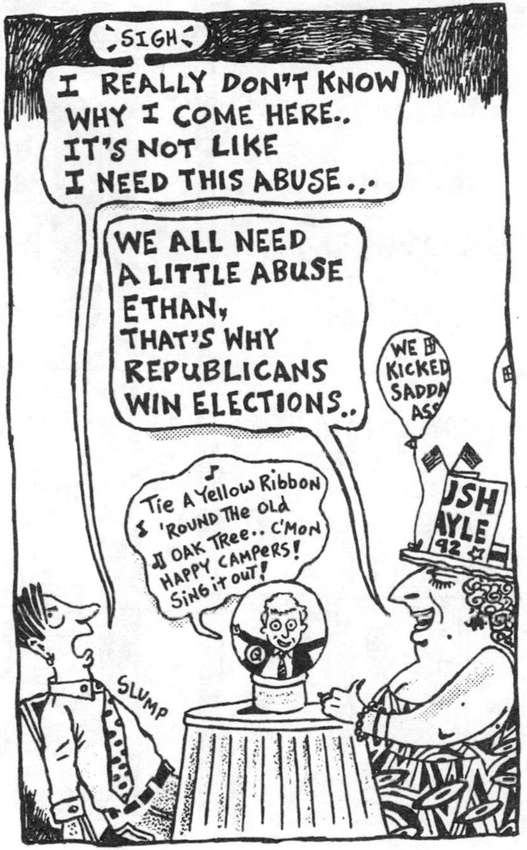
SIGH
I REALLY DON'T KNOW WHY I COME HERE.. IT'S NOT LIKE I NEED THIS ABUSE...
WE ALL NEED A LITTLE ABUSE ETHAN, THAT'S WHY REPUBLICANS WIN ELECTIONS..
Tie A Yellow Ribbon 'Round The Old Oak Tree.. C'MON HAPPY CAMPERS! SiNG it OUT!
SLUMP

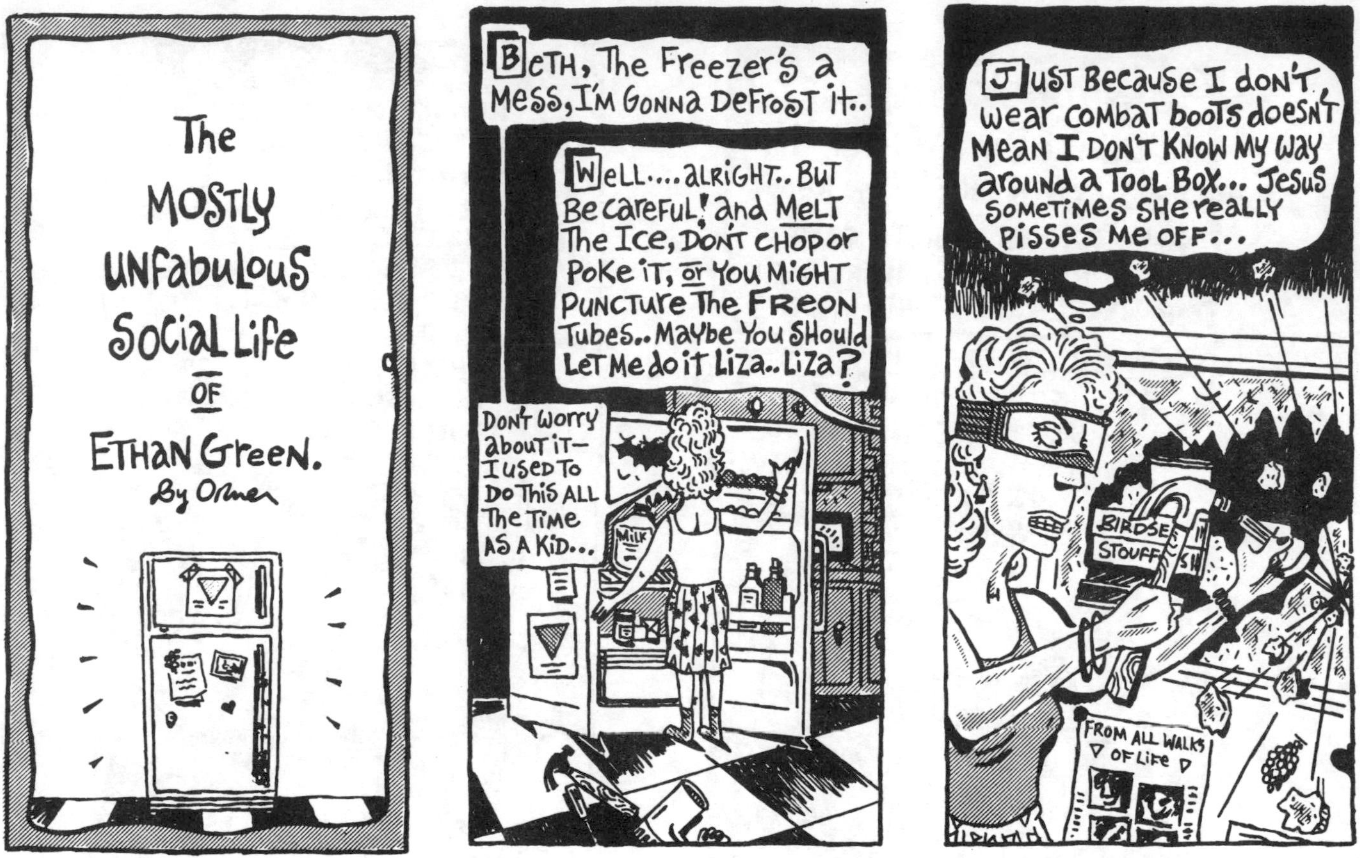

The MOSTLY UNFabuLous SociaL Life OF ETHAN Green.
By Orner
BETH, The Freezer's a Mess, I'M GoNNA DeFrosT it..
WELL.... ALRIGHT.. BUT Be careful! and MELT The Ice, DON'T CHOP or Poke iT, or You MiGHT PUNCTURE The FREON Tubes.. MaYbe You SHould LeT Me do it Liza.. LiZa?
DON'T WORRY about IT— I USED To DO THIS ALL The TiME AS A KiD...
MILK
JUST Because I don't wear combaT boots doesN'T Mean I DON'T KNOW My way around a TooL Box... JeSuS SOMETIMES SHE really PiSSeS Me OFF...
BIRDSE
STOUFF
FROM ALL WALKS OF LiFe

BANG oh shit...

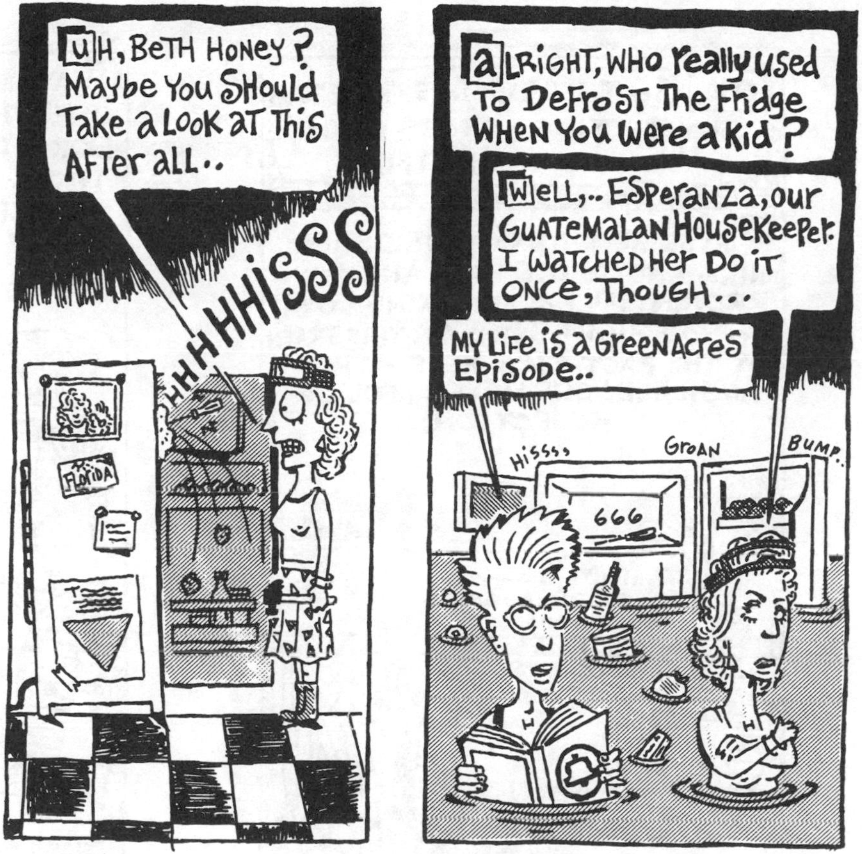
UH, BETH HONEY? Maybe You Should Take a Look at This After all..
HHHHHHISSSS
FLORIDA
ALRIGHT, WHO really used To Defrost The Fridge WHEN You were a Kid?
WELL,.. ESperanza, our GUATEMALAN HouseKeeper. I WATCHED Her DO IT ONCE, THOUGH...
MY LIFE IS a GREEN ACRES EPISODE..
HISSSS
GROAN
BUMP..
666

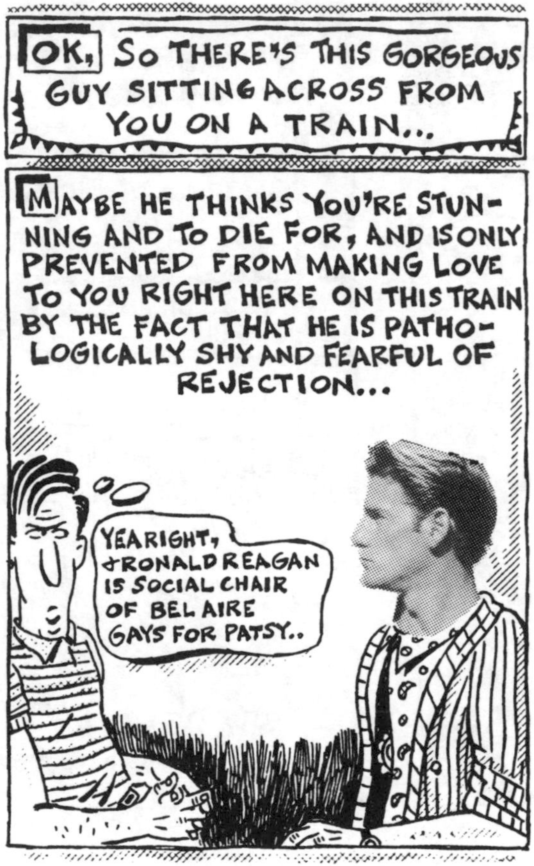
OK, SO THERE'S THIS GORGEOUS GUY SITTING ACROSS FROM YOU ON A TRAIN...
MAYBE HE THINKS YOU'RE STUNNING AND TO DIE FOR, AND IS ONLY PREVENTED FROM MAKING LOVE TO YOU RIGHT HERE ON THIS TRAIN BY THE FACT THAT HE IS PATHOLOGICALLY SHY AND FEARFUL OF REJECTION...
YEA RIGHT, & RONALD REAGAN IS SOCIAL CHAIR OF BEL AIRE GAYS FOR PATSY..

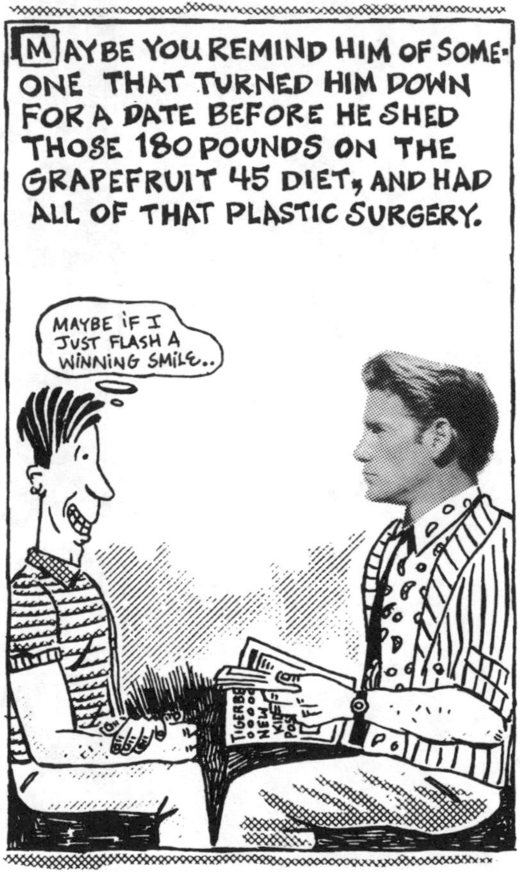
MAYBE YOU REMIND HIM OF SOMEONE THAT TURNED HIM DOWN FOR A DATE BEFORE HE SHED THOSE 180 POUNDS ON THE GRAPEFRUIT 45 DIET, AND HAD ALL OF THAT PLASTIC SURGERY.
MAYBE IF I JUST FLASH A WINNING SMILE..

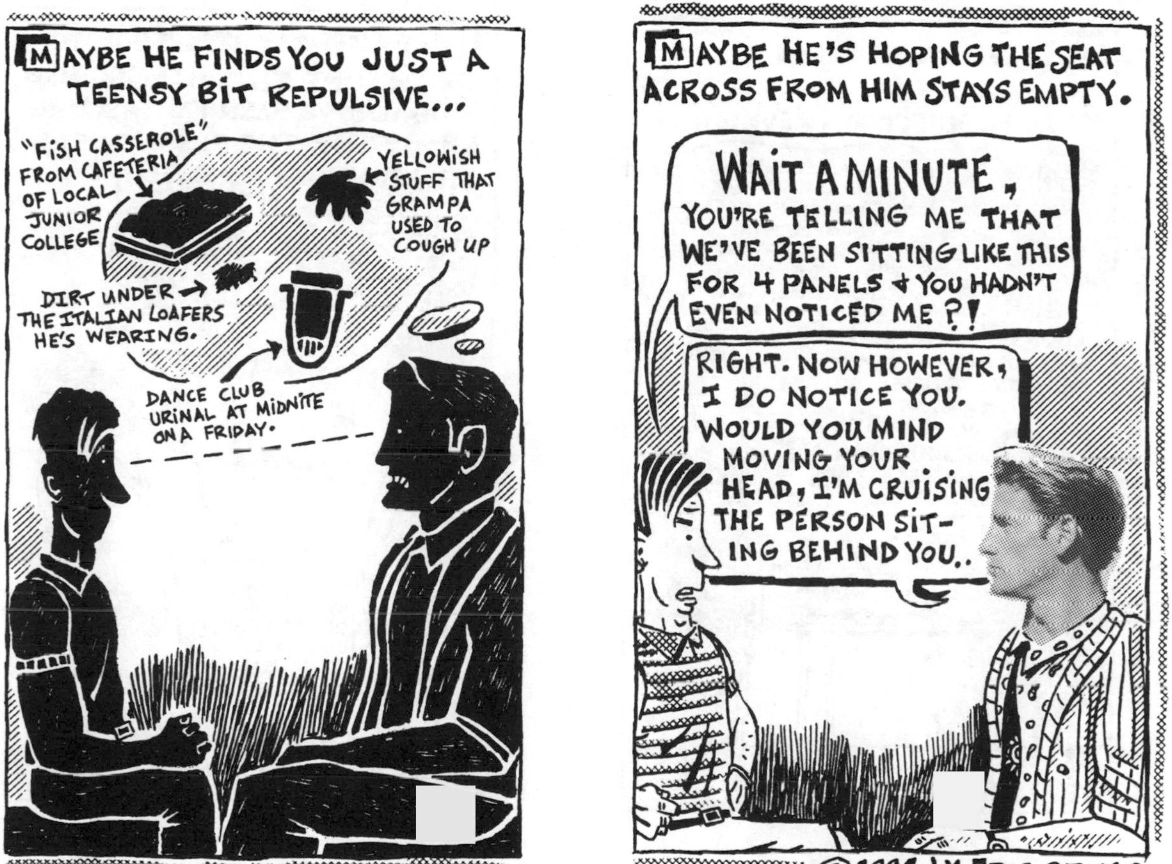
MAYBE HE FINDS YOU JUST A TEENSY BIT REPULSIVE...
"FISH CASSEROLE" FROM CAFETERIA OF LOCAL JUNIOR COLLEGE
YELLOWISH STUFF THAT GRAMPA USED TO COUGH UP
DIRT UNDER THE ITALIAN LOAFERS HE'S WEARING.
DANCE CLUB URINAL AT MIDNITE ON A FRIDAY.
MAYBE HE'S HOPING THE SEAT ACROSS FROM HIM STAYS EMPTY.
WAIT A MINUTE, YOU'RE TELLING ME THAT WE'VE BEEN SITTING LIKE THIS FOR 4 PANELS & YOU HADN'T EVEN NOTICED ME ?!
RIGHT. NOW HOWEVER, I DO NOTICE YOU. WOULD YOU MIND MOVING YOUR HEAD, I'M CRUISING THE PERSON SITTING BEHIND YOU..

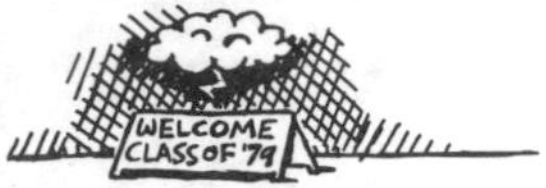

WELCOME CLASS OF '79

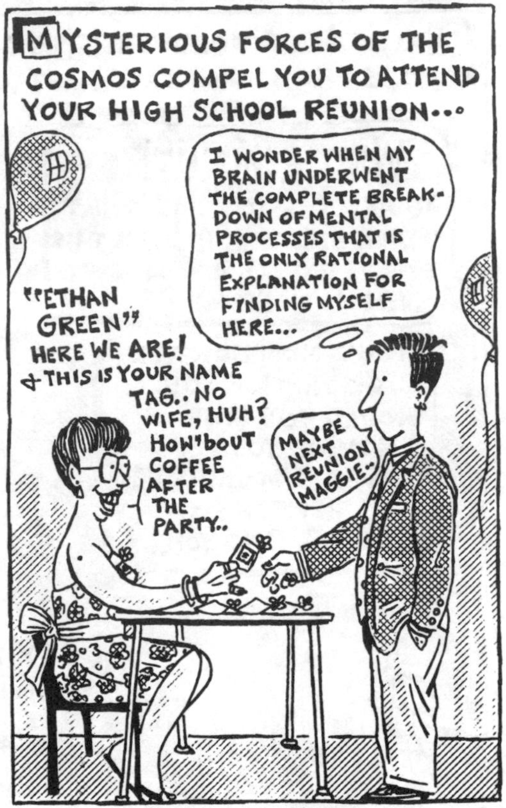

MYSTERIOUS FORCES OF THE COSMOS COMPEL YOU TO ATTEND YOUR HIGH SCHOOL REUNION...
"ETHAN GREEN" HERE WE ARE! & THIS IS YOUR NAME TAG.. NO WIFE, HUH? HOW'BOUT COFFEE AFTER THE PARTY..
I WONDER WHEN MY BRAIN UNDERWENT THE COMPLETE BREAK-DOWN OF MENTAL PROCESSES THAT IS THE ONLY RATIONAL EXPLANATION FOR FINDING MYSELF HERE...
MAYBE NEXT REUNION MAGGIE..

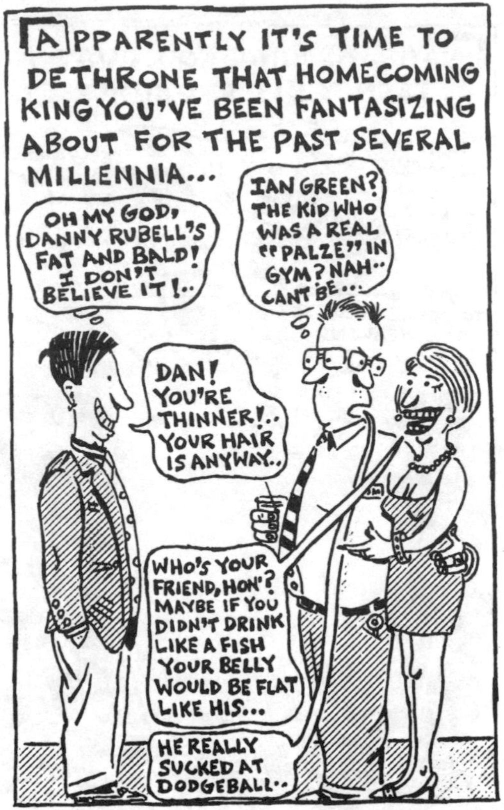

APPARENTLY IT'S TIME TO DETHRONE THAT HOMECOMING KING YOU'VE BEEN FANTASIZING ABOUT FOR THE PAST SEVERAL MILLENNIA...
OH MY GOD, DANNY RUBELL'S FAT AND BALD! I DON'T BELIEVE IT!..
IAN GREEN? THE KID WHO WAS A REAL "PALZE" IN GYM? NAH.. CANT BE...
DAN! YOU'RE THINNER!.. YOUR HAIR IS ANYWAY..
WHO'S YOUR FRIEND, HON'? MAYBE IF YOU DIDN'T DRINK LIKE A FISH YOUR BELLY WOULD BE FLAT LIKE HIS...
HE REALLY SUCKED AT DODGEBALL..

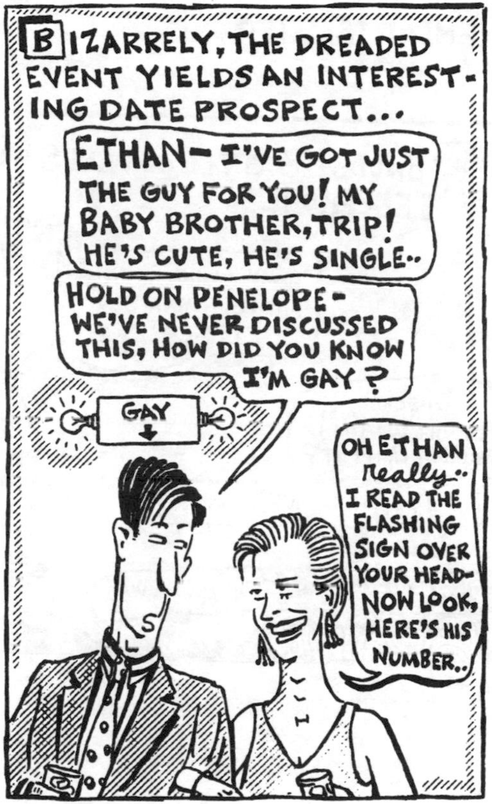
BIZARRELY, THE DREADED EVENT YIELDS AN INTERESTING DATE PROSPECT...
ETHAN– I'VE GOT JUST THE GUY FOR YOU! MY BABY BROTHER, TRIP! HE'S CUTE, HE'S SINGLE..
HOLD ON PENELOPE– WE'VE NEVER DISCUSSED THIS, HOW DID YOU KNOW I'M GAY?
GAY
OH ETHAN really.. I READ THE FLASHING SIGN OVER YOUR HEAD– NOW LOOK, HERE'S HIS NUMBER..

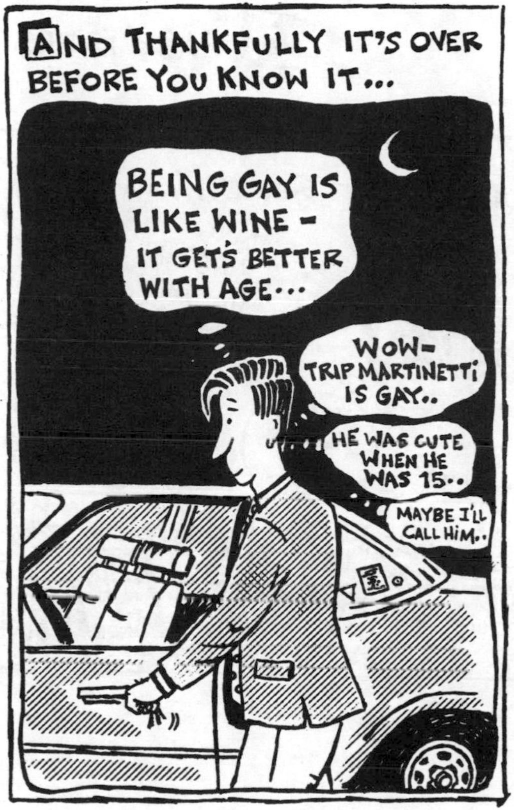
AND THANKFULLY IT'S OVER BEFORE YOU KNOW IT...
BEING GAY IS LIKE WINE – IT GETS BETTER WITH AGE...
WOW– TRIP MARTINETTI IS GAY..
HE WAS CUTE WHEN HE WAS 15..
MAYBE I'LL CALL HIM..

6 EASY STEPS TO WEEKEND DISASTER.

HOLD OUT FOR SOMETHING BETTER.
RING
RING click... PAUSE...
Hi ETHAN, THIS IS TED
I WAS HOPING YOU'D
LIKE TO SEE A MOVIE
WITH ME ON FRIDAY-
CALL ME, OK? I'D LOVE
TO SEE YOU... BYE...
MAYBE LEO WILL CALL..
HEALTH CRISIS SURVEY.
CHEAT ON YOUR LOVER? YES NO DEFINE CHEAT
RIGHT.
CONDUCT BATTLE OF WILLS WITH TELEPHONE.
YOU'RE GONNA RING, AND IT'S GONNA BE LEO..
SHEESH- ALL THIS WAITIN' IS MURDER, AIN'T IT?
HEY, HOWBOUT A SMOKE?
HUM HUM HUM

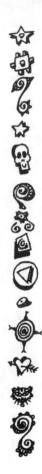

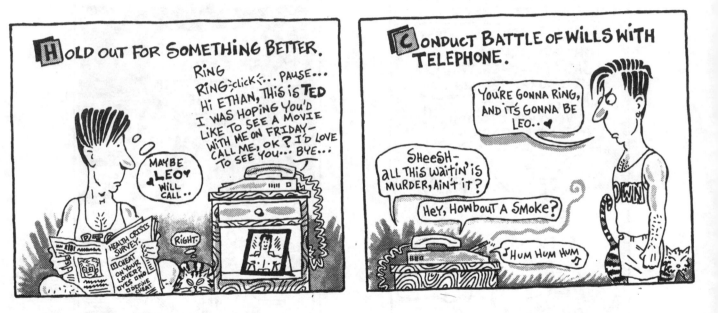

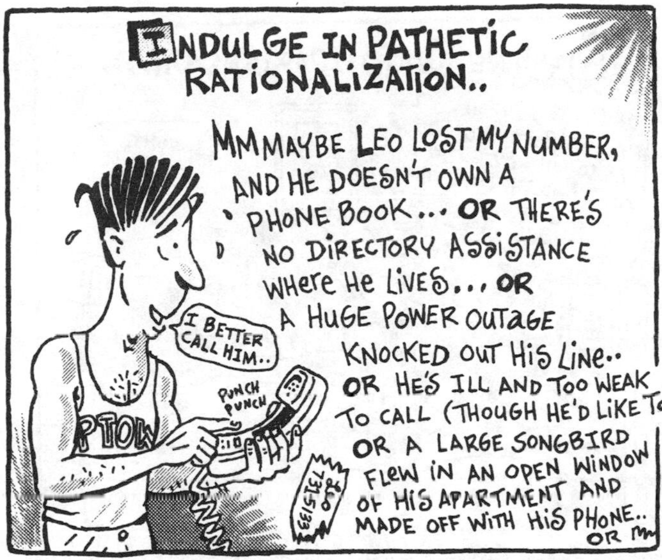
INDULGE IN PATHETIC RATIONALIZATION..
MMMAYBE LEO LOST MY NUMBER, AND HE DOESN'T OWN A PHONE BOOK... OR THERE'S NO DIRECTORY ASSISTANCE WHERE HE LIVES... OR A HUGE POWER OUTAGE KNOCKED OUT HIS LINE.. OR HE'S ILL AND TOO WEAK TO CALL (THOUGH HE'D LIKE TO) OR A LARGE SONGBIRD FLEW IN AN OPEN WINDOW OF HIS APARTMENT AND MADE OFF WITH HIS PHONE.. OR
I BETTER CALL HIM..
PUNCH PUNCH

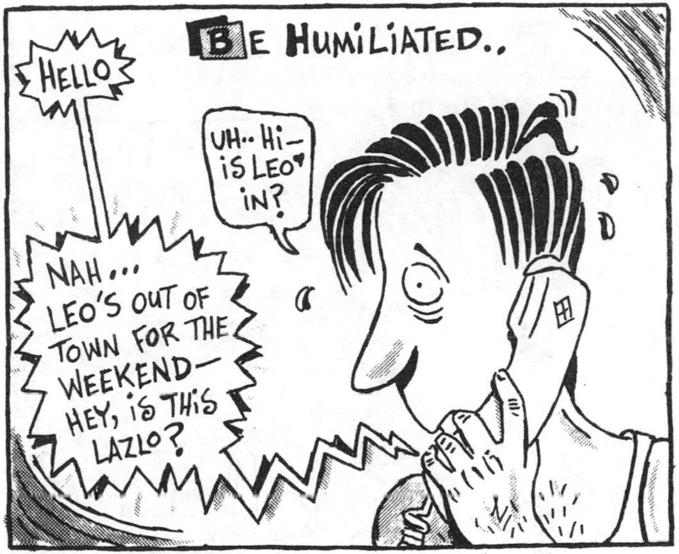
BE HUMILIATED..
HELLO
UH.. HI- IS LEO IN?
NAH... LEO'S OUT OF TOWN FOR THE WEEKEND- HEY, IS THIS LAZLO?

CONTINUED →

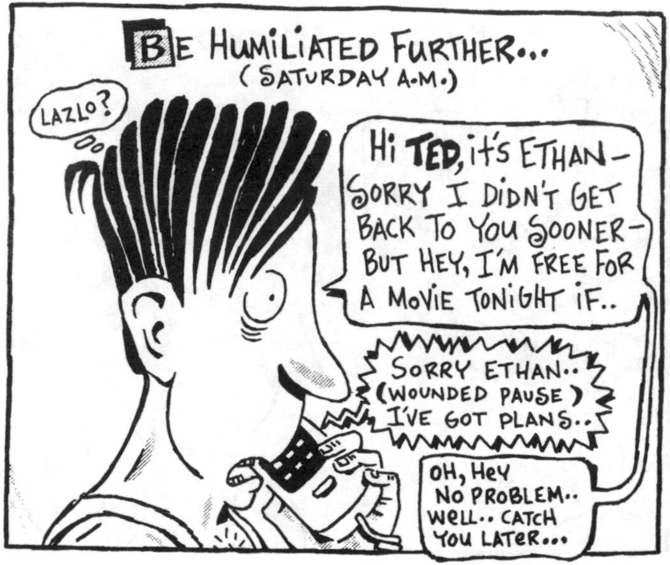
BE HUMILIATED FURTHER...
(SATURDAY A.M.)
LAZLO?
Hi TED, it's ETHAN- SORRY I DIDN'T GET BACK TO YOU SOONER- BUT HEY, I'M FREE FOR A MOVIE TONIGHT IF..
SORRY ETHAN.. (WOUNDED PAUSE) I'VE GOT PLANS..
OH, HEY NO PROBLEM.. WELL.. CATCH YOU LATER...

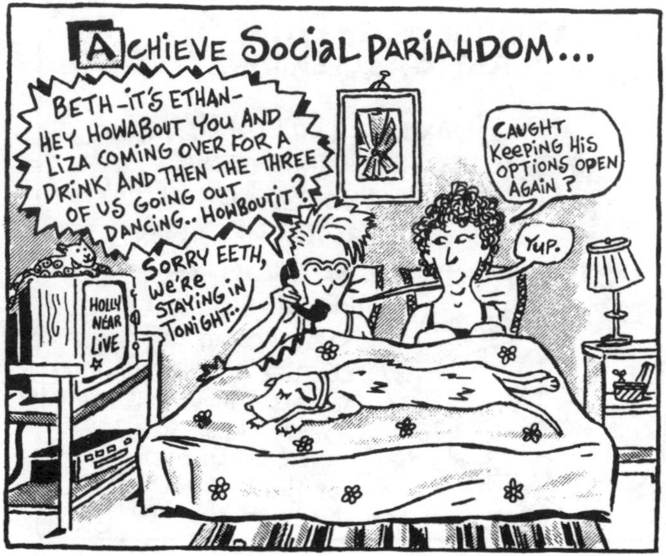
ACHIEVE SOCIAL PARIAHDOM...
BETH-IT'S ETHAN- HEY HOWABOUT YOU AND LIZA COMING OVER FOR A DRINK AND THEN THE THREE OF US GOING OUT DANCING.. HOWBOUTIT?
CAUGHT KEEPING HIS OPTIONS OPEN AGAIN?
YUP.
SORRY EETH, WE'RE STAYING IN TONIGHT..
HOLLY NEAR LIVE

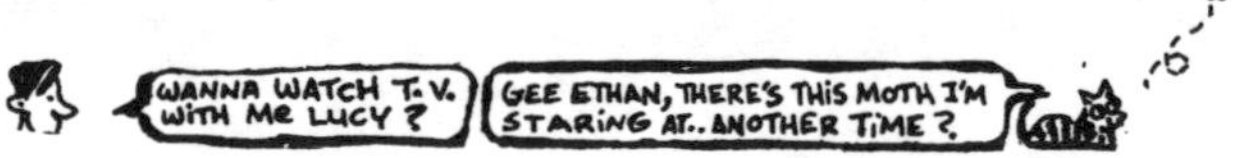
WANNA WATCH T.V. WITH ME LUCY?
GEE ETHAN, THERE'S THIS MOTH I'M STARING AT.. ANOTHER TIME?

SINGLEHOOD...

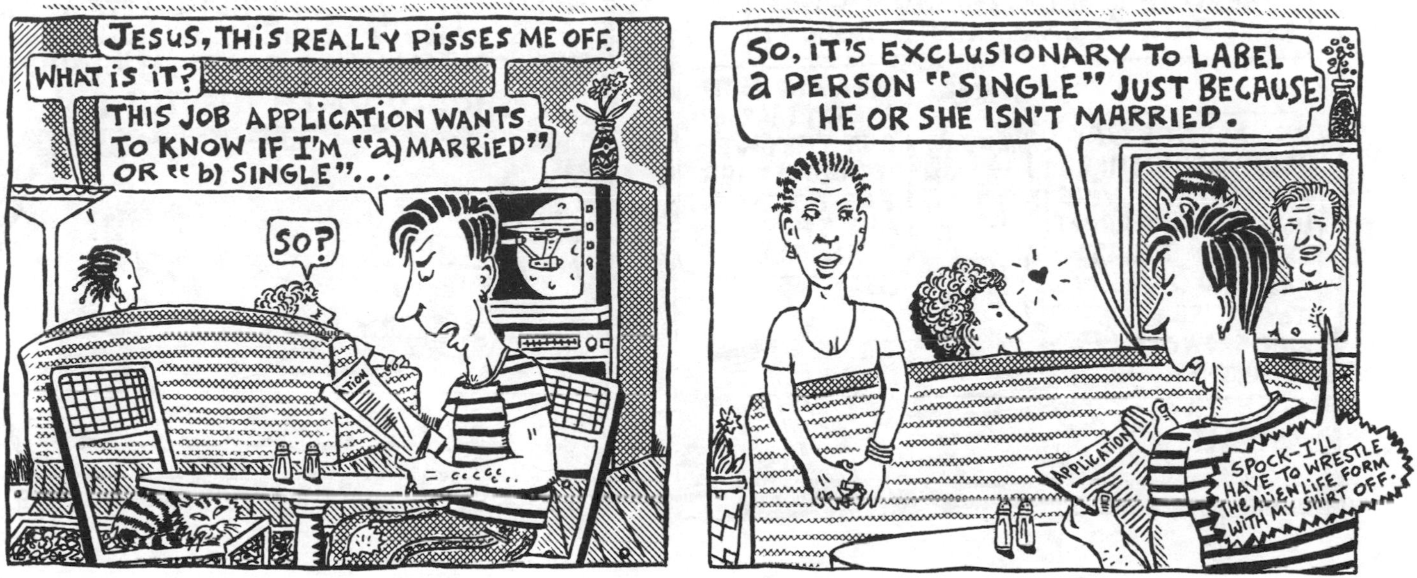
JESUS, THIS REALLY PISSES ME OFF.
WHAT IS IT?
THIS JOB APPLICATION WANTS TO KNOW IF I'M "a) MARRIED" OR "b) SINGLE"...
SO?
ATION
SO, IT'S EXCLUSIONARY TO LABEL A PERSON "SINGLE" JUST BECAUSE HE OR SHE ISN'T MARRIED.
APPLICATION
SPOCK–I'LL HAVE TO WRESTLE THE ALIEN LIFE FORM WITH MY SHIRT OFF.

CONTINUED

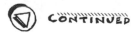

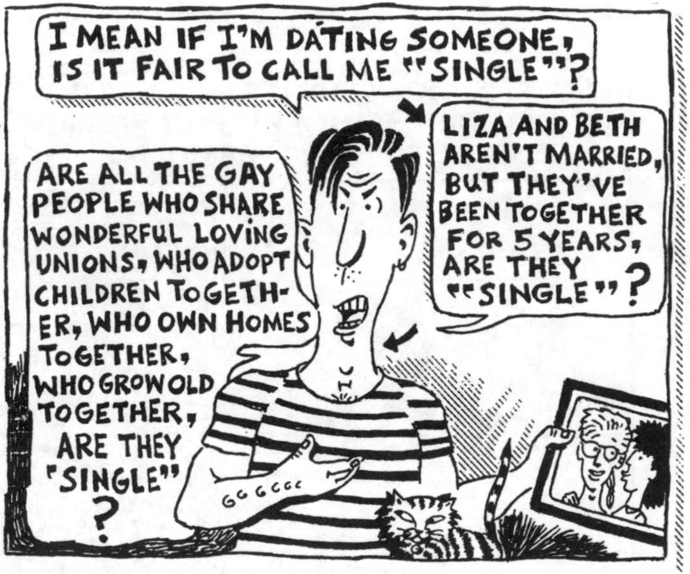
I MEAN IF I'M DATING SOMEONE, IS IT FAIR TO CALL ME "SINGLE"?
ARE ALL THE GAY PEOPLE WHO SHARE WONDERFUL LOVING UNIONS, WHO ADOPT CHILDREN TOGETHER, WHO OWN HOMES TOGETHER, WHO GROW OLD TOGETHER, ARE THEY "SINGLE"?
LIZA AND BETH AREN'T MARRIED, BUT THEY'VE BEEN TOGETHER FOR 5 YEARS, ARE THEY "SINGLE"?

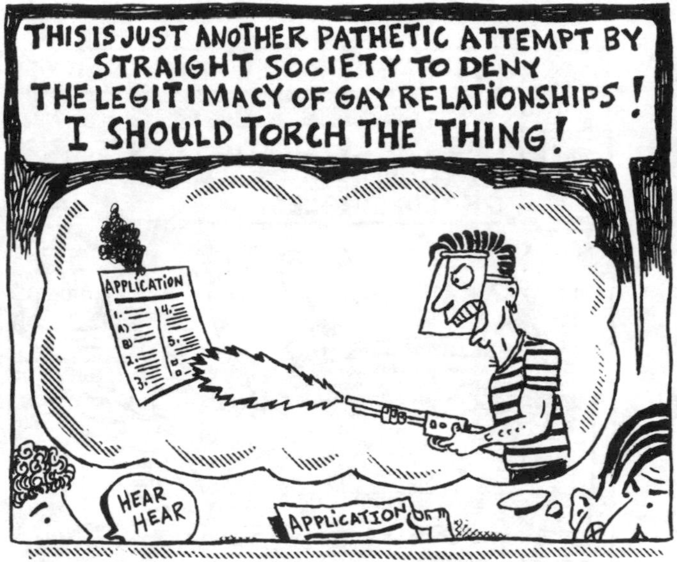
THIS IS JUST ANOTHER PATHETIC ATTEMPT BY STRAIGHT SOCIETY TO DENY THE LEGITIMACY OF GAY RELATIONSHIPS! I SHOULD TORCH THE THING!
APPLICATION
HEAR HEAR
APPLICATION

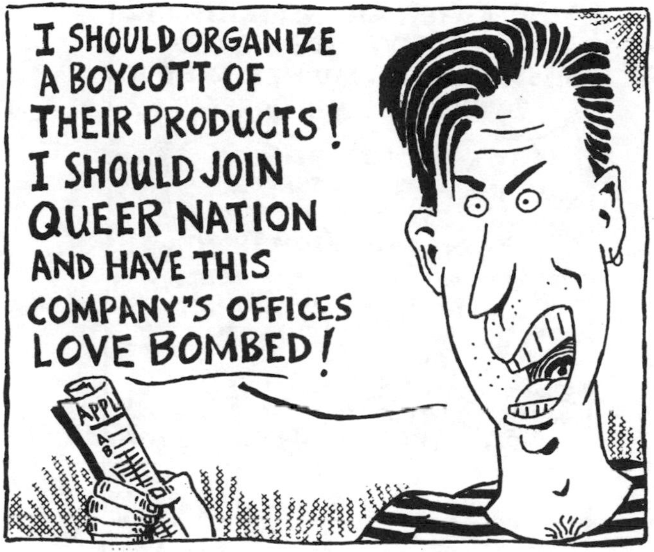
I SHOULD ORGANIZE A BOYCOTT OF THEIR PRODUCTS! I SHOULD JOIN QUEER NATION AND HAVE THIS COMPANY'S OFFICES LOVE BOMBED!
APPL
A
B

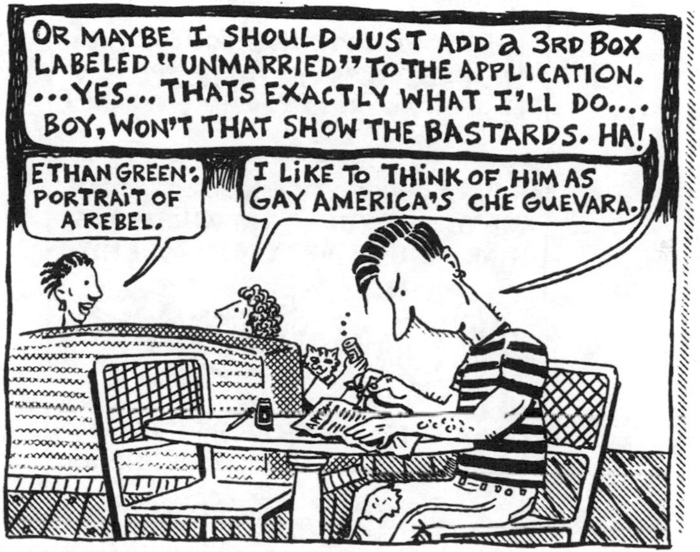
OR MAYBE I SHOULD JUST ADD A 3RD BOX LABELED "UNMARRIED" TO THE APPLICATION. ...YES... THATS EXACTLY WHAT I'LL DO.... BOY, WON'T THAT SHOW THE BASTARDS. HA!
ETHAN GREEN: PORTRAIT OF A REBEL.
I LIKE TO THINK OF HIM AS GAY AMERICA'S CHÉ GUEVARA.

©1991 Eric Orner

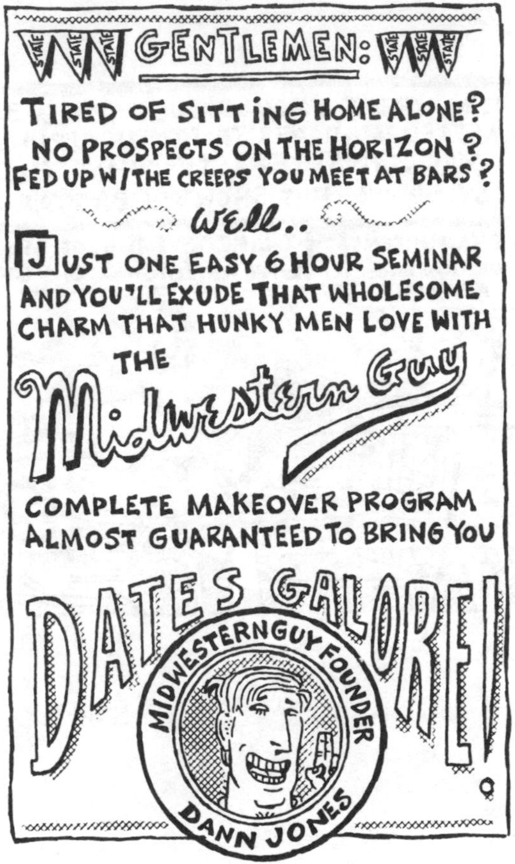
STATE STATE STATE
GENTLEMEN:
STATE STATE
TIRED OF SITTING HOME ALONE?
NO PROSPECTS ON THE HORIZON?
FED UP W/THE CREEPS YOU MEET AT BARS?
WELL..
JUST ONE EASY 6 HOUR SEMINAR AND YOU'LL EXUDE THAT WHOLESOME CHARM THAT HUNKY MEN LOVE WITH
THE Midwestern Guy
COMPLETE MAKEOVER PROGRAM ALMOST GUARANTEED TO BRING YOU
DATES GALORE!
MIDWESTERNGUY FOUNDER
DANN JONES

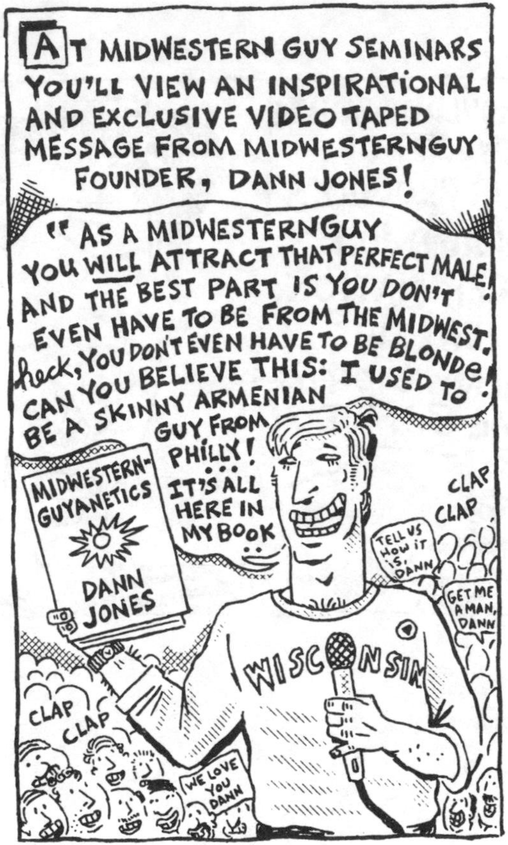
AT MIDWESTERN GUY SEMINARS YOU'LL VIEW AN INSPIRATIONAL AND EXCLUSIVE VIDEO TAPED MESSAGE FROM MIDWESTERNGUY FOUNDER, DANN JONES!
"AS A MIDWESTERNGUY YOU WILL ATTRACT THAT PERFECT MALE! AND THE BEST PART IS YOU DON'T EVEN HAVE TO BE FROM THE MIDWEST. heck, YOU DON'T EVEN HAVE TO BE BLONDE! CAN YOU BELIEVE THIS: I USED TO BE A SKINNY ARMENIAN GUY FROM PHILLY! ... IT'S ALL HERE IN MY BOOK ..
MIDWESTERN-GUYANETICS
DANN JONES
WISCONSIN
CLAP CLAP
TELL US HOW IT IS, DANN
GET ME A MAN, DANN
CLAP CLAP
WE LOVE YOU DANN

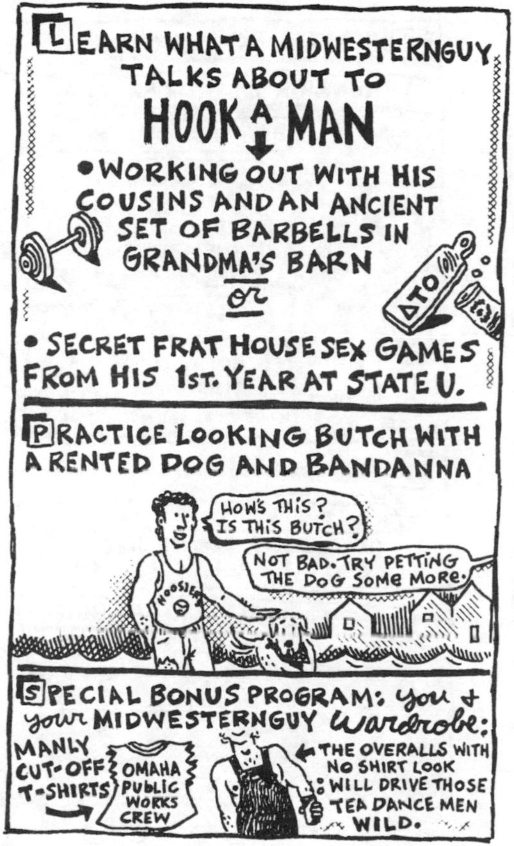
LEARN WHAT A MIDWESTERNGUY TALKS ABOUT TO
HOOK A MAN
• WORKING OUT WITH HIS COUSINS AND AN ANCIENT SET OF BARBELLS IN GRANDMA'S BARN
or
• SECRET FRAT HOUSE SEX GAMES FROM HIS 1ST. YEAR AT STATE U.
ΔΤΟ
PRACTICE LOOKING BUTCH WITH A RENTED DOG AND BANDANNA
HOW'S THIS? IS THIS BUTCH?
NOT BAD. TRY PETTING THE DOG SOME MORE.
HOOSIER
SPECIAL BONUS PROGRAM: you & your MIDWESTERNGUY Wardrobe:
MANLY CUT-OFF T-SHIRTS
OMAHA PUBLIC WORKS CREW
THE OVERALLS WITH NO SHIRT LOOK WILL DRIVE THOSE TEA DANCE MEN WILD.

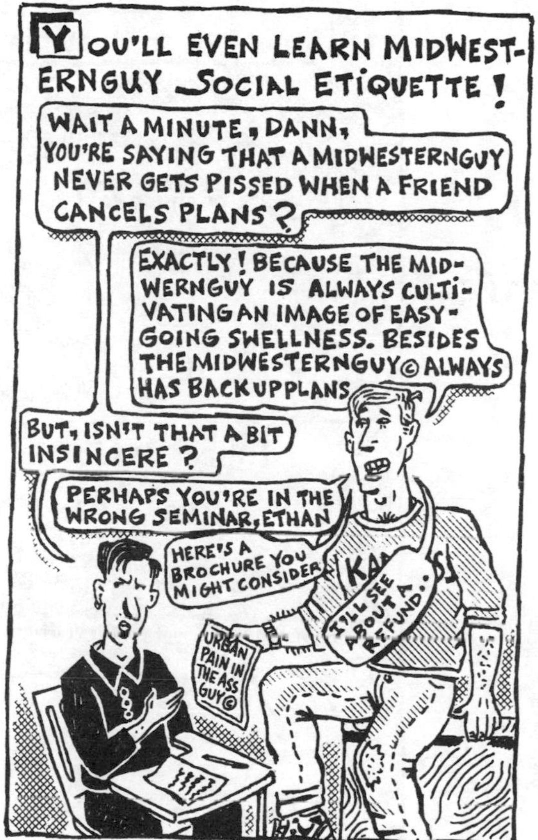
YOU'LL EVEN LEARN MIDWESTERNGUY SOCIAL ETIQUETTE!
WAIT A MINUTE, DANN, YOU'RE SAYING THAT A MIDWESTERNGUY NEVER GETS PISSED WHEN A FRIEND CANCELS PLANS?
EXACTLY! BECAUSE THE MIDWERNGUY IS ALWAYS CULTIVATING AN IMAGE OF EASY-GOING SWELLNESS. BESIDES THE MIDWESTERNGUY© ALWAYS HAS BACKUPPLANS
BUT, ISN'T THAT A BIT INSINCERE?
PERHAPS YOU'RE IN THE WRONG SEMINAR, ETHAN
HERE'S A BROCHURE YOU MIGHT CONSIDER
URBAN PAIN IN THE ASS GUY©
I'LL SEE ABOUT A REFUND...
KA

by ERIC ORNER, 1991.

NOTES FROM THE BEACH...

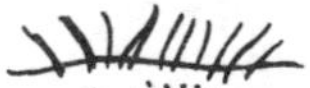

*LITTLE DUNE PREDATOR

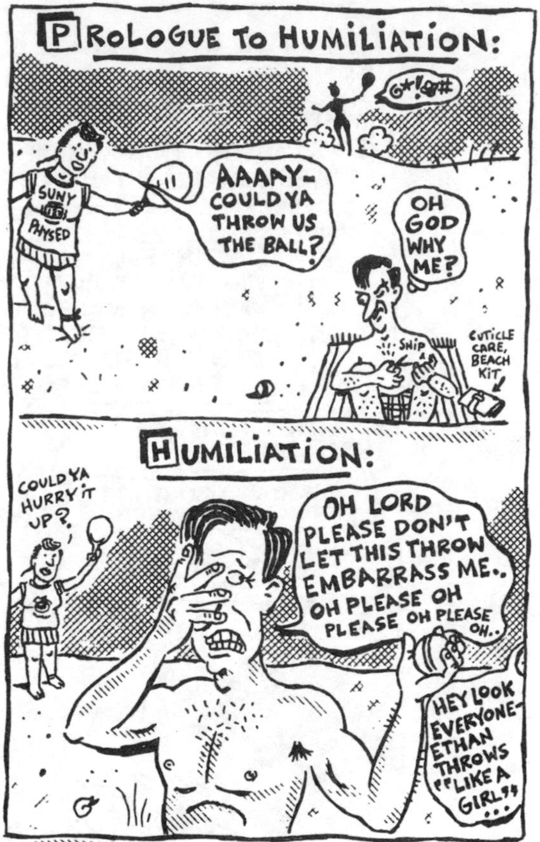
PROLOGUE TO HUMILIATION:
@*!@#
AAAAY- COULD YA THROW US THE BALL?
SUNY PHYSED
OH GOD WHY ME?
SNIP
CUTICLE CARE, BEACH KIT
HUMILIATION:
COULD YA HURRY IT UP?
OH LORD PLEASE DON'T LET THIS THROW EMBARRASS ME.. OH PLEASE OH PLEASE OH PLEASE OH PLEASE OH..
HEY LOOK EVERYONE- ETHAN THROWS "LIKE A GIRL"...

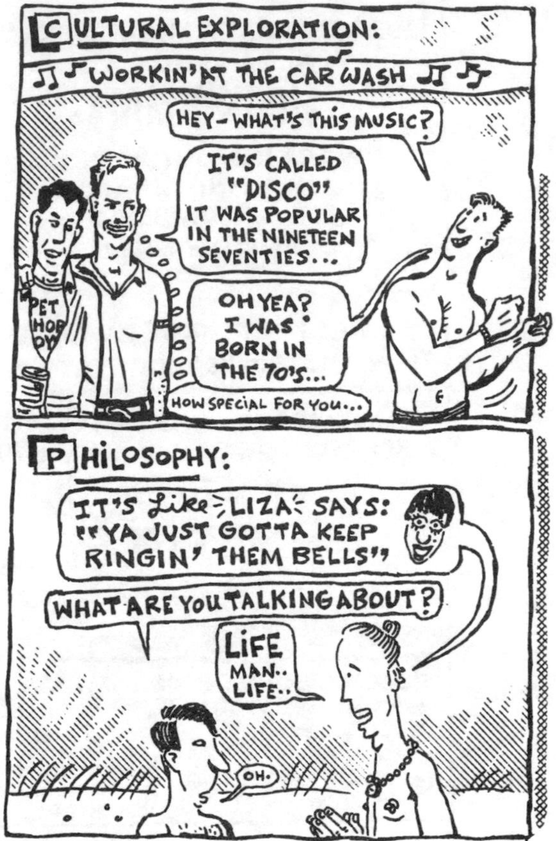
CULTURAL EXPLORATION:
WORKIN' AT THE CAR WASH
HEY- WHAT'S THIS MUSIC?
IT'S CALLED "DISCO" IT WAS POPULAR IN THE NINETEEN SEVENTIES...
OH YEA? I WAS BORN IN THE 70'S...
HOW SPECIAL FOR YOU...
PHILOSOPHY:
IT'S Like LIZA SAYS: "YA JUST GOTTA KEEP RINGIN' THEM BELLS"
WHAT ARE YOU TALKING ABOUT?
LIFE MAN.. LIFE..
OH.

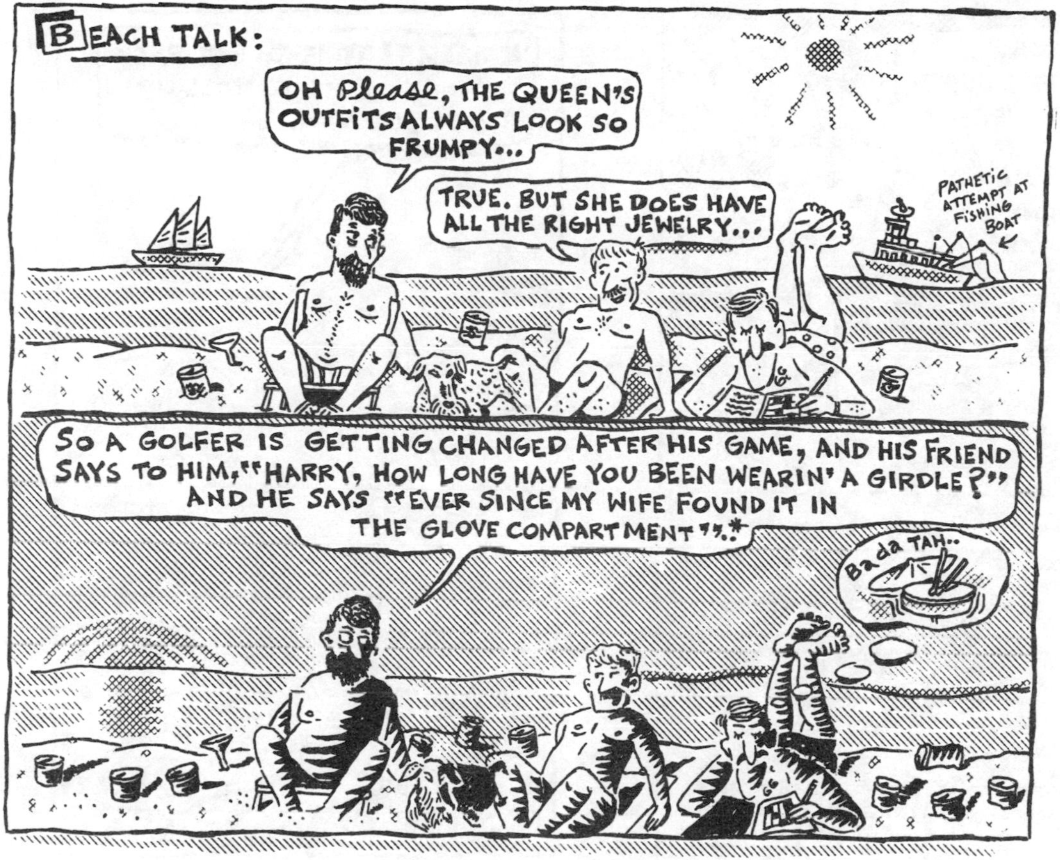
BEACH TALK:
OH Please, THE QUEEN'S OUTFITS ALWAYS LOOK SO FRUMPY...
TRUE. BUT SHE DOES HAVE ALL THE RIGHT JEWELRY...
PATHETIC ATTEMPT AT FISHING BOAT
SO A GOLFER IS GETTING CHANGED AFTER HIS GAME, AND HIS FRIEND SAYS TO HIM, "HARRY, HOW LONG HAVE YOU BEEN WEARIN' A GIRDLE?" AND HE SAYS "EVER SINCE MY WIFE FOUND IT IN THE GLOVE COMPARTMENT".*
Ba da TAH..

*THANKS TO MARK NEWELL

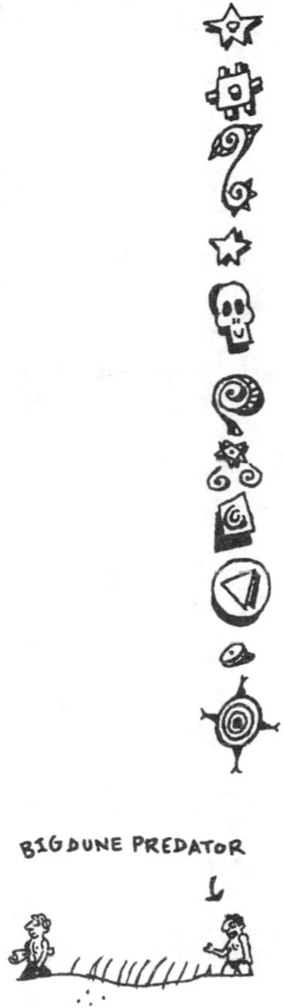
BIG DUNE PREDATOR

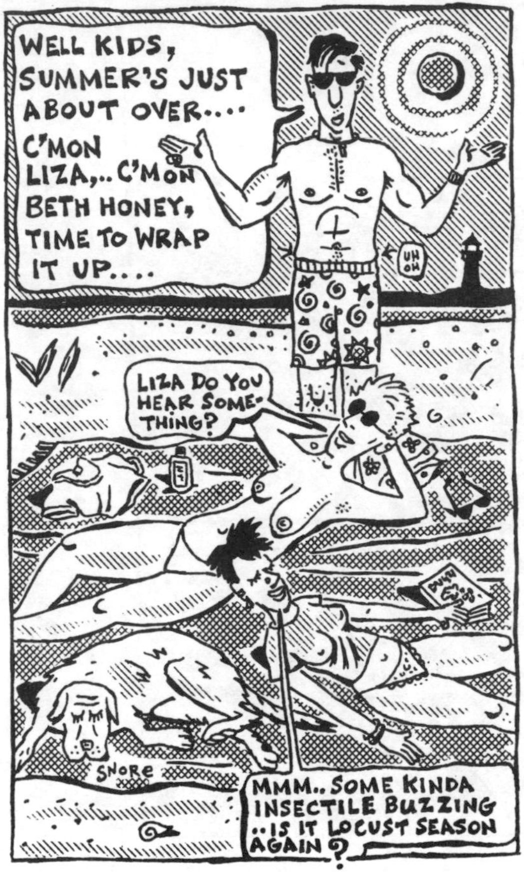
WELL KIDS, SUMMER'S JUST ABOUT OVER.... C'MON LIZA,.. C'MON BETH HONEY, TIME TO WRAP IT UP....
UH OH
LIZA DO YOU HEAR SOME-THING?
SNORE
MMM.. SOME KINDA INSECTILE BUZZING ..IS IT LOCUST SEASON AGAIN?

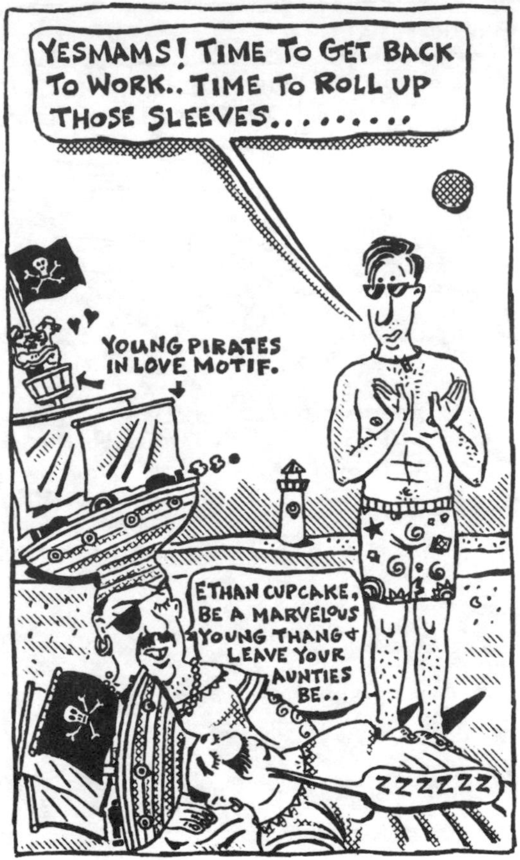
YESMAMS! TIME TO GET BACK TO WORK.. TIME TO ROLL UP THOSE SLEEVES........
YOUNG PIRATES IN LOVE MOTIF.
ETHAN CUPCAKE, BE A MARVELOUS YOUNG THANG & LEAVE YOUR AUNTIES BE..
ZZZZZZ

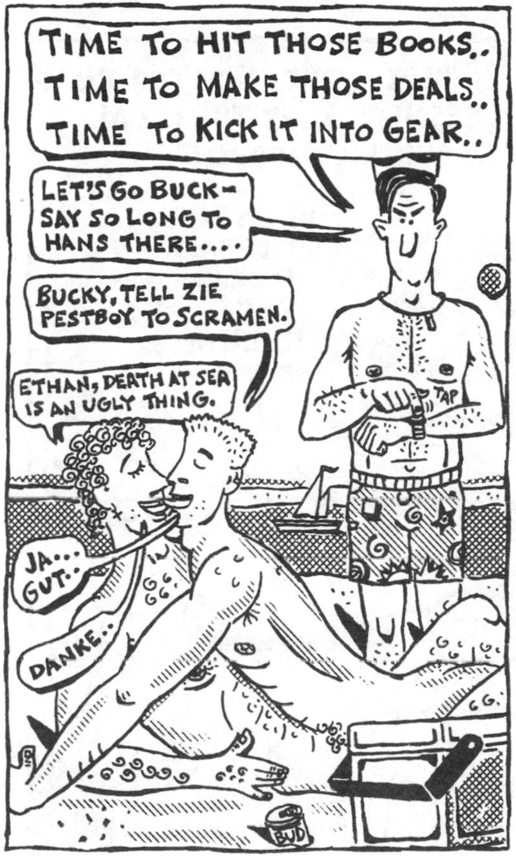
TIME TO HIT THOSE BOOKS..
TIME TO MAKE THOSE DEALS..
TIME TO KICK IT INTO GEAR..
LET'S GO BUCK- SAY SO LONG TO HANS THERE....
BUCKY, TELL ZIE PESTBOY TO SCRAMEN.
ETHAN, DEATH AT SEA IS AN UGLY THING.
TAP
JA... GUT..
DANKE..
BUD

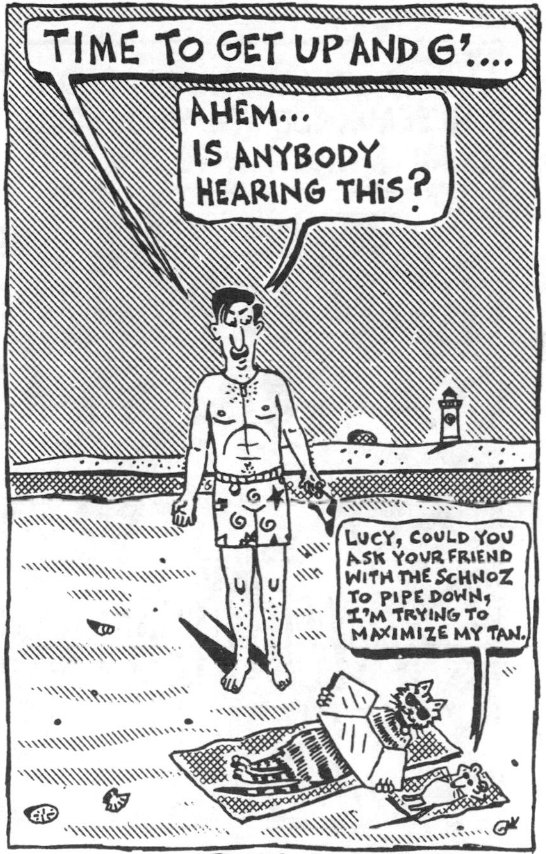
TIME TO GET UP AND G'....
AHEM... IS ANYBODY HEARING THIS?
LUCY, COULD YOU ASK YOUR FRIEND WITH THE SCHNOZ TO PIPE DOWN, I'M TRYING TO MAXIMIZE MY TAN.

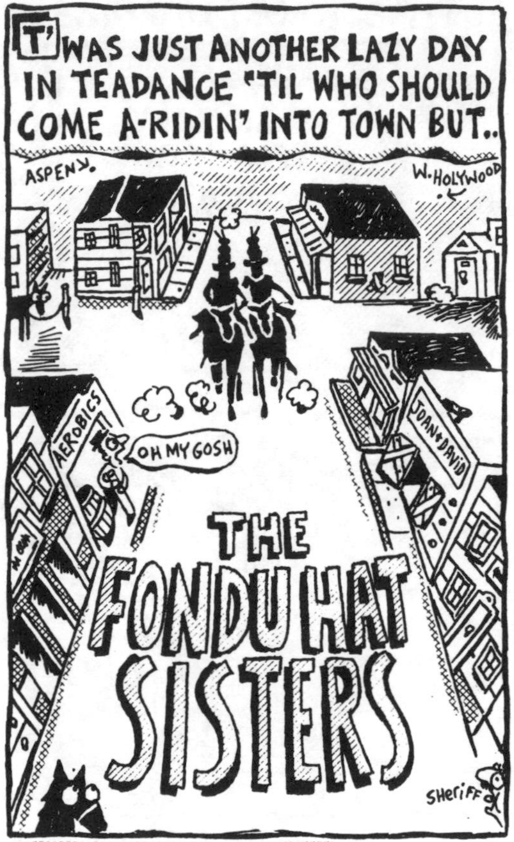
T'WAS JUST ANOTHER LAZY DAY IN TEADANCE 'TIL WHO SHOULD COME A-RIDIN' INTO TOWN BUT..
W. HOLYWOOD
AEROBICS
OH MY GOSH
JOAN+DAVID
THE FONDU HAT SISTERS
SHERIFF

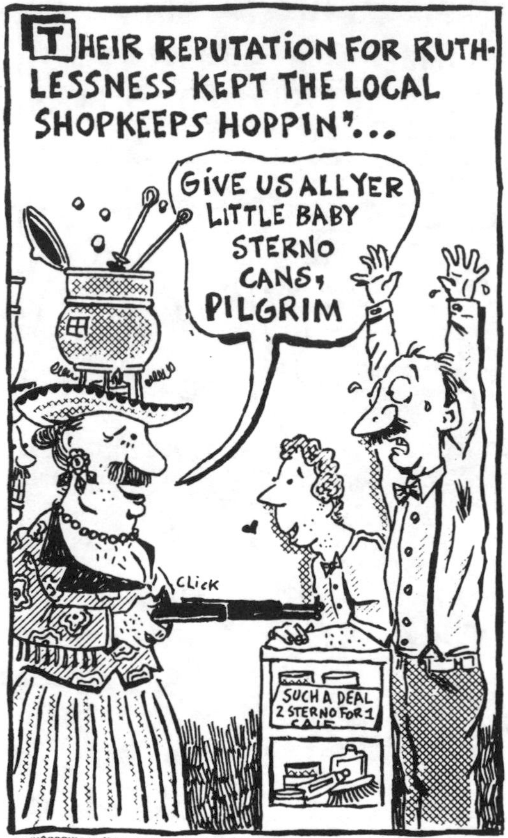
THEIR REPUTATION FOR RUTHLESSNESS KEPT THE LOCAL SHOPKEEPS HOPPIN'...
GIVE US ALL YER LITTLE BABY STERNO CANS, PILGRIM
CLICK
SUCH A DEAL 2 STERNO FOR 1

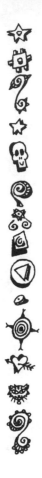

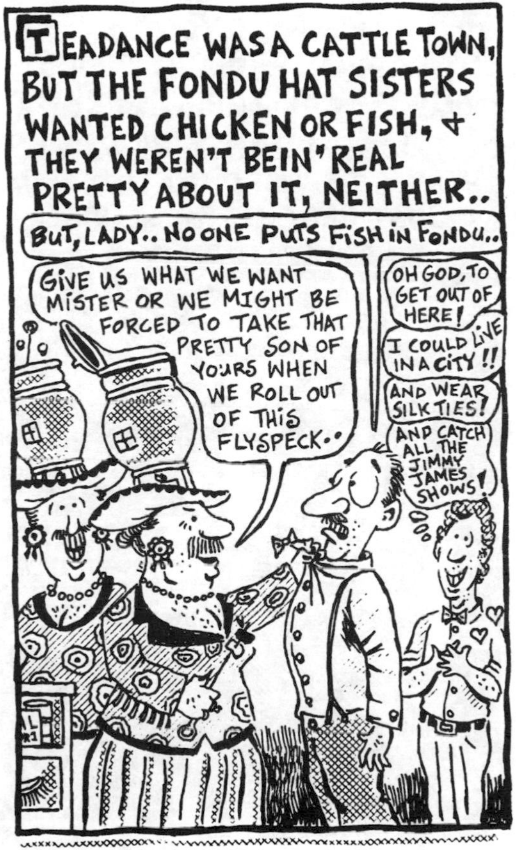
TEADANCE WAS A CATTLE TOWN, BUT THE FONDU HAT SISTERS WANTED CHICKEN OR FISH, + THEY WEREN'T BEIN' REAL PRETTY ABOUT IT, NEITHER..
BUT, LADY.. NO ONE PUTS FISH IN FONDU..
GIVE US WHAT WE WANT MISTER OR WE MIGHT BE FORCED TO TAKE THAT PRETTY SON OF YOURS WHEN WE ROLL OUT OF THIS FLYSPECK..
OH GOD, TO GET OUT OF HERE!
I COULD LIVE IN A CITY!!
AND WEAR SILK TIES!
AND CATCH ALL THE JIMMY JAMES SHOWS!

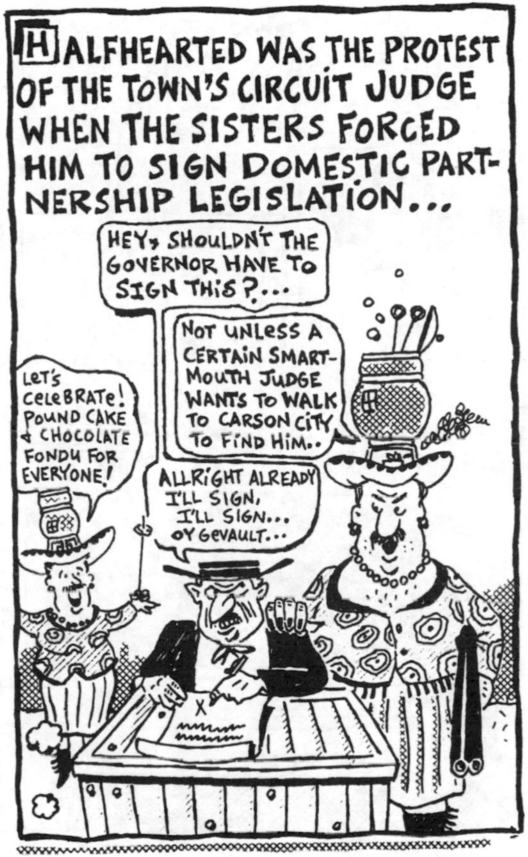
HALFHEARTED WAS THE PROTEST OF THE TOWN'S CIRCUIT JUDGE WHEN THE SISTERS FORCED HIM TO SIGN DOMESTIC PARTNERSHIP LEGISLATION...
HEY, SHOULDN'T THE GOVERNOR HAVE TO SIGN THIS?...
NOT UNLESS A CERTAIN SMART-MOUTH JUDGE WANTS TO WALK TO CARSON CITY TO FIND HIM..
LET'S CELEBRATE! POUND CAKE + CHOCOLATE FONDU FOR EVERYONE!
ALLRIGHT ALREADY I'LL SIGN, I'LL SIGN... OY GEVAULT...

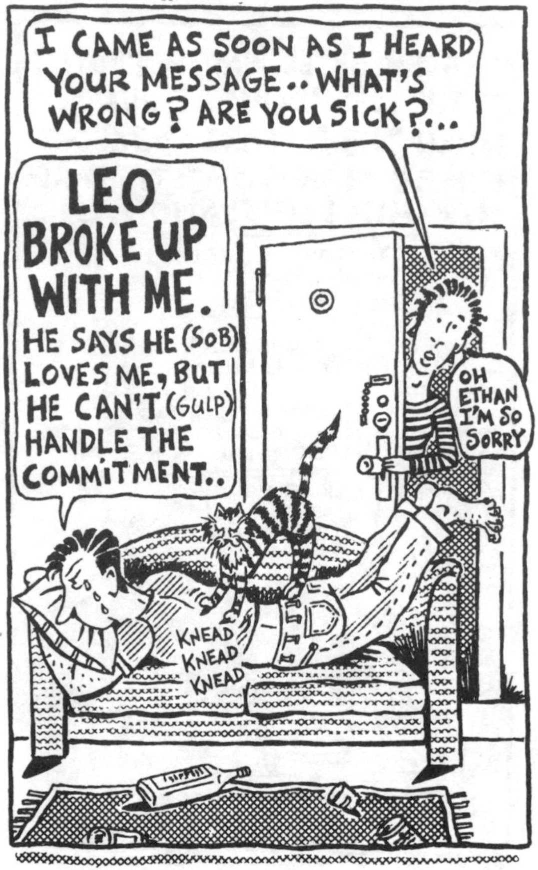
I CAME AS SOON AS I HEARD YOUR MESSAGE.. WHAT'S WRONG? ARE YOU SICK?...
LEO BROKE UP WITH ME. HE SAYS HE (SOB) LOVES ME, BUT HE CAN'T (GULP) HANDLE THE COMMITMENT..
OH ETHAN I'M SO SORRY
KNEAD KNEAD KNEAD

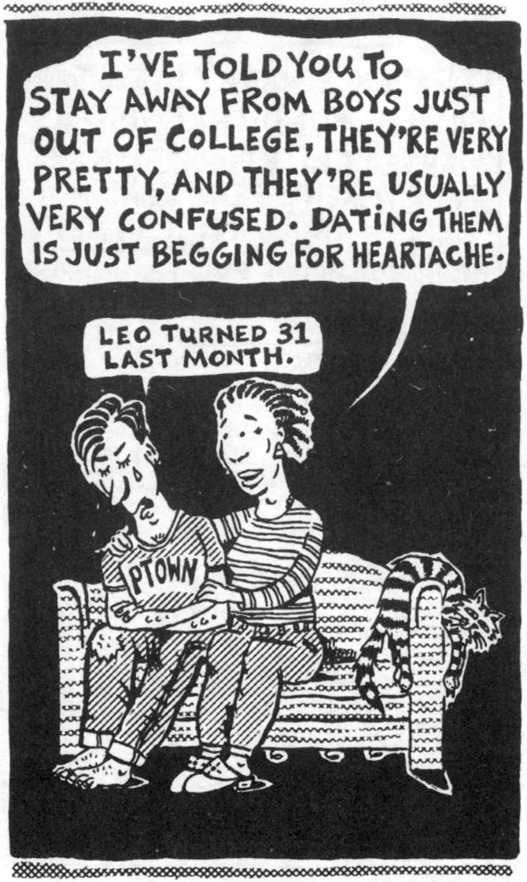
I'VE TOLD YOU TO STAY AWAY FROM BOYS JUST OUT OF COLLEGE, THEY'RE VERY PRETTY, AND THEY'RE USUALLY VERY CONFUSED. DATING THEM IS JUST BEGGING FOR HEARTACHE.
LEO TURNED 31 LAST MONTH.
PTOWN

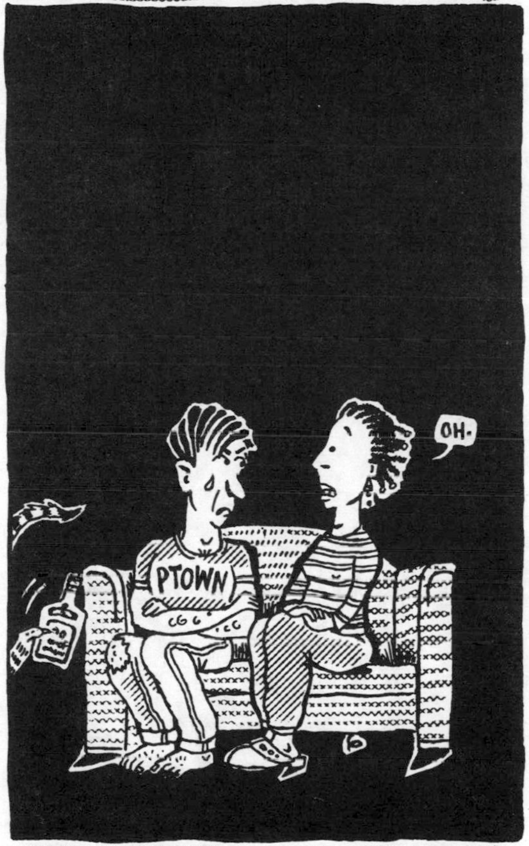
OH.
PTOWN

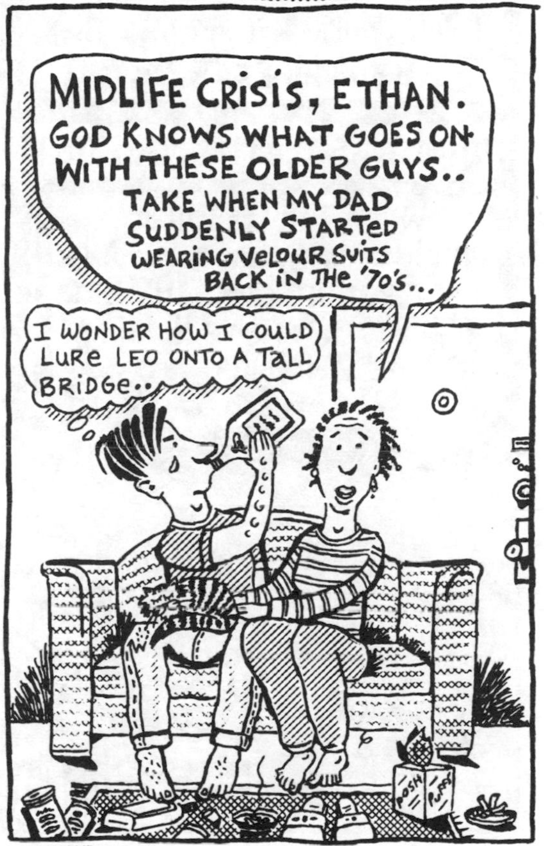
MIDLIFE CRISIS, ETHAN. GOD KNOWS WHAT GOES ON WITH THESE OLDER GUYS.. TAKE WHEN MY DAD SUDDENLY STARTED WEARING VELOUR SUITS BACK IN THE '70'S...
I WONDER HOW I COULD LURE LEO ONTO A TALL BRIDGE..

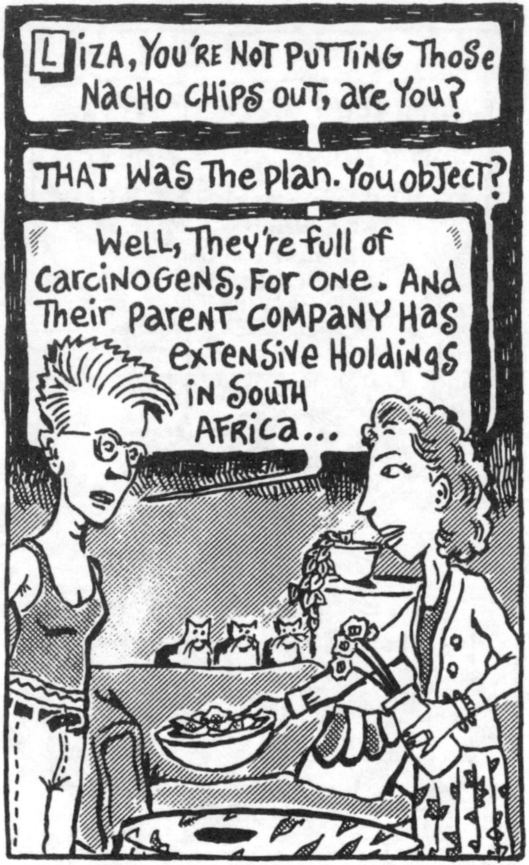
LIZA, YOU'RE NOT PUTTING THOSE NACHO CHIPS OUT, ARE YOU?
THAT WAS THE PLAN. YOU OBJECT?
WELL, THEY'RE FULL OF CARCINOGENS, FOR ONE. AND THEIR PARENT COMPANY HAS EXTENSIVE HOLDINGS IN SOUTH AFRICA...

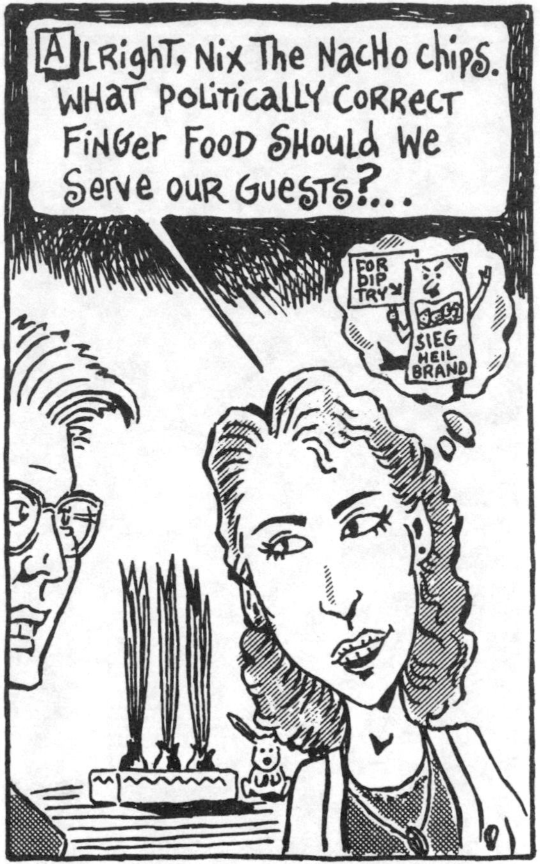
ALRIGHT, NIX THE NACHO CHIPS. WHAT POLITICALLY CORRECT FINGER FOOD SHOULD WE SERVE OUR GUESTS?...
FOR DIP TRY
SIEG HEIL BRAND

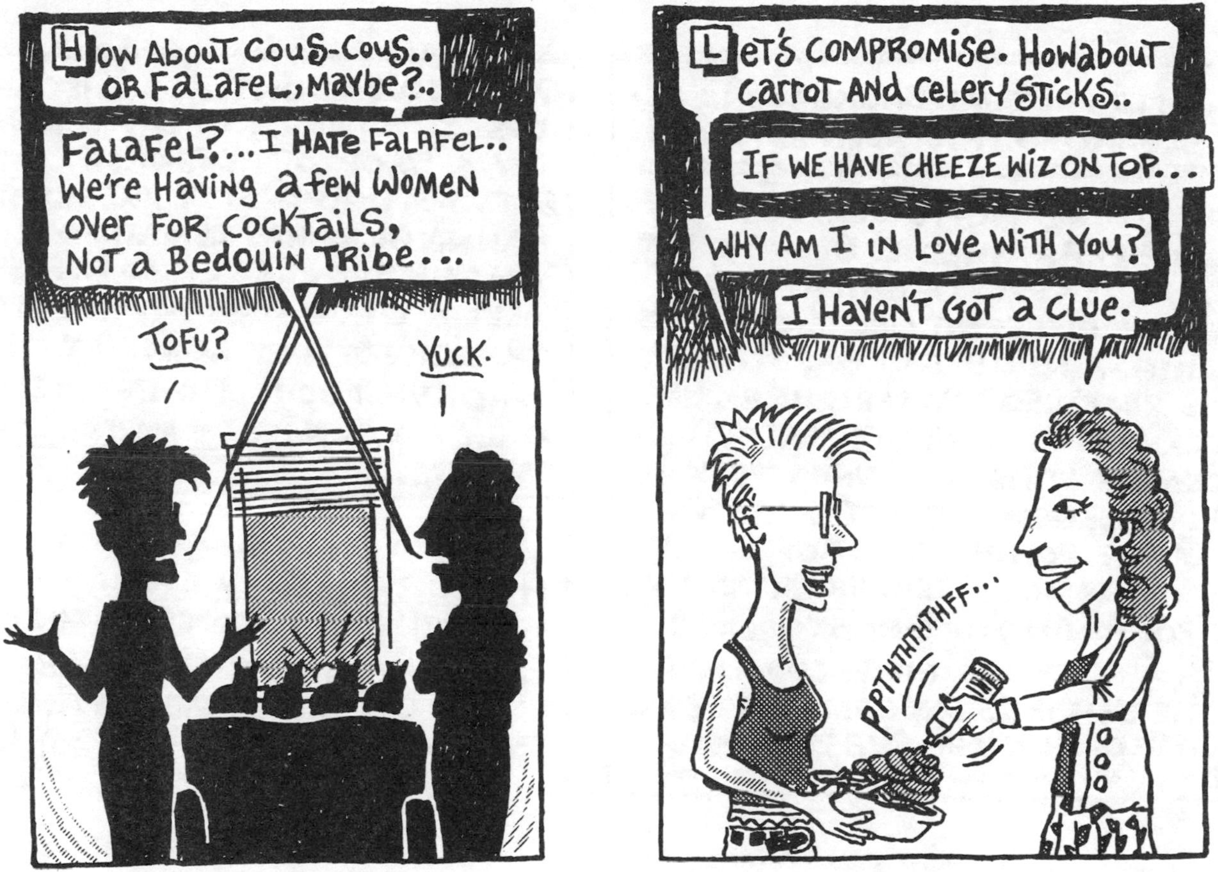
How about cous-cous.. or falafel, maybe?..
Falafel?... I hate falafel.. We're having a few women over for cocktails, not a Bedouin tribe...
Tofu?
Yuck.
Let's compromise. Howabout carrot and celery sticks..
If we have Cheeze Wiz on top...
Why am I in love with you?
I haven't got a clue.
PPTHTHTHTHTHFF...

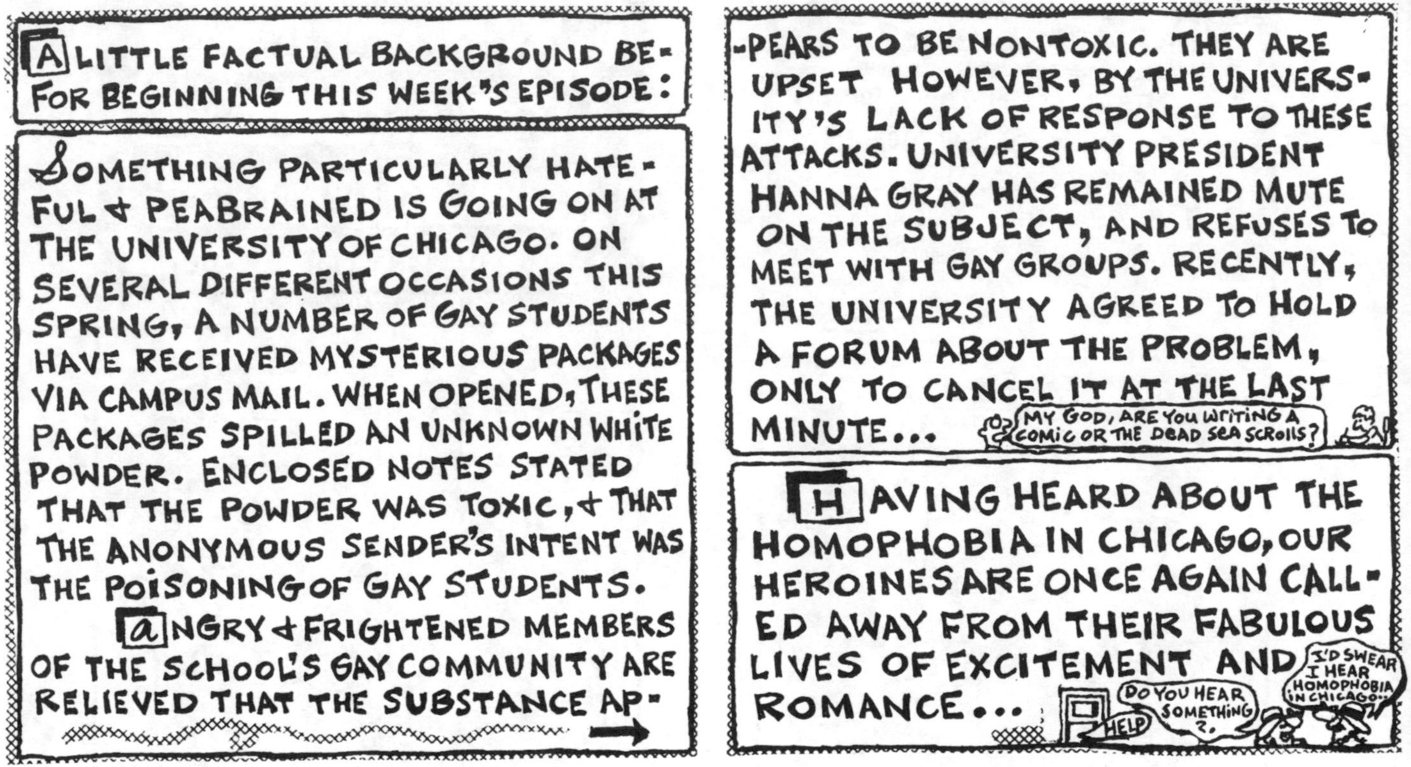
A LITTLE FACTUAL BACKGROUND BEFOR BEGINNING THIS WEEK'S EPISODE:
SOMETHING PARTICULARLY HATEFUL & PEABRAINED IS GOING ON AT THE UNIVERSITY OF CHICAGO. ON SEVERAL DIFFERENT OCCASIONS THIS SPRING, A NUMBER OF GAY STUDENTS HAVE RECEIVED MYSTERIOUS PACKAGES VIA CAMPUS MAIL. WHEN OPENED, THESE PACKAGES SPILLED AN UNKNOWN WHITE POWDER. ENCLOSED NOTES STATED THAT THE POWDER WAS TOXIC, & THAT THE ANONYMOUS SENDER'S INTENT WAS THE POISONING OF GAY STUDENTS.
ANGRY & FRIGHTENED MEMBERS OF THE SCHOOL'S GAY COMMUNITY ARE RELIEVED THAT THE SUBSTANCE APPEARS TO BE NONTOXIC. THEY ARE UPSET HOWEVER, BY THE UNIVERSITY'S LACK OF RESPONSE TO THESE ATTACKS. UNIVERSITY PRESIDENT HANNA GRAY HAS REMAINED MUTE ON THE SUBJECT, AND REFUSES TO MEET WITH GAY GROUPS. RECENTLY, THE UNIVERSITY AGREED TO HOLD A FORUM ABOUT THE PROBLEM, ONLY TO CANCEL IT AT THE LAST MINUTE...
MY GOD, ARE YOU WRITING A COMIC OR THE DEAD SEA SCROLLS?
HAVING HEARD ABOUT THE HOMOPHOBIA IN CHICAGO, OUR HEROINES ARE ONCE AGAIN CALLED AWAY FROM THEIR FABULOUS LIVES OF EXCITEMENT AND ROMANCE...
HELP
DO YOU HEAR SOMETHING?
I'D SWEAR I HEAR HOMOPHOBIA IN CHICAGO...

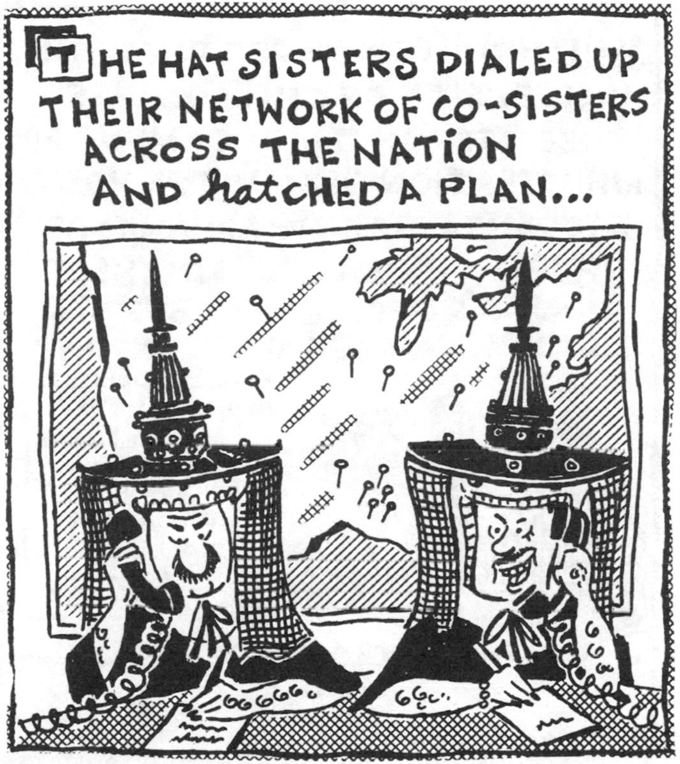
THE HAT SISTERS DIALED UP THEIR NETWORK OF CO-SISTERS ACROSS THE NATION AND hatCHED A PLAN...

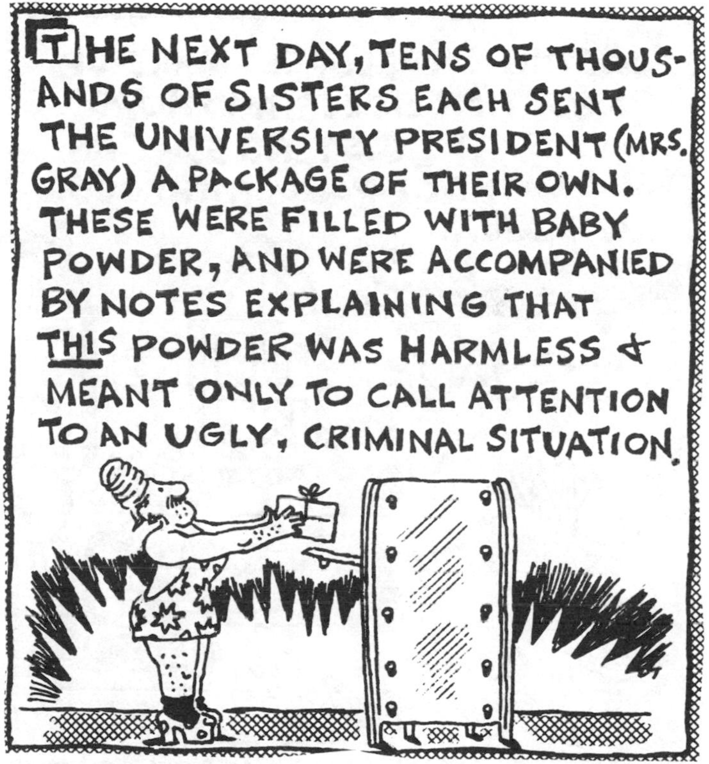
THE NEXT DAY, TENS OF THOUSANDS OF SISTERS EACH SENT THE UNIVERSITY PRESIDENT (MRS. GRAY) A PACKAGE OF THEIR OWN. THESE WERE FILLED WITH BABY POWDER, AND WERE ACCOMPANIED BY NOTES EXPLAINING THAT THIS POWDER WAS HARMLESS & MEANT ONLY TO CALL ATTENTION TO AN UGLY, CRIMINAL SITUATION.

Continued →

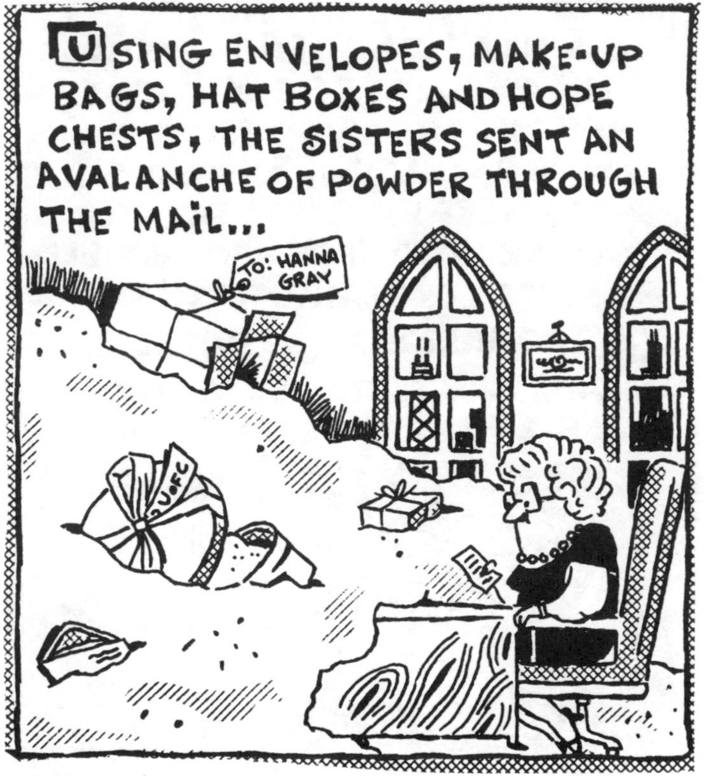
USING ENVELOPES, MAKE-UP BAGS, HAT BOXES AND HOPE CHESTS, THE SISTERS SENT AN AVALANCHE OF POWDER THROUGH THE MAIL...
TO: HANNA GRAY

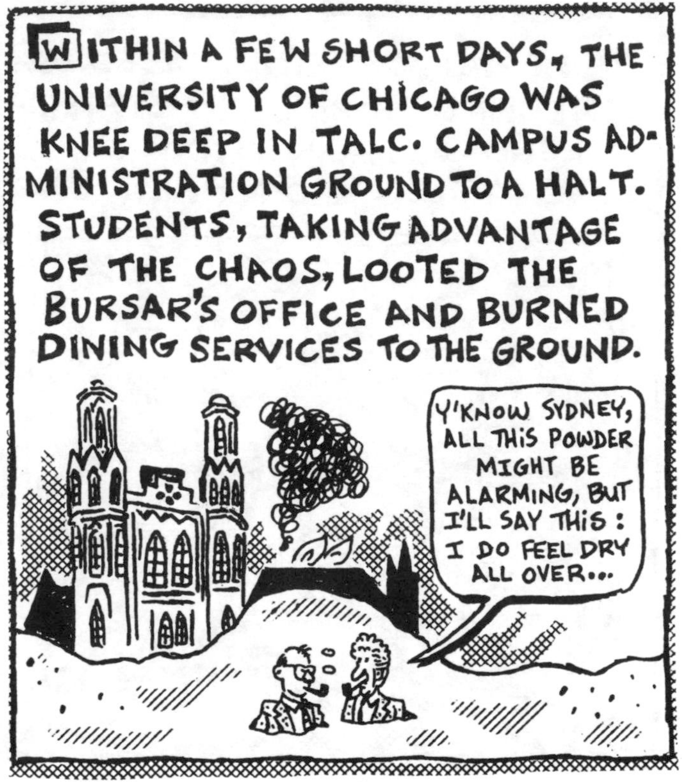
WITHIN A FEW SHORT DAYS, THE UNIVERSITY OF CHICAGO WAS KNEE DEEP IN TALC. CAMPUS ADMINISTRATION GROUND TO A HALT. STUDENTS, TAKING ADVANTAGE OF THE CHAOS, LOOTED THE BURSAR'S OFFICE AND BURNED DINING SERVICES TO THE GROUND.
Y'KNOW SYDNEY, ALL THIS POWDER MIGHT BE ALARMING, BUT I'LL SAY THIS: I DO FEEL DRY ALL OVER...

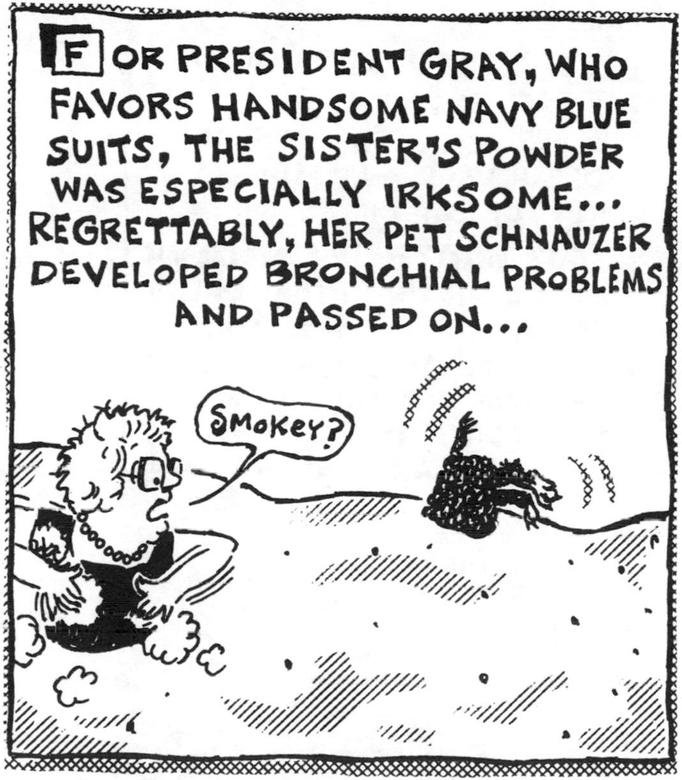
FOR PRESIDENT GRAY, WHO FAVORS HANDSOME NAVY BLUE SUITS, THE SISTER'S POWDER WAS ESPECIALLY IRKSOME... REGRETTABLY, HER PET SCHNAUZER DEVELOPED BRONCHIAL PROBLEMS AND PASSED ON...
SMOKEY?

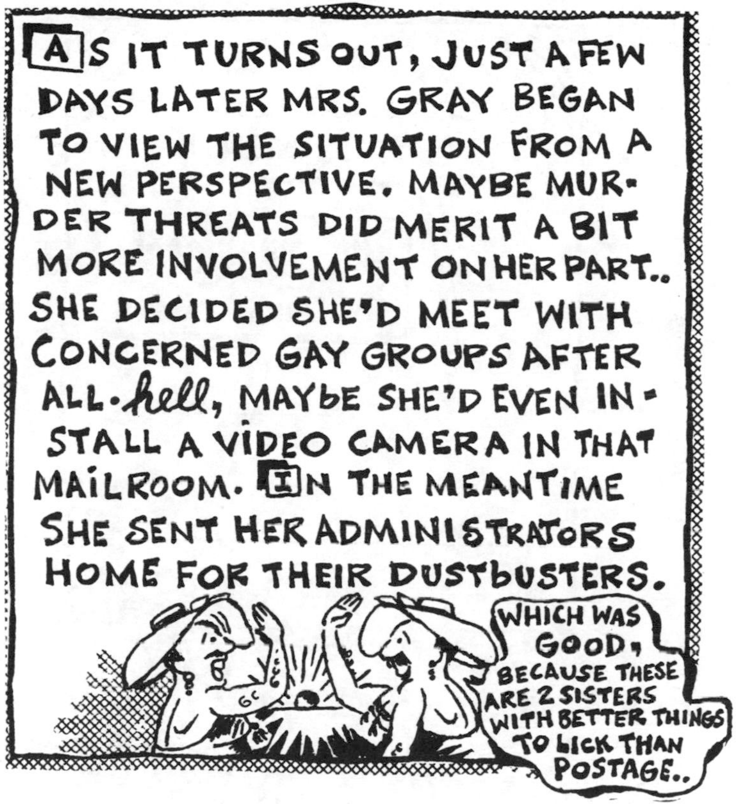
AS IT TURNS OUT, JUST A FEW DAYS LATER MRS. GRAY BEGAN TO VIEW THE SITUATION FROM A NEW PERSPECTIVE. MAYBE MUR-DER THREATS DID MERIT A BIT MORE INVOLVEMENT ON HER PART.. SHE DECIDED SHE'D MEET WITH CONCERNED GAY GROUPS AFTER ALL. hell, MAYBE SHE'D EVEN IN-STALL A VIDEO CAMERA IN THAT MAILROOM. IN THE MEANTIME SHE SENT HER ADMINISTRATORS HOME FOR THEIR DUSTBUSTERS.
GC
WHICH WAS GOOD, BECAUSE THESE ARE 2 SISTERS WITH BETTER THINGS TO LICK THAN POSTAGE..

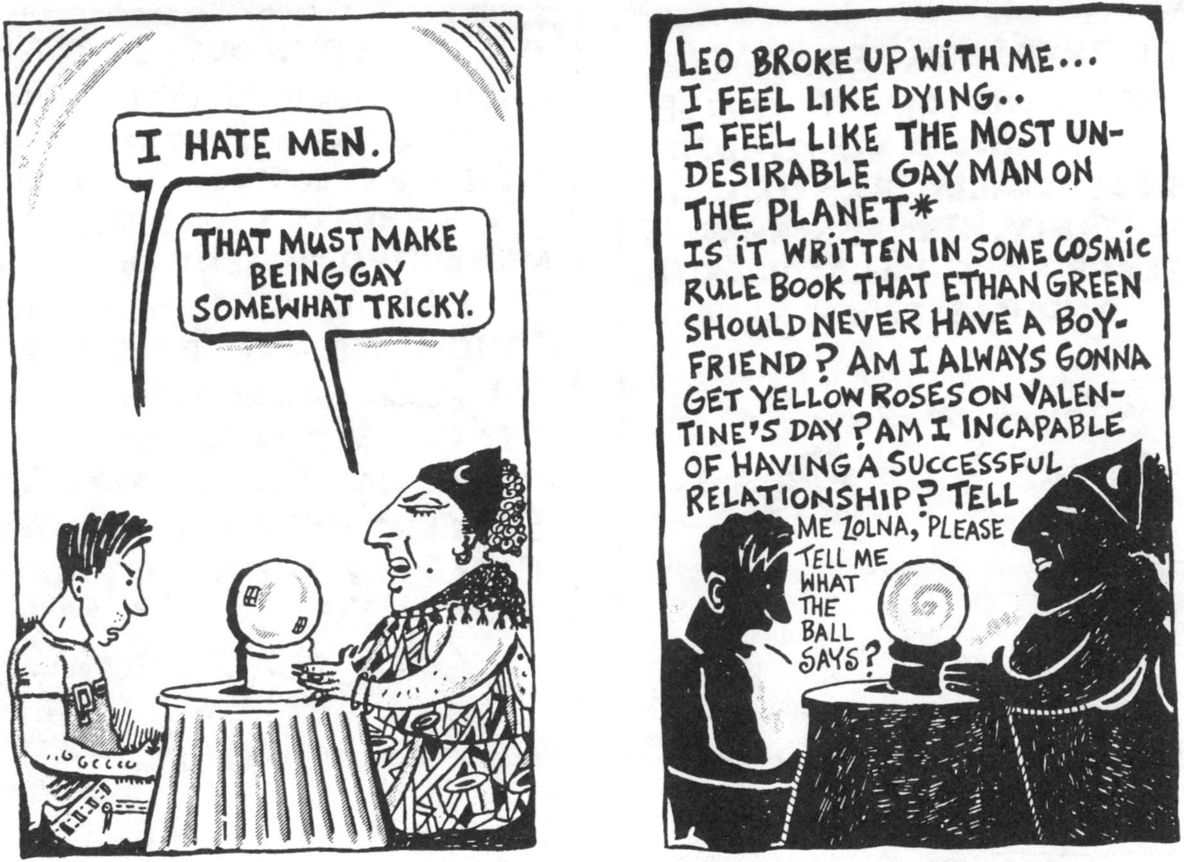
I HATE MEN.
THAT MUST MAKE BEING GAY SOMEWHAT TRICKY.
LEO BROKE UP WITH ME... I FEEL LIKE DYING.. I FEEL LIKE THE MOST UN-DESIRABLE GAY MAN ON THE PLANET* IS IT WRITTEN IN SOME COSMIC RULE BOOK THAT ETHAN GREEN SHOULD NEVER HAVE A BOY-FRIEND? AM I ALWAYS GONNA GET YELLOW ROSES ON VALEN-TINE'S DAY? AM I INCAPABLE OF HAVING A SUCCESSFUL RELATIONSHIP? TELL ME ZOLNA, PLEASE TELL ME WHAT THE BALL SAYS?

* WITH THE POSSIBLE EXCEPTION OF GEORGE MICHAEL...

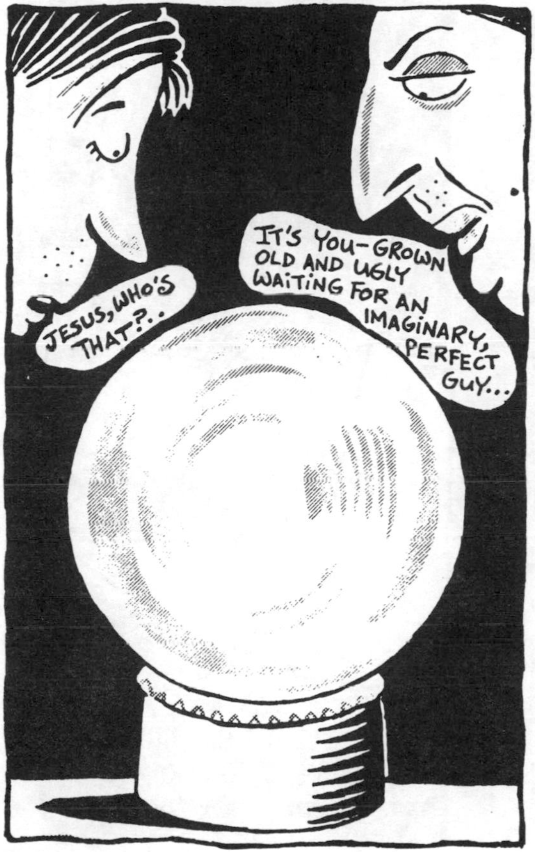
JESUS, WHO'S THAT?..
IT'S YOU-GROWN OLD AND UGLY WAITING FOR AN IMAGINARY, PERFECT GUY...

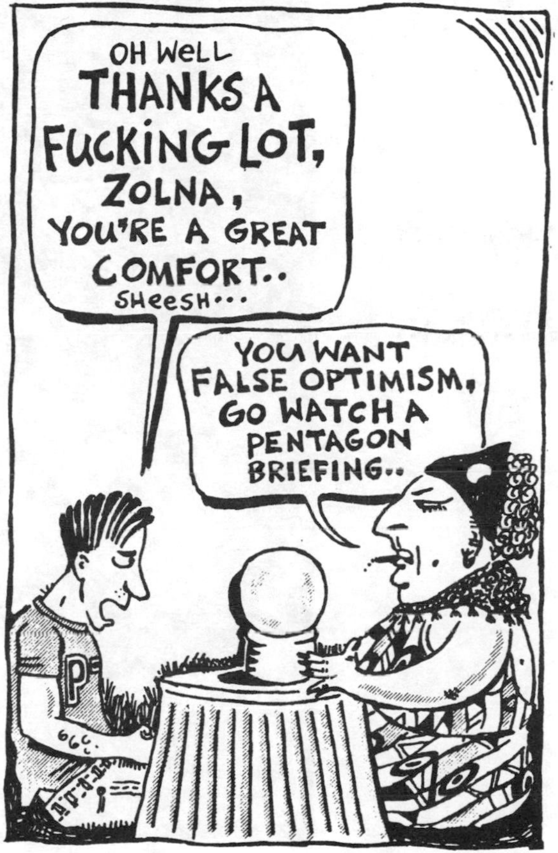
OH WELL THANKS A FUCKING LOT, ZOLNA, YOU'RE A GREAT COMFORT.. SHEESH...
YOU WANT FALSE OPTIMISM, GO WATCH A PENTAGON BRIEFING..
P

ASTRONAUT

MISSION

OF

LOVE..

♡

TEADANCE
COPA NEPTUNE NEXT LEFT
TETHERED TO THE CAPSULE BY A THIN FIBERGLASS CABLE, ASTRONAUT PHIL EMBARKS UPON HIS DARING MISSION.

THIS OLD SPACE CAPSULE
THE "TEADANCE" MUST RECEIVE A FAINT BUT VITAL TRANSMISSION FROM EARTH.

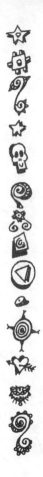

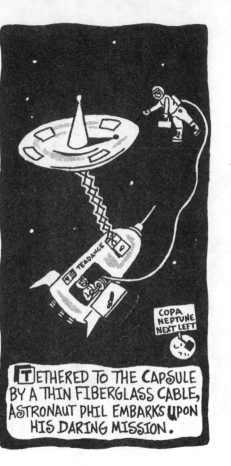

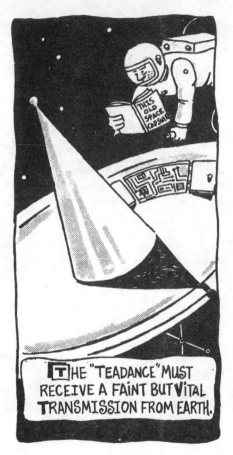

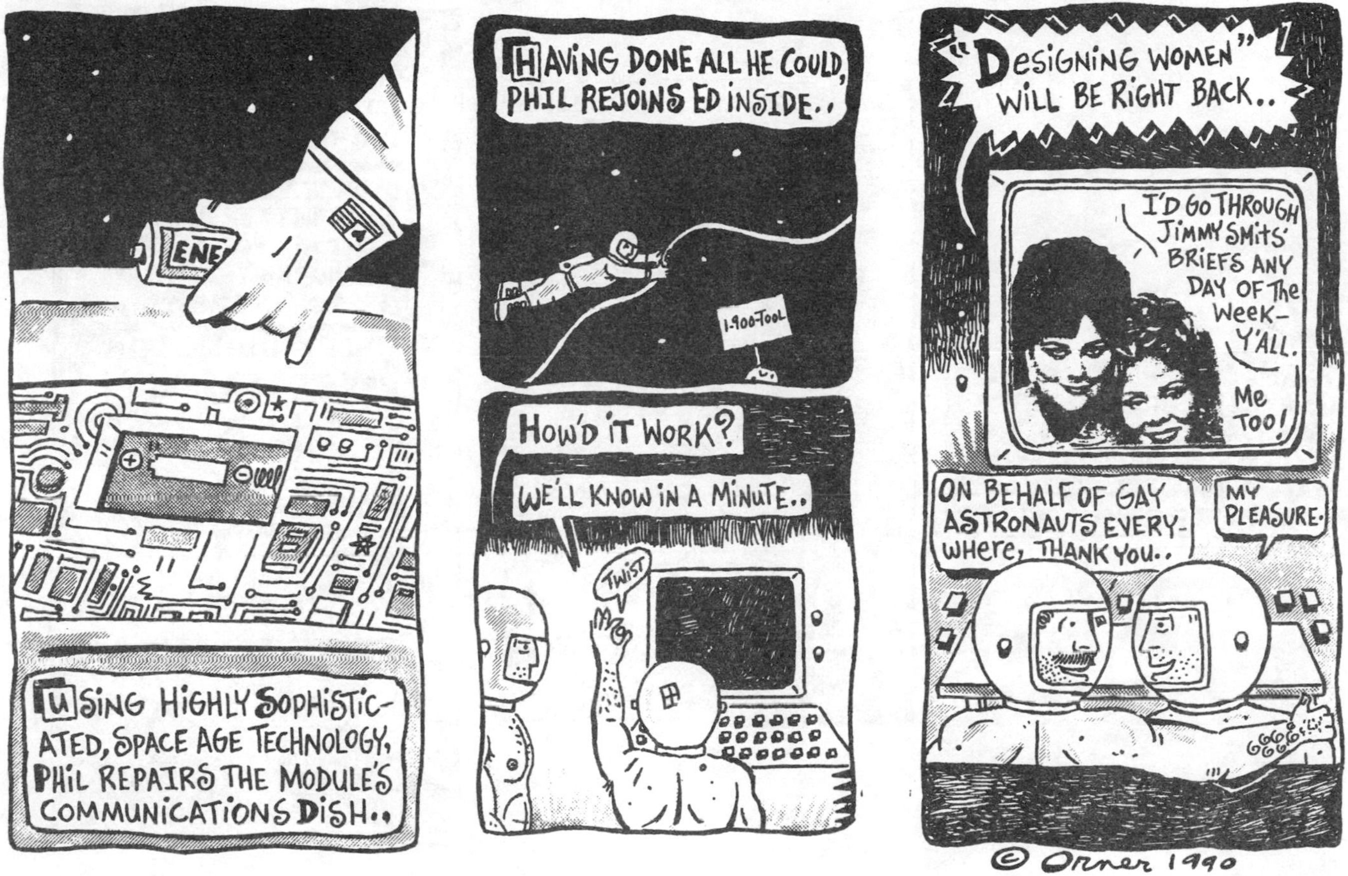
ENE
USING HIGHLY SOPHISTIC-
ATED, SPACE AGE TECHNOLOGY,
PHIL REPAIRS THE MODULE'S
COMMUNICATIONS DISH..
HAVING DONE ALL HE COULD,
PHIL REJOINS ED INSIDE..
1-900-TOOL
HOW'D IT WORK?
WE'LL KNOW IN A MINUTE..
TWIST
"DESIGNING WOMEN"
WILL BE RIGHT BACK..
I'D GO THROUGH
JIMMY SMITS'
BRIEFS ANY
DAY OF THE
WEEK—
Y'ALL.
Me
TOO!
ON BEHALF OF GAY
ASTRONAUTS EVERY-
WHERE, THANK YOU..
MY
PLEASURE.
© Orner 1990

ETHAN, STILL DEPRESSED BY HIS RECENT BREAK UP WITH LEO, TAKES UP A LONGSTANDING OFFER TO VISIT TERRY, AN OLD COLLEGE PAL. HE ARRIVES FRIDAY NIGHT FOR A WEEKEND STAY.

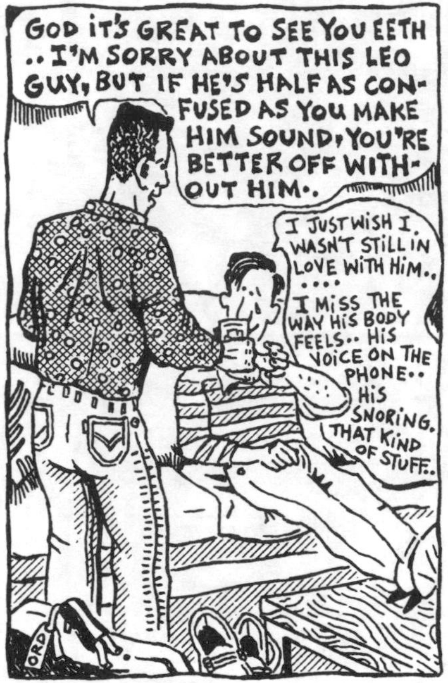

GOD IT'S GREAT TO SEE YOU EETH .. I'M SORRY ABOUT THIS LEO GUY, BUT IF HE'S HALF AS CONFUSED AS YOU MAKE HIM SOUND, YOU'RE BETTER OFF WITHOUT HIM..
I JUST WISH I WASN'T STILL IN LOVE WITH HIM.. .... I MISS THE WAY HIS BODY FEELS.. HIS VOICE ON THE PHONE.. HIS SNORING. THAT KIND OF STUFF..

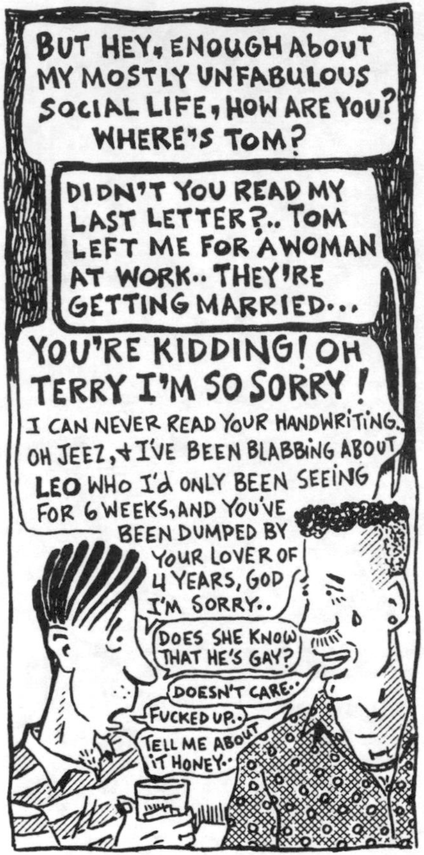

BUT HEY, ENOUGH ABOUT MY MOSTLY UNFABULOUS SOCIAL LIFE, HOW ARE YOU? WHERE'S TOM?
DIDN'T YOU READ MY LAST LETTER?.. TOM LEFT ME FOR A WOMAN AT WORK.. THEY'RE GETTING MARRIED...
YOU'RE KIDDING! OH TERRY I'M SO SORRY! I CAN NEVER READ YOUR HANDWRITING. OH JEEZ, & I'VE BEEN BLABBING ABOUT LEO WHO I'd ONLY BEEN SEEING FOR 6 WEEKS, AND YOU'VE BEEN DUMPED BY YOUR LOVER OF 4 YEARS, GOD I'M SORRY..
DOES SHE KNOW THAT HE'S GAY?
DOESN'T CARE..
FUCKED UP..
TELL ME ABOUT IT HONEY..

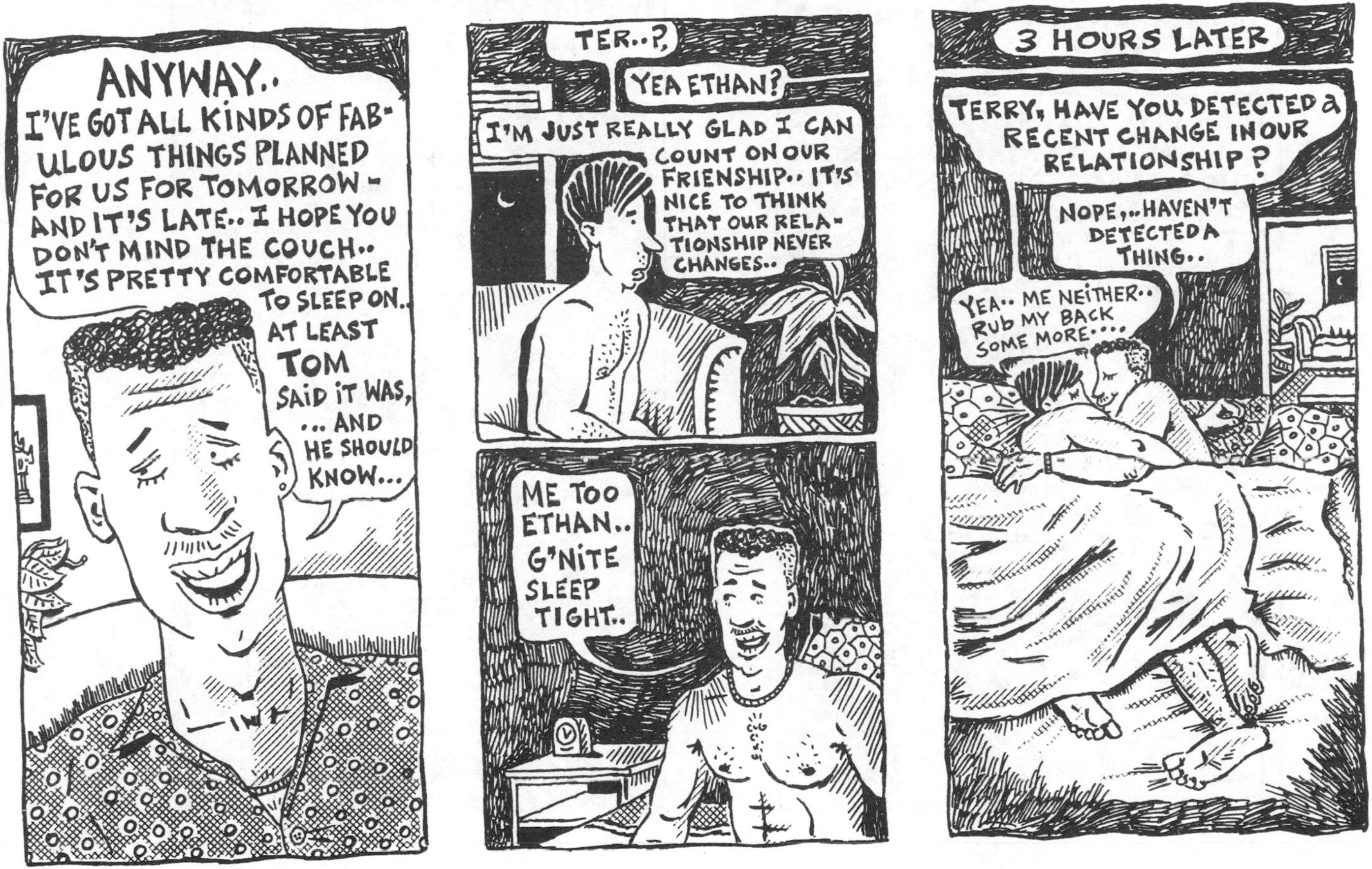
ANYWAY.. I'VE GOT ALL KINDS OF FABULOUS THINGS PLANNED FOR US FOR TOMORROW – AND IT'S LATE.. I HOPE YOU DON'T MIND THE COUCH.. IT'S PRETTY COMFORTABLE TO SLEEP ON.. AT LEAST TOM SAID IT WAS, ... AND HE SHOULD KNOW...
TER..?,
YEA ETHAN?
I'M JUST REALLY GLAD I CAN COUNT ON OUR FRIENSHIP.. IT'S NICE TO THINK THAT OUR RELATIONSHIP NEVER CHANGES..
ME TOO ETHAN.. G'NITE SLEEP TIGHT..
3 HOURS LATER
TERRY, HAVE YOU DETECTED a RECENT CHANGE IN OUR RELATIONSHIP?
NOPE,...HAVEN'T DETECTED A THING..
YEA.. ME NEITHER.. Rub MY BACK SOME MORE....

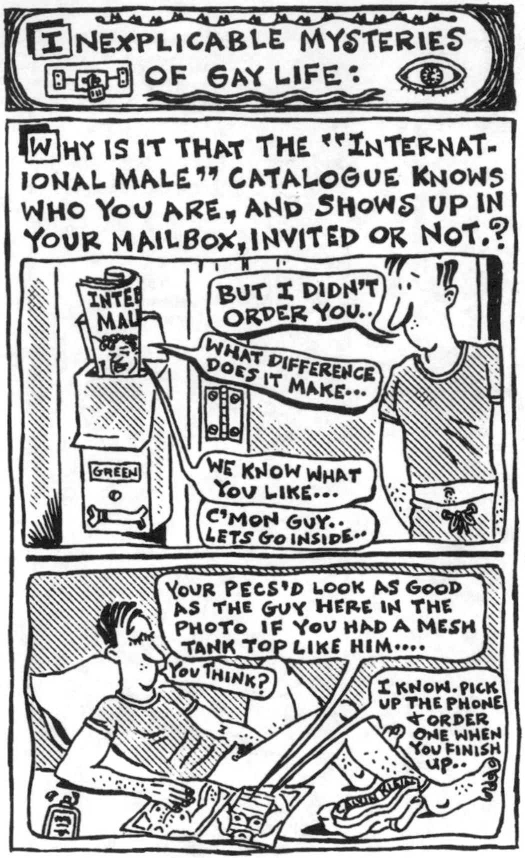
INEXPLICABLE MYSTERIES OF GAY LIFE:
WHY IS IT THAT THE "INTERNATIONAL MALE" CATALOGUE KNOWS WHO YOU ARE, AND SHOWS UP IN YOUR MAILBOX, INVITED OR NOT.?
BUT I DIDN'T ORDER YOU..
WHAT DIFFERENCE DOES IT MAKE...
WE KNOW WHAT YOU LIKE...
C'MON GUY.. LETS GO INSIDE..
GREEN
YOUR PECS'D LOOK AS GOOD AS THE GUY HERE IN THE PHOTO IF YOU HAD A MESH TANK TOP LIKE HIM....
YOU THINK?
I KNOW. PICK UP THE PHONE & ORDER ONE WHEN YOU FINISH UP..

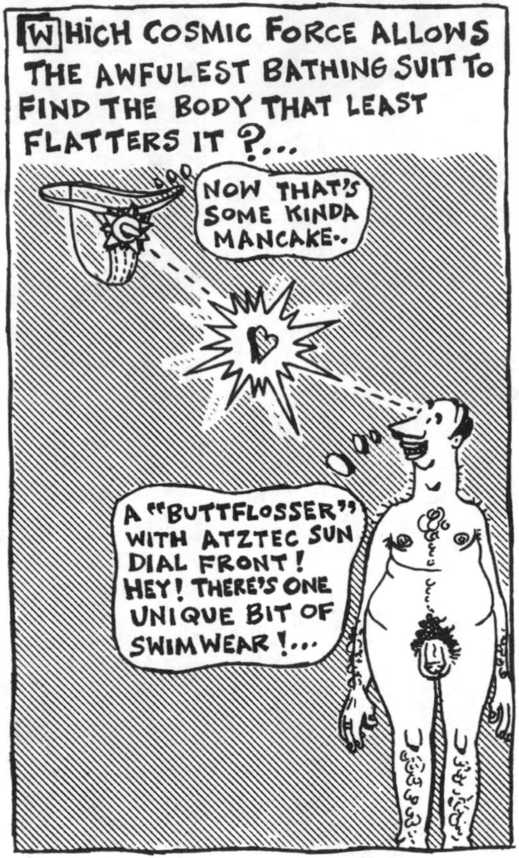
WHICH COSMIC FORCE ALLOWS THE AWFULEST BATHING SUIT TO FIND THE BODY THAT LEAST FLATTERS IT ?...
NOW THAT'S SOME KINDA MANCAKE..
A "BUTTFLOSSER" WITH ATZTEC SUN DIAL FRONT! HEY! THERE'S ONE UNIQUE BIT OF SWIMWEAR!...

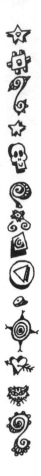

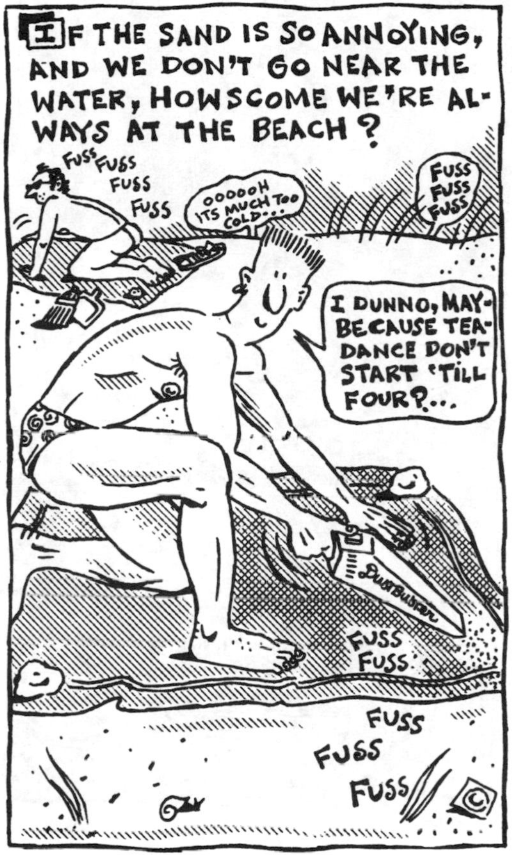
IF THE SAND IS SO ANNOYING, AND WE DON'T GO NEAR THE WATER, HOWSCOME WE'RE ALWAYS AT THE BEACH?
FUSS FUSS FUSS FUSS
OOOOOOH ITS MUCH TOO COLD...
FUSS FUSS FUSS
I DUNNO, MAYBE BECAUSE TEA-DANCE DON'T START 'TILL FOUR?...
DUSTBUSTER
FUSS FUSS
FUSS FUSS FUSS

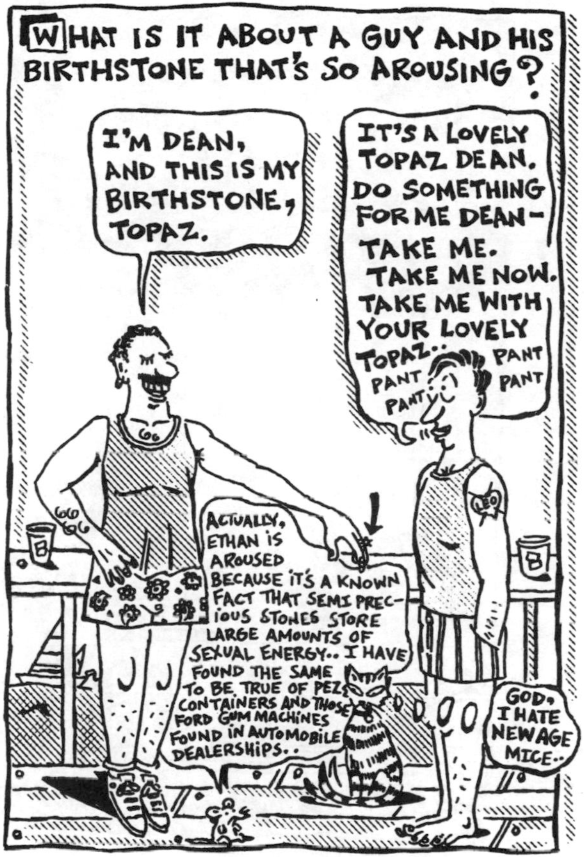
WHAT IS IT ABOUT A GUY AND HIS BIRTHSTONE THAT'S SO AROUSING?
I'M DEAN, AND THIS IS MY BIRTHSTONE, TOPAZ.
IT'S A LOVELY TOPAZ DEAN. DO SOMETHING FOR ME DEAN- TAKE ME. TAKE ME NOW. TAKE ME WITH YOUR LOVELY TOPAZ..
PANT PANT PANT PANT PANT
ACTUALLY, ETHAN IS AROUSED BECAUSE IT'S A KNOWN FACT THAT SEMI PRECIOUS STONES STORE LARGE AMOUNTS OF SEXUAL ENERGY.. I HAVE FOUND THE SAME TO BE TRUE OF PEZ CONTAINERS AND THOSE FORD GUM MACHINES FOUND IN AUTOMOBILE DEALERSHIPS..
GOD, I HATE NEWAGE MICE..

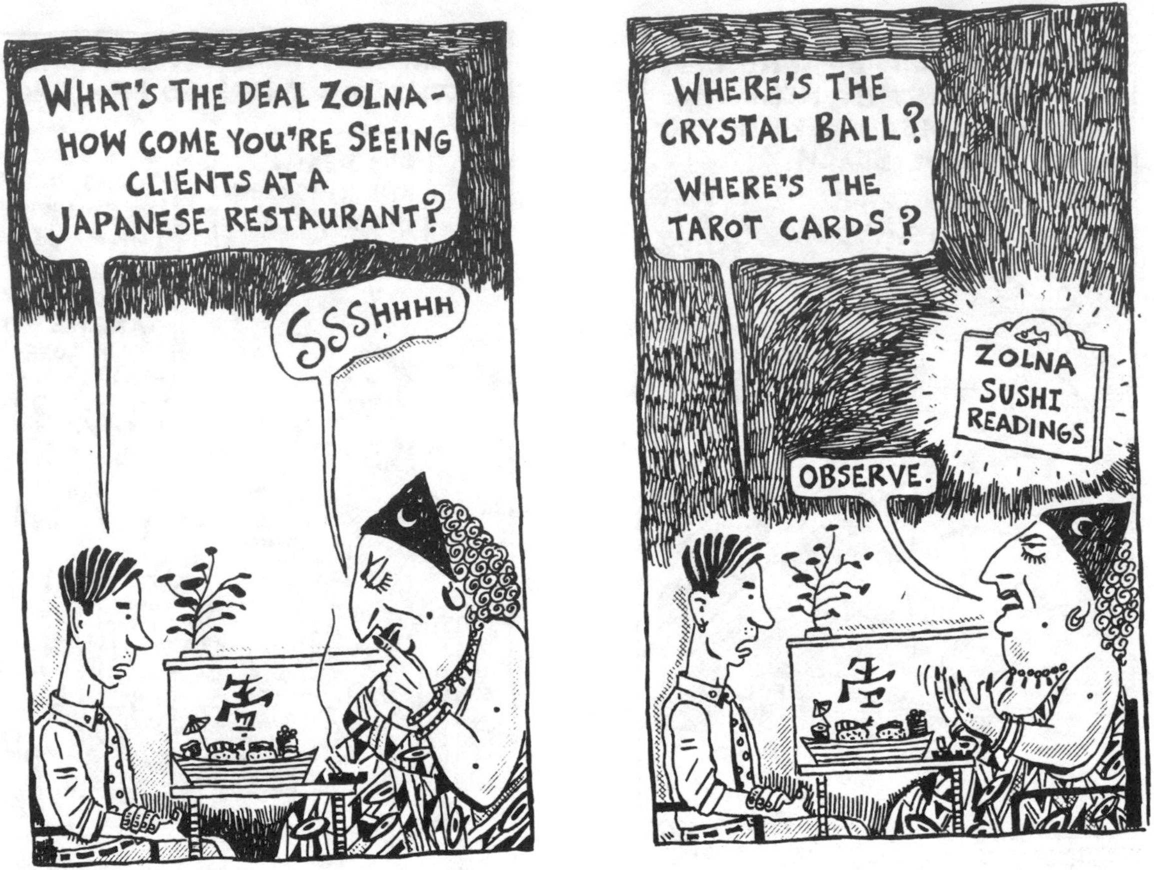
WHAT'S THE DEAL ZOLNA- HOW COME YOU'RE SEEING CLIENTS AT A JAPANESE RESTAURANT?
SSSHHHH
WHERE'S THE CRYSTAL BALL? WHERE'S THE TAROT CARDS?
ZOLNA SUSHI READINGS
OBSERVE.

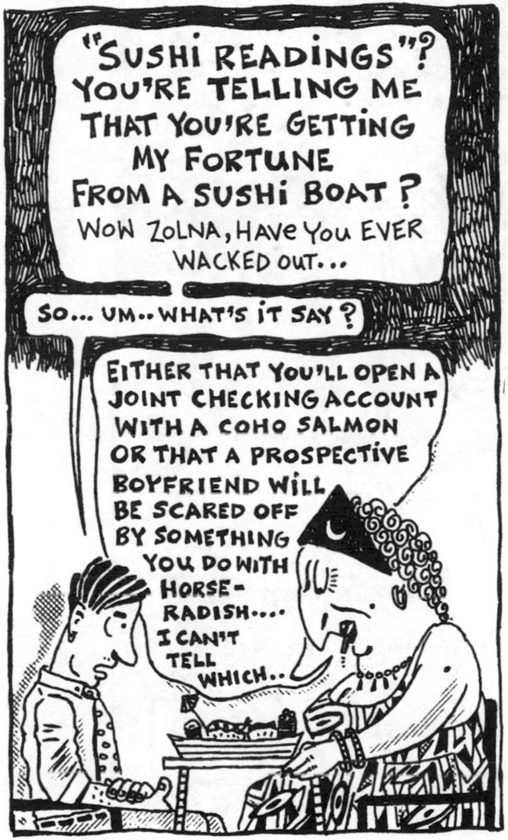
"SUSHI READINGS"? YOU'RE TELLING ME THAT YOU'RE GETTING MY FORTUNE FROM A SUSHI BOAT? WOW ZOLNA, HAVE YOU EVER WACKED OUT...
SO... UM.. WHAT'S IT SAY?
EITHER THAT YOU'LL OPEN A JOINT CHECKING ACCOUNT WITH A COHO SALMON OR THAT A PROSPECTIVE BOYFRIEND WILL BE SCARED OFF BY SOMETHING YOU DO WITH HORSE-RADISH.... I CAN'T TELL WHICH..

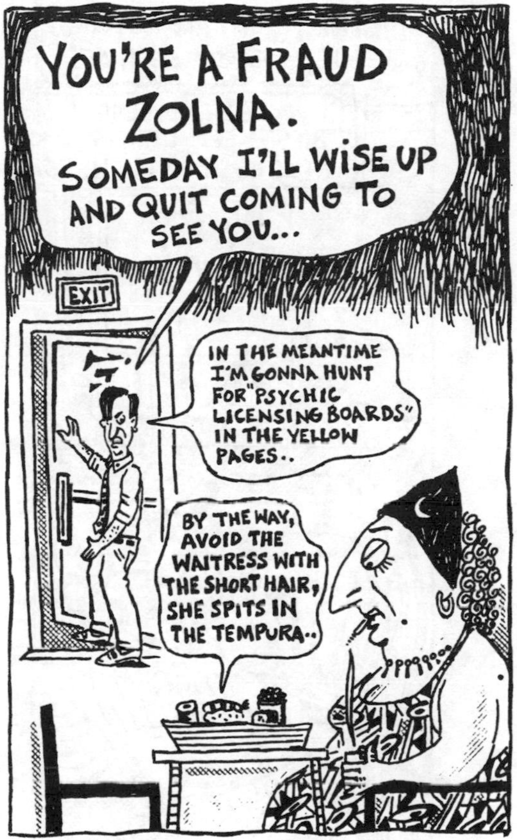
YOU'RE A FRAUD ZOLNA. SOMEDAY I'LL WISE UP AND QUIT COMING TO SEE YOU...
EXIT
IN THE MEANTIME I'M GONNA HUNT FOR "PSYCHIC LICENSING BOARDS" IN THE YELLOW PAGES..
BY THE WAY, AVOID THE WAITRESS WITH THE SHORT HAIR, SHE SPITS IN THE TEMPURA..

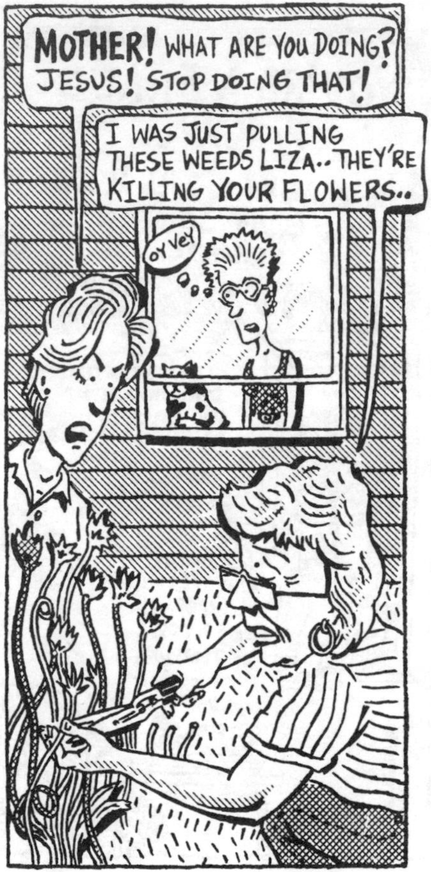
MOTHER! WHAT ARE YOU DOING? JESUS! STOP DOING THAT!
I WAS JUST PULLING THESE WEEDS LIZA.. THEY'RE KILLING YOUR FLOWERS..
OY VEY

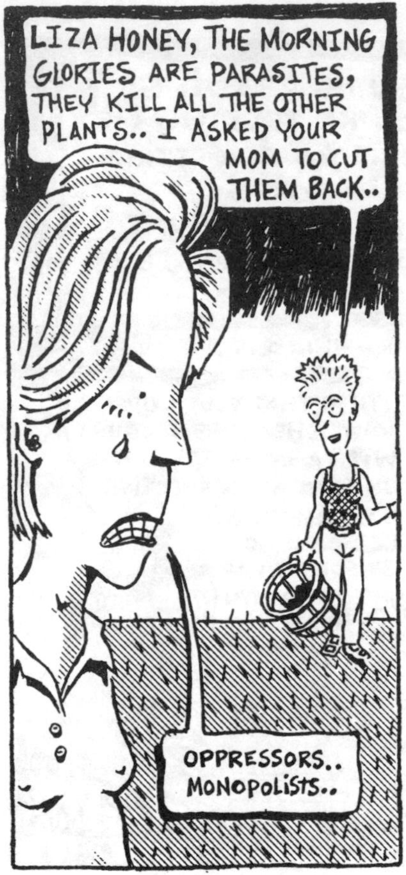
LIZA HONEY, THE MORNING GLORIES ARE PARASITES, THEY KILL ALL THE OTHER PLANTS.. I ASKED YOUR MOM TO CUT THEM BACK..
OPPRESSORS.. MONOPOLISTS..

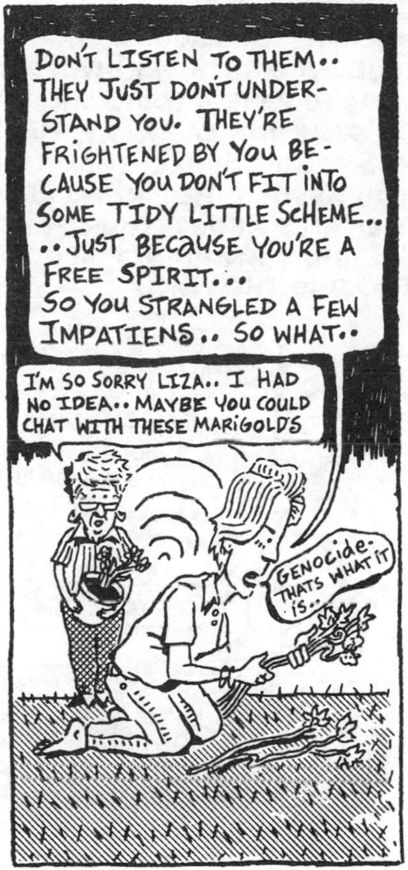
DON'T LISTEN TO THEM.. THEY JUST DON'T UNDER-STAND YOU. THEY'RE FRIGHTENED BY YOU BE-CAUSE YOU DON'T FIT INTO SOME TIDY LITTLE SCHEME.. ..JUST BECAUSE YOU'RE A FREE SPIRIT... SO YOU STRANGLED A FEW IMPATIENS.. SO WHAT..
I'M SO SORRY LIZA.. I HAD NO IDEA.. MAYBE YOU COULD CHAT WITH THESE MARIGOLD'S
GENOCIDE. THATS WHAT IT IS..

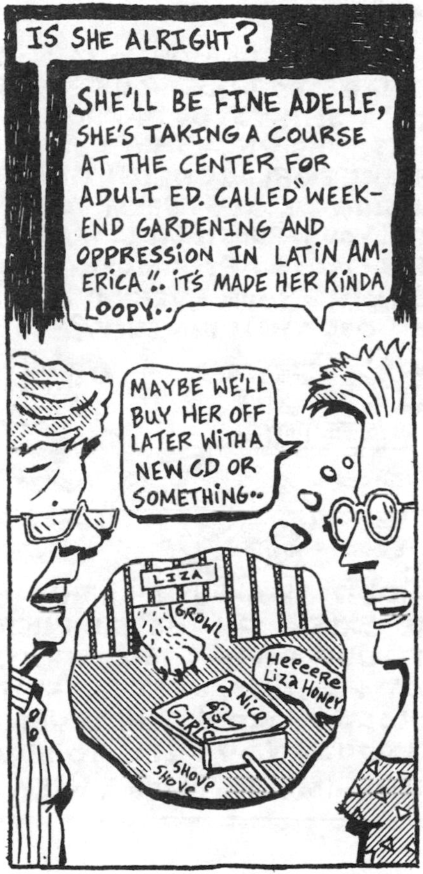
IS SHE ALRIGHT?
SHE'LL BE FINE ADELLE, SHE'S TAKING A COURSE AT THE CENTER FOR ADULT ED. CALLED "WEEK-END GARDENING AND OPPRESSION IN LATIN AM-ERICA".. IT'S MADE HER KINDA LOOPY..
MAYBE WE'LL BUY HER OFF LATER WITH A NEW CD OR SOMETHING..
LIZA
GROWL
Heeeere Liza Honey
2 Nice GIRLS
SHOVE SHOVE

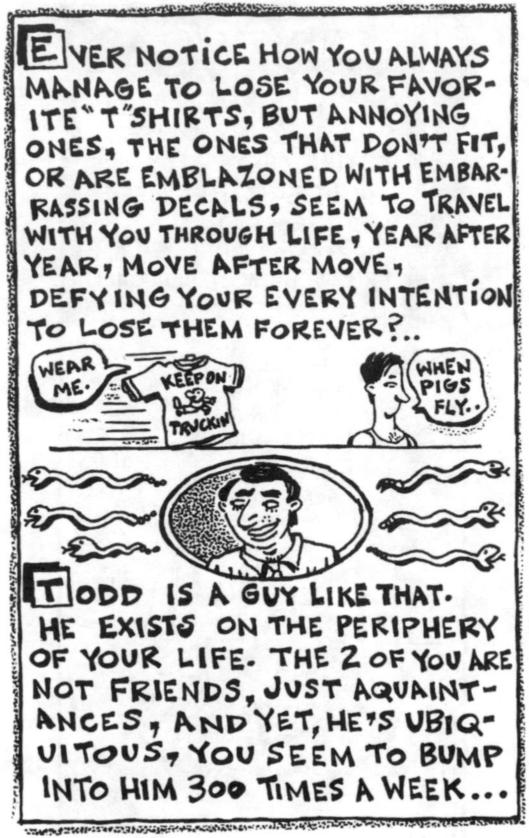
EVER NOTICE HOW YOU ALWAYS MANAGE TO LOSE YOUR FAVORITE "T" SHIRTS, BUT ANNOYING ONES, THE ONES THAT DON'T FIT, OR ARE EMBLAZONED WITH EMBARRASSING DECALS, SEEM TO TRAVEL WITH YOU THROUGH LIFE, YEAR AFTER YEAR, MOVE AFTER MOVE, DEFYING YOUR EVERY INTENTION TO LOSE THEM FOREVER?..
WEAR ME.
KEEP ON TRUCKIN
WHEN PIGS FLY..
TODD IS A GUY LIKE THAT. HE EXISTS ON THE PERIPHERY OF YOUR LIFE. THE 2 OF YOU ARE NOT FRIENDS, JUST AQUAINTANCES, AND YET, HE'S UBIQUITOUS, YOU SEEM TO BUMP INTO HIM 300 TIMES A WEEK...

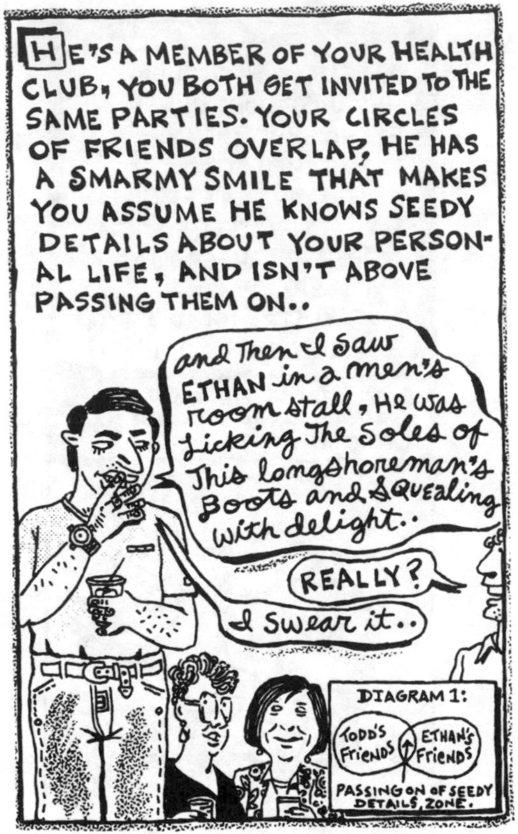
HE'S A MEMBER OF YOUR HEALTH CLUB, YOU BOTH GET INVITED TO THE SAME PARTIES. YOUR CIRCLES OF FRIENDS OVERLAP, HE HAS A SMARMY SMILE THAT MAKES YOU ASSUME HE KNOWS SEEDY DETAILS ABOUT YOUR PERSONAL LIFE, AND ISN'T ABOVE PASSING THEM ON..
and Then I Saw ETHAN in a men's room stall, He was Licking The Soles of This longshoreman's Boots and Squealing with delight..
REALLY?
I Swear it..
DIAGRAM 1:
TODD'S Friends
ETHAN'S Friends
PASSING ON OF SEEDY DETAILS, ZONE.

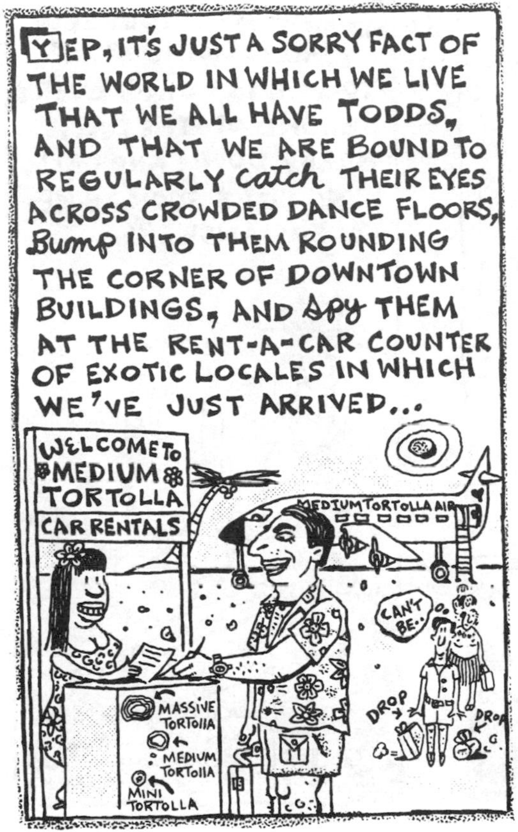
YEP, IT'S JUST A SORRY FACT OF THE WORLD IN WHICH WE LIVE THAT WE ALL HAVE TODDS, AND THAT WE ARE BOUND TO REGULARLY catch THEIR EYES ACROSS CROWDED DANCE FLOORS, Bump INTO THEM ROUNDING THE CORNER OF DOWNTOWN BUILDINGS, AND spy THEM AT THE RENT-A-CAR COUNTER OF EXOTIC LOCALES IN WHICH WE'VE JUST ARRIVED...
WELCOME TO MEDIUM TORTOLLA
CAR RENTALS
MEDIUM TORTOLLA AIR
CAN'T BE..
DROP
DROP
MASSIVE TORTOLLA
MEDIUM TORTOLLA
MINI TORTOLLA

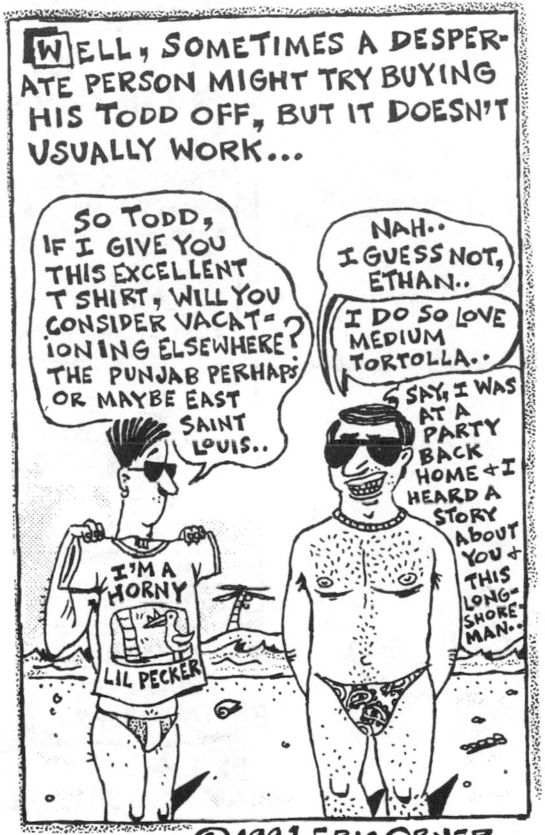
WELL, SOMETIMES A DESPERATE PERSON MIGHT TRY BUYING HIS TODD OFF, BUT IT DOESN'T USUALLY WORK...
SO TODD, IF I GIVE YOU THIS EXCELLENT T SHIRT, WILL YOU CONSIDER VACATIONING ELSEWHERE? THE PUNJAB PERHAPS OR MAYBE EAST SAINT LOUIS..
NAH.. I GUESS NOT, ETHAN..
I DO SO LOVE MEDIUM TORTOLLA..
SAY, I WAS AT A PARTY BACK HOME & I HEARD A STORY ABOUT YOU & THIS LONGSHOREMAN..
I'M A HORNY
LIL PECKER

HOW TO BE DEPRESSED AND BROKEN HEARTED

a Guide For The recently Broken up upon

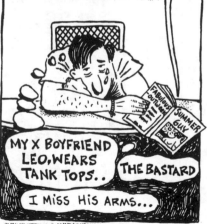

1. IDENTIFY WITH VAPID NOVELS ABOUT FAILED ROMANCE...
"KENT WAS BEAUTIFUL, WITH A FLAT STOMACH AND AQUILINE FEATURES. HE WORRIED ABOUT BRINGING JUST THE RIGHT TANK TOP FOR THIS, HIS FIRST FIRE ISLAND WEEKEND"
FABULOUS OUTLOOK
SUMMER GUY
MY X BOYFRIEND LEO, WEARS TANK TOPS..
THE BASTARD
I MISS HIS ARMS...
2. DISGUST YOURSELF BY WONDERING WHAT YOUR X IS DOING EVERY SECOND OF THE DAY. BREAK DOWN AND CALL. HANG UP AS SOON AS HE OR SHE ANSWERS...
CLICK
SLAM
2B COMMISERATE WITH YOUR CAT, WHO ALWAYS THOUGHT YOUR "X" WAS A BIT OF A JERK ANYWAY.

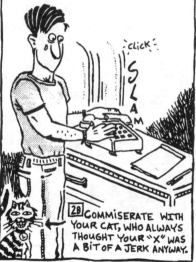

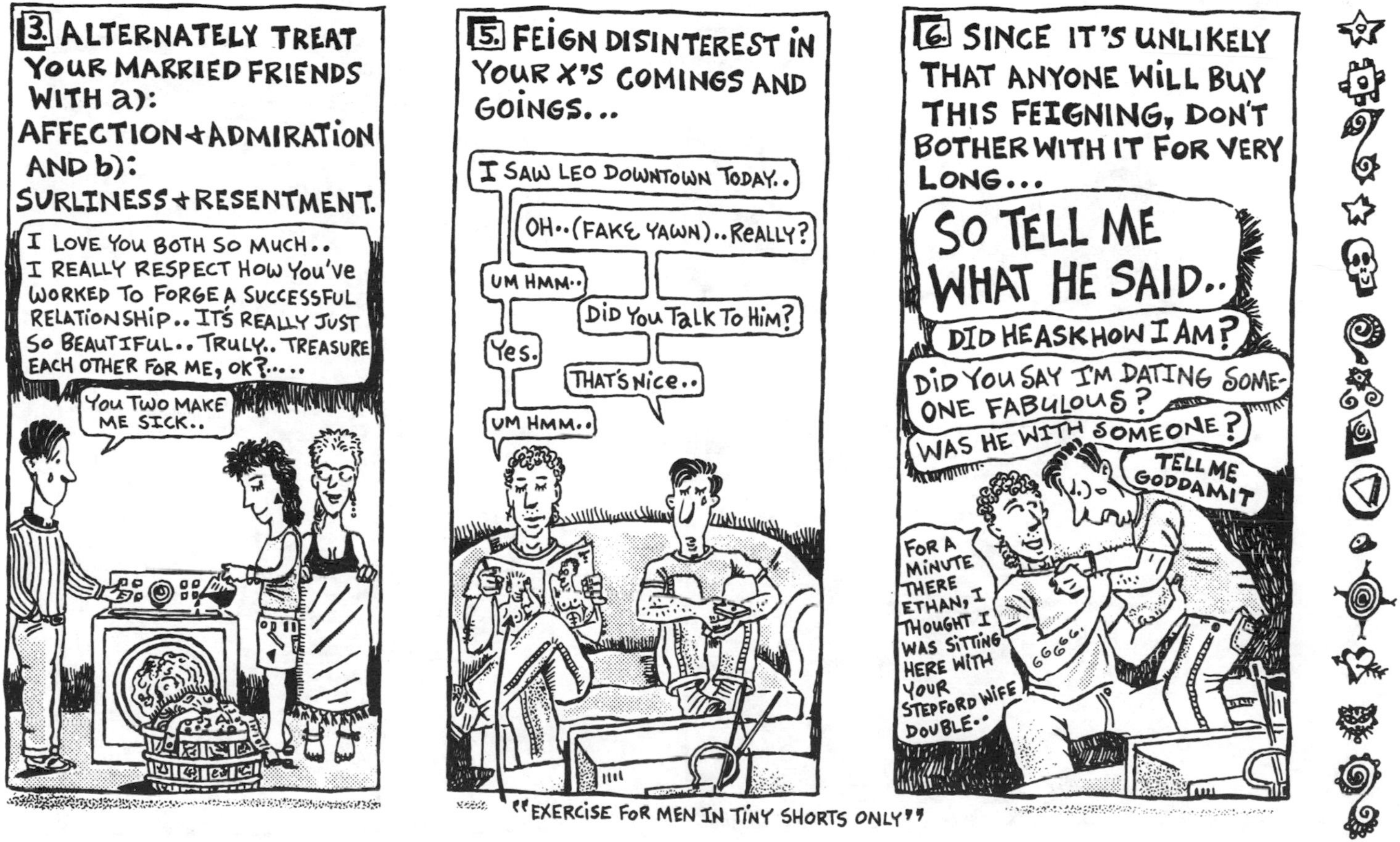
3. ALTERNATELY TREAT YOUR MARRIED FRIENDS WITH a): AFFECTION + ADMIRATION AND b): SURLINESS + RESENTMENT.
I LOVE YOU BOTH SO MUCH.. I REALLY RESPECT HOW YOU'VE WORKED TO FORGE A SUCCESSFUL RELATIONSHIP.. IT'S REALLY JUST SO BEAUTIFUL.. TRULY.. TREASURE EACH OTHER FOR ME, OK?....
YOU TWO MAKE ME SICK..
5. FEIGN DISINTEREST IN YOUR X'S COMINGS AND GOINGS...
I SAW LEO DOWNTOWN TODAY..
OH..(FAKE YAWN)..REALLY?
UM HMM..
DID YOU TALK TO HIM?
YES.
THAT'S NICE..
UM HMM..
"EXERCISE FOR MEN IN TINY SHORTS ONLY"
6. SINCE IT'S UNLIKELY THAT ANYONE WILL BUY THIS FEIGNING, DON'T BOTHER WITH IT FOR VERY LONG...
SO TELL ME WHAT HE SAID..
DID HE ASK HOW I AM?
DID YOU SAY I'M DATING SOMEONE FABULOUS?
WAS HE WITH SOMEONE?
TELL ME GODDAMIT
FOR A MINUTE THERE ETHAN, I THOUGHT I WAS SITTING HERE WITH YOUR STEPFORD WIFE DOUBLE..

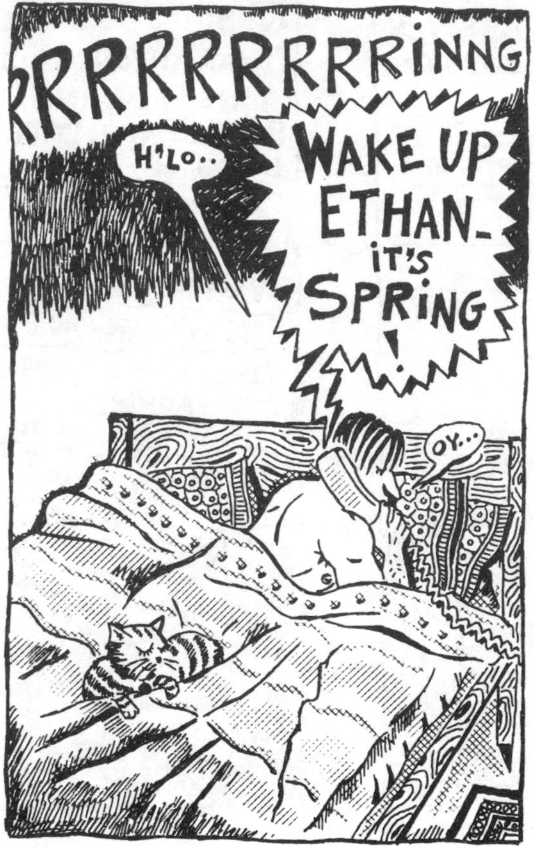
RRRRRRRRRINNG
H'LO..
WAKE UP ETHAN_ IT'S SPRING !
OY...

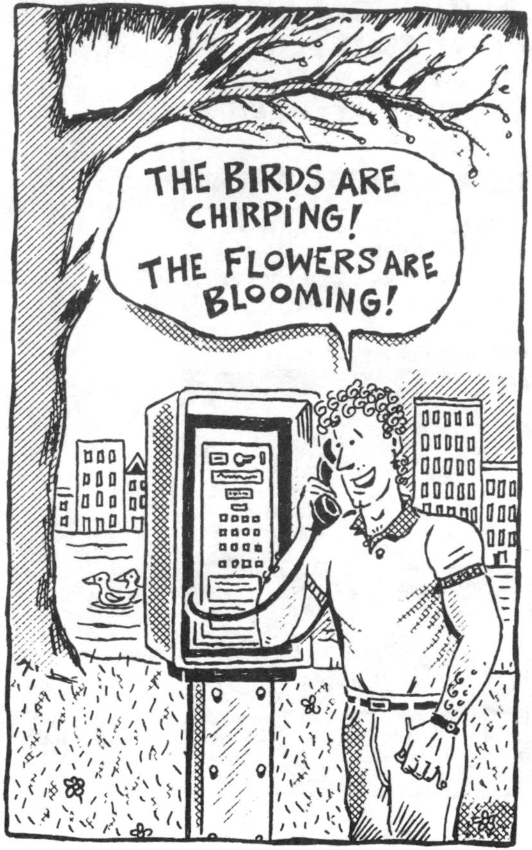
THE BIRDS ARE CHIRPING!
THE FLOWERS ARE BLOOMING!

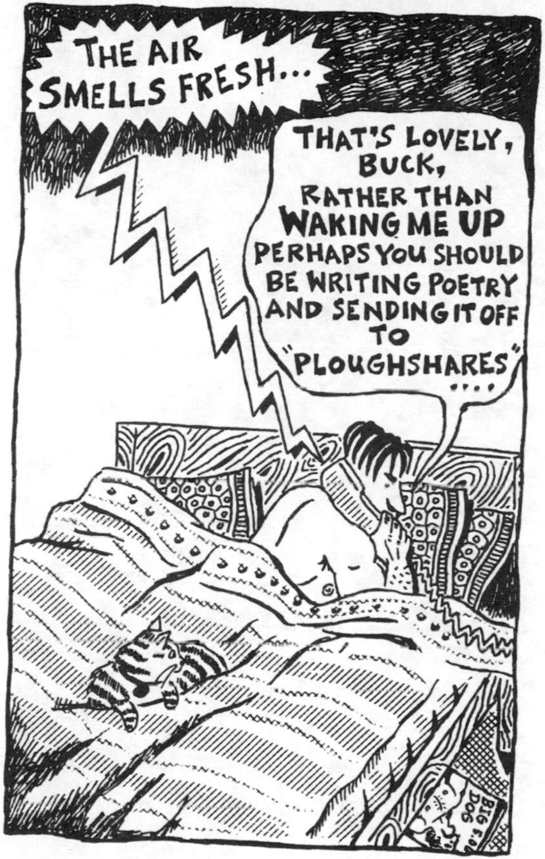
THE AIR SMELLS FRESH...
THAT'S LOVELY, BUCK, RATHER THAN WAKING ME UP PERHAPS YOU SHOULD BE WRITING POETRY AND SENDING IT OFF TO "PLOUGHSHARES"....

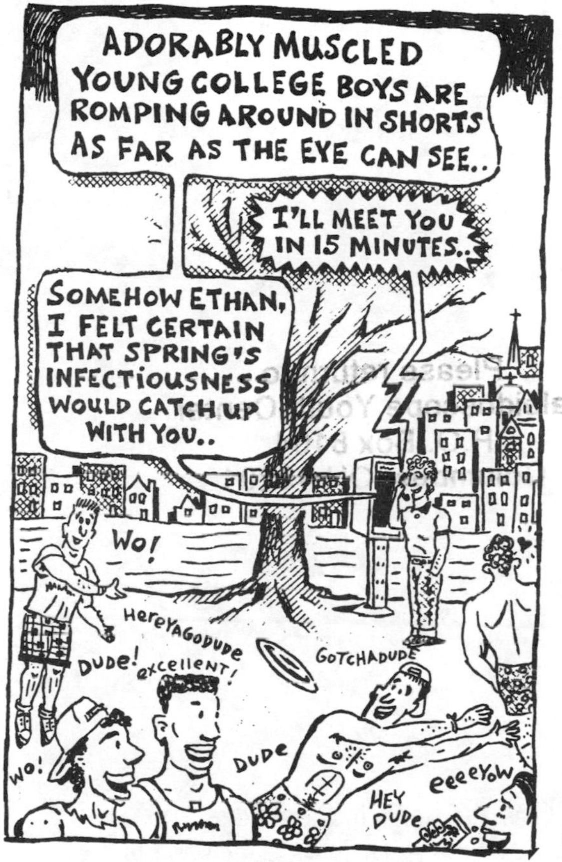
ADORABLY MUSCLED YOUNG COLLEGE BOYS ARE ROMPING AROUND IN SHORTS AS FAR AS THE EYE CAN SEE..
I'LL MEET YOU IN 15 MINUTES..
SOMEHOW ETHAN, I FELT CERTAIN THAT SPRING'S INFECTIOUSNESS WOULD CATCH UP WITH YOU..
Wo!
HereYaGoDude
Dude!
excellent!
GOTCHADUDE
Wo!
DUDE
HEY DUDE
eeeeYow

Stella Johnson

Please return to
Kaleidoscope Youth Center
P.O. Box 8104
Columbus, OH 43201

Eric Orner lives and works in Cambridge,
Massachusetts. His cartoons appear regularly in
newspapers across the U.S. and Canada.